Disney Devotionals

Book Two

100 Daily Devotionals Based on the Disneyland Attractions, Resort Hotels, and More

Albert Thweatt

Theme Park Press
The Happiest Books on Earth
www.ThemeParkPress.com

Editor: Bob McLain
Layout: Artisanal Text
ISBN 978-1-68390-237-9
Printed in the United States of America

Theme Park Press | www.ThemeParkPress.com
ddress queries to bob@themeparkpress.com

This book is dedicated to my six nieces and nephews:
Kaylee, Tucker, Luke, Amelia, Levi, and Tristen.

Second only to being a father, being your uncle is one of God's greatest blessings. Your dedication to God, along with your obvious servant hearts are a blessing to many. I pray for strong faith and a healthy relationship with Him throughout your lives. I love you all and I'm so proud of you!

Contents

Introduction

Here we go again! I can't believe I'm sitting here writing a second book. I didn't even plan on writing a first book! I just submitted an idea to a website on a whim never expecting it would turn into what it became. But the family devotionals that I just happened to save on my computer for some reason became a book. An actual book! Like when I Google myself, an Amazon link pops up! Say what? And by the way, yes I tried it. I Googled myself. I have no shame. You've all done it too. Right? I hope. But back to the point....this has truly been an amazing ride! I cannot believe what the first book has given me. There have been so many compliments, congratulations, kind words, and contacts made because of the book. I can't count the number of people that have told me they are enjoying it. I had one friend who told me it was like reading Harry Potter...he couldn't put it down (shout out to Mark). I'm not sure it's quite up to Harry Potter standards, but I was humbled by the remark. I had another friend at church come up and talk to me all about the book, repeating many of the fun facts I shared because he loves reading it. Oh, by the way, this friend is 5 years old! (Shout out to Jack). I got to do an incredible book signing complete with Disney decorations galore (shout out to Heather, Susan S., Jennifer and Susan P.). I got to do an extremely fun podcast where for an hour we talked about my life and the book (shout out to Amy, Katie and Kerry of the "Sunday Lunch" podcast). I've had so many wonderful opportunities because of this book, and I repeat....it's been an amazing ride! I want to make clear that I give all the credit and glory to God. I am but His humble servant and this is all part of His plan. I believe that with all my heart. This all happened because He wanted it to. My constant prayer for years has been for Him to give me an avenue to talk to others and share my faith. After I wrote the devotionals for my family, I also prayed that there would be a way to be able to share them with others. And He made it happen! He gave me a way to share them! Do you think after those prayers my wife just happened to buy a book published by Theme Park Press? And I just happened to read it too? And I just happened to look on their website? And I just happened to see the link to submit a book? And I just happened to have the idea to submit my devotionals to be published? And they just happened to agree to publish them? You can believe what you want, but I have no doubts that it was God's plan. God answers prayer!! He allowed my thoughts and words to be published as an answer to my prayer and so I could share with others. He has truly blessed my life and continues to surprise me with wonderful gifts. And now He's doing it again!

As I mentioned, the first book brought so many conversations. I was humbled and honored to talk to so many about it, and I was genuinely flattered by all the kind words. I also had several people ask me when book two was coming out. My first instinct was to laugh it off, which I did. There were no plans for book two. I was still enjoying the moment that was book one. But then that question kept coming up. So I thought about it. Book two? Really? That would be great and all, but I just don't know if I'm up for doing this all over again. It was such a long process. The first book took over a year to write and then over a year to publish once submitted. Do I really want to do that again? Wait...that brought another question. Would Theme Park Press even publish another book from me or is it a "one and done" kind of thing? So I figured I'd send an email. It wouldn't hurt to just ask, right? Theme Park Press has been very good to me. The publisher (shout out to Bob) always answers my emails pretty much instantaneously. So I told him I was maybe, possibly, perhaps, perchance, just entertaining the possibility of writing another book, and would he be interested in publishing again. As expected, I got a response in less than five minutes. And I couldn't believe what it said. He said he had been meaning to email me and ask, "When are you starting book 2?" Not only that but he extended an offer...get me a draft in 45 days and I'll publish a couple months after that. Say what now? I had to read that again. Write a whole book in 45 days and publish in 2 months!?! What happened to that three year process I was so used to? My first thought was...ain't gonna happen! Disney may be magical, but I am not. But then I talked to God. He is magical. And I got the strong feeling that He wanted me to give it a shot. My family agreed. So here I am writing book two. It's going to be a lot of late nights and early mornings, but that's the life of a paramedic anyways. We don't need sleep!

So what do I write about? I've already done all the attractions at Disney World. What now? The restaurants? The shops? The cast members? Universal? Oops, sorry Disney. That may be blasphemy...I'm not sure. Anyways, I had a friend or two suggest I switch coasts and take on Disneyland. Not a bad idea! I love Disneyland. However, I've only been there three times. Not nearly as much as the World, but I could still write about it, right? One problem I quickly realized. A lot of the attractions at Disneyland have copycats at Disney World. I can't write about the same attractions again. I've already given all the fun facts. I don't want redundancy. So I did some quick research and counting. There are a little over fifty attractions at Disneyland that are unique in that fact that they don't have a repeat at WDW. But I need 100 devotionals. That number worked well in the first book, and I want to keep the same format. What about the resorts? Quick count. There are over 30 of them if you count both coasts. Getting close to 100. What else? Cruise ships! Love those! Almost to 100. Surely I can just fill in from there. And that's exactly what I did.

So here it is! I present to you a new set of 100 daily devotionals based on the attractions of Disneyland, the Disney resorts, and some bonus material as well. I hope once again you enjoy it and can learn a little something about Disney. Most importantly though, I hope you learn a little something about God. I hope you can once again read these devotionals with your families. Share them together, discuss them, read the passages presented, ask questions, learn and grow closer to God. That's my wish, my dream and my prayer.

I wear a blue rubber bracelet on my right arm. I've been wearing it for several years now. It was a free gift from a Bible class teacher (shout out to Darrell). It has one word etched on it. The word is "Perissos." It's a Greek word which means exceeding abundantly, beyond what is expected, imagined, or hoped for. We were told when given the bracelets that it is a reminder of how much we have been blessed by God. I have definitely been blessed abundantly, beyond what is expected, imagined or hoped for. Anytime I get upset, down, worried or scared, I have a reminder on my arm that I don't need to be any of those things. Despite my many faults and sins; despite the reality that I mess up and disappoint God a lot; despite the fact that I don't deserve a thing, He still continues to graciously bless me. I am still on the narrow path to Heaven. I still plan on being there to see my son, my Father and His Son. And I still want you to join me there. I am still praying for everyone reading these books. God has chosen you. He wants you. He gave His Son for you. He's prepared the way for you. So take advantage. The best is yet to be! (Shout out to my wife, Susan who always says that). May God bless you all!

Disneyland Park

As mentioned in the introduction, the first half of this book will be dedicated to Disneyland in California and all the unique attractions there that weren't discussed in the first book of Disney World devotionals. We're going to begin, well, at the beginning. The first and original Disney park is simply called Disneyland Park, and that's where we'll start our journey. However, before we even step foot into the park, let's discuss this park in general.

Disneyland Park was originally called simply "Disneyland." However, in the late 1990's when a new park began to be built as well as several resorts and a downtown Disney area, it was renamed "Disneyland Park" to distinguish it from the entire property which is often called "Disneyland." Disneyland Park opened on July 17, 1955 and is of course the oldest Disney park in the world. In 2018, it was the 2nd most visited theme park in the world with 18.7 million guests. (#1 of course was the Magic Kingdom at WDW.) Disneyland Park was of course created by Walt Disney, who had already established a movie studio having produced several successful films. However, despite the fact that he wanted to create a park of sorts where families could visit, he lacked the funds to do so. Therefore, he created a new TV show called "Disneyland" that aired on ABC. In return, the network helped to finance the project. The park took one year and one day to build and cost 17 million dollars. 28,000 people attended on opening day which was three times more than expected. However, many of those had purchased counterfeit tickets or even snuck into the park climbing over fences. For years, Walt Disney referred to that day as "Black Sunday." The park officially opened with twenty attractions but was plagued with several problems including inoperable drinking fountains, too few staff, lack of enough food, and asphalt that had not yet hardened.

Today, Disneyland Park consists of nine different themed lands and nearly sixty attractions, and it's had nearly a billion cumulative visitors in its nearly 65 year history. There are so many fun facts about this park that I could dedicate this whole book just to it. However, I'll just pick a few of my favorites which include the fact that there are a large group of cats that make their home at the park to help minimize the rodent population. Cast members weren't allowed to have mustaches until the year 2000. And during the park's early years, Walt Disney would often emerge and wait in line with guests just to spend time with them.

Since its birth in 1955, this one park has blossomed into twelve parks around the world not counting the various water parks, resorts, restaurants and shopping areas. Disneyland has turned into a massive and very successful company, but if you read above, it didn't start out that way. The first day at Disneyland was a disaster. That day was mainly set up for the press as they were invited to hopefully spread many positive comments about this park which would in turn entice many visitors to come. Unfortunately, due to all the mishaps and unexpected problems, Disneyland did not get a glowing review. Therefore it would've been very easy for Walt Disney and all of the Disney executives to become very discouraged. They could have easily felt like failures or even given up. Thankfully, they did the exact opposite. They pressed on and continued to work hard despite the problems, bad reviews and complaints. They realized that to be a success, it was going to take some time, effort, patience and persistence which leads to our very first devotional thought.

One of my favorite Biblical characters of the Old Testament is Joseph. I love his story! I even love the popular Broadway musical about his life. Even though Joseph's story takes up several chapters of Genesis (chapters 37-50), I enjoy re-reading about him from time to time, and I encourage you to do the same. His story is the ultimate story of determination. Despite the fact that he was hated by his own brothers, he didn't give up on God. Despite the fact that he was sold into slavery and taken away from his family, he didn't give up on God. Despite the fact that he was falsely accused of a crime and thrown into prison, he didn't give up on God. It would have been very easy for Joseph to become angry with God for all the struggles he went through, but he instead realized that it was all part of God's ultimate plan. He trusted God and never quit serving Him, and in the end it ultimately paid off. We have to do the same.

Galatians 6:9 says, "And let us not grow weary of doing good, for in due season we will reap, if we do not give up." Romans 12:12 tells us to be patient in tribulation. We are on God's time, not our own. We may go through years of hard times. We may think that things are never going to get better, but we have to keep in mind that God is in control. We must be patient with Him. Jeremiah 29:11 reminds us that God has a plan for all of us. Always keep that in mind and never give up on God. Disneyland may have had a rough start, but because of persistence and determination, it has become an amazing phenomenon. God will do the same with you if you can just be patient and wait on Him. Never give up on God. He certainly won't give up on you!

"Walk in Walt's Disneyland Footsteps"

So now that we've talked about the Disneyland Park in general, let's get to the attractions, right? Not so fast! I think we owe at least one devotional to the man who started it all. As I mentioned in the last devotional, there are so many fun facts about Disneyland, but also about the man, Walt Disney himself. There have been many biographies written about this fascinating individual because he was such an interesting person with an incredible history. I could probably do a devotional book based just on him and his life. However, I know you are probably anxious to get into the park so allow me just this one to talk about something very cool you can take advantage of at Disneyland related to Walt Disney. There is a tour available for all guests called Walk in Walt's Disneyland Footsteps. I have never actually done the tour myself, although I want to very badly. We almost took advantage of it on our last trip but unfortunately had to change our plans. It's definitely on my bucket list, however, and one day I'll get around to it.

As you probably know, there are many tours available both at Disneyland and Disney World. If space allows, we might talk about some of the WDW ones toward the end of this book since we didn't have space in the first book. Today I'd like to discuss the main one available at Disneyland. Walk in Walt's Disneyland Footsteps is a 3 hour guided tour around Disneyland Park. The tour typically costs around $110 although you can get a discount if you are an annual passholder or DVC member. The tour is typically offered at various times during the day depending on time of year and crowd level. Everyone who signs up for the tour gets a special name badge, as well as a provided meal at the end of the tour and a special collectable pin. At the beginning of the tour, you are presented with a special headset that allows you to hear your tour guide as you roam throughout the park looking at various attractions and points of interest. You are essentially walking in Walt's footsteps around the park as your guide tells you about him and the history of the park. You will also get to experience a few attractions that were particularly significant to Walt as you hear about his vision for the park. What I think is the best part of the tour, and the main reason I want to do it, happens at the end. All tour guests get to enter Walt's apartment which is above the fire station at the front of the park. I devoted an entry in the last book to this apartment, and while I've certainly seen the window of the apartment from the outside and the light that forever shines there, to see it in person from the inside would be a dream come true.

Walt Disney died in 1966 and although he knew Disney World in Florida was coming, he never got to step foot inside that completed park as it opened in 1971. Therefore Disneyland is the only one of the 12 worldwide Disney parks he ever got to walk in and experience. He obviously even lived there in the tiny apartment where he could overlook Town Square as people entered and enjoyed what he'd created. As I mentioned in the introduction of this book, I was able to do a podcast about the first book, and I was specifically asked if I could meet anyone past or present for lunch, who would it be? I chose Walt Disney of course. I would love to have been able to talk to this great man and ask him personally about his dreams. I would love to know what he thinks of what Disney is today, and how it compares with his vision. There are probably a lot of business executives today that do indeed try to follow in Walt's footsteps. After all, he was a very successful businessman that showed great determination and stamina in everything he did. While I certainly admire and would love to have known him, his footsteps are not the ones I try the hardest to follow.

Walt Disney was a great man, but he was just that...a man. He wasn't perfect and made mistakes, as we all do. I instead try hard every day to follow in the footsteps of Jesus Christ. He WAS perfect. He came to this world to show us how to live. That was one of the main reasons God sent Him here. Look at these verses: "Whoever says he abides in him ought to walk in the same way in which he walked." (I John 2:6) "For to this you have been called, because Christ also suffered for you, leaving you an example, so that you might follow in his steps." (I Peter 2:21-22) Those verses literally tell us to walk in the steps of Jesus. Ephesians 5:1 also tells us to be imitators of God. Jesus was God in human form so if we want to indeed imitate God, we should live like Jesus lived and walk as He walked. I'm certainly not perfect by any means, but I try hard each day to follow Jesus. Any time I have to make a decision, I try to think about what Jesus would do. I try to pattern my life after His and do what He did. I want to invite and challenge you to do the same. This is what we are called to do as God's children. He sent Jesus here as our example. Let's all try hard to take advantage of this amazing gift we were given and walk in the footsteps of Jesus!

"Disneyland Railroad"

Ok, enough waiting! Let's get into the park already! Just like the Magic Kingdom at Disney World, the first thing you see walking into Disneyland Park is that beautiful train station. As you probably know, Walt Disney loved trains. When planning this park, he definitely wanted to include a train encircling the park which was of course copied at Disney World. I realize that there was a devotional in the first book dedicated to the Disney World railroad so you may think we would just skip the railroad here as it's not really a ride unique to Disneyland. However, you would be mistaken. While the path it follows and the ride itself is virtually the same, there is a lot of special history and facts about this railroad that make it quite special. After all, Walt Disney rode this one himself several times. Therefore, I think a devotional dedicated to this special attraction is important. Let's talk about the Disneyland Railroad!

The Disneyland Railroad is a 1.2 mile loop around the park with four stops at subsequent train stations, one more than at Disney World. On average there are three trains that are running at the same time although sometimes a fourth is added depending on park crowds. Altogether it is an 18-20 minute ride around the park. This attraction opened with the park in 1955 and Walt Disney himself sat in the steam engine and drove the train into the Main Street station to open the park, with the governor of California on board as well. Within a week of the park's opening, one of the workers on the train made a mistake causing the caboose to derail and collide with a concrete slab. The worker quickly left the scene, most likely to avoid disciplinary action, and was never seen again. Luckily, nobody was injured. As you travel around the park on this attraction, you will see two diorama scenes, one resembling the Grand Canyon and another dedicated to the Primeval World. Both of these scenes are from the 1964-1965 New York World's Fair.

There is no doubt that Walt Disney loved trains. He even dreamed about being a train engineer as a child, just like his father's cousin who told him all about his experiences driving a train across the country. Walt purchased several model train sets growing up and when he and his family moved to Los Angeles in 1949, he started construction on a train in his own backyard that he called the Carolwood Pacific Railroad. This personal train featured a set of freight cars pulled by the "Lilly Belle," an engine he named after his wife Lillian. This backyard attraction attracted neighbors and visitors which Walt allowed to ride and even drive the train. It's fairly obvious that Walt's trains were his pride and joy. He worked hard to build them and was proud of his accomplishments. His decision to drive the train into the station on opening day was evidence of this and put an exclamation point on his hard work.

What are you proud of? Have you ever worked really hard on something and felt pride when you got to display it or show it off? Maybe it was a big project at school, a presentation at your job or even a personal goal that you met. Have you ever been congratulated or been given compliments for your accomplishments? It probably felt pretty good, right? While the Bible does speak negatively of pride on several occasions, there is nothing wrong with being proud of yourself and your hard work. The kind of pride scripture frowns upon is when you let it go to your head and abuse it. We have to remember to stay humble like Jesus in all we do. However, the Bible also speaks very positively of working hard to achieve goals. Galatians 6:4 says, "But let each one test his own work, and then his reason to boast will be in himself alone and not in his neighbor." Colossians 3:23 reminds us that in whatever we do, we should work hard for the Lord. God is proud of us when we work hard and use the many talents he's given us. Jesus reminded us of that in the parable of the talents in Matthew 25.

I'm sure that Walt Disney was very proud of his accomplishments. There are many photos of him in his park smiling with guests. I also have no doubt that as he drove that railroad into the station on that first day, he had a big smile on his face as well. He had a right to be proud. He had accomplished a wonderful goal and worked very hard. Let's all commit to working hard in whatever we are doing to show God that we appreciate the many gifts he's given us. After all, Proverbs 16:3 reminds us, "Commit your work to the Lord, and your plans will be established."

"Great Moments with Mr. Lincoln"

Now that we've completed our first official ride with a loop on the train, where should we head next? Well, if we did indeed do a complete circle, we are back at the front of the park and heading down Main Street. There is a very important attraction here on Main Street that the sister park in Orlando doesn't have. And it's an attraction that was very special and important to Walt Disney, so we have to stop and discuss it. It's called Great Moments with Mr. Lincoln.

This is a stage show that has been running at Disneyland Park since 1965. It features an audio-animatronic representation of President Abraham Lincoln. It was originally part of the 1964 World's Fair in New York. Walt Disney originally wanted a stage show dedicated to all the US Presidents but the technology available at the time would not allow a show on that grand of a scale so Disney settled for a show dedicated to his boyhood hero, President Lincoln. The Hall of Presidents at Disney World would later be created to fulfill the original dream of Disney, although he never got to see it. This attraction has changed some over the years and has been called by several different names. Technically the current name is "The Disneyland Story presenting Great Moments with Mr. Lincoln." That's quite a name! Just as the name has changed several times, the version of Lincoln has as well. The current version is one of the most advanced audio animatronics in the park. The original that was on display at the World's Fair was packed in a crate and forgotten about for decades. It was later discovered and is at the Walt Disney: One Man's Dream display at Hollywood Studios in Orlando. The current version of the show features an excerpt from Lincoln's autobiography, a small portion of the Gettysburg Address and a song. When this attraction first came to Disneyland, it was completely free. Guests didn't need a special A-E ticket as they did for other attractions. Walt Disney wanted all guests to be able to experience this special show with simply the low cost of park admission.

Walt Disney was always fascinated by the life of Abraham Lincoln. As a boy, he even memorized the Gettysburg Address and recited it to his elementary class. He would also dress up like Lincoln wearing his father's frock coat and wearing a homemade stovepipe hat. I think it's safe to say that Abraham Lincoln was one of Walt Disney's heroes. He respected him, looked up to him, studied him and had a great admiration of his life. What about you? Do you have somebody in your life like that? Who is your hero? I know it would be easy to say that Jesus is our hero as he should be, but what about someone you've actually met and look up to? Think about someone past or present that has had a positive and profound impact on your life.

In I Samuel 17, we find the famous story of David and Goliath. In verse 51, after David kills Goliath, the Bible says that when the Philistines saw that their hero was dead, they fled. The NIV version of the Bible actually uses that word "hero." It's pretty obvious that the Philistines had picked the wrong hero. They based their hero decision on size, strength and victories. They clearly didn't base it on God. However, that's exactly what we need to do. I want to encourage you today to do two things. First I invite you to choose Godly heroes while you live your life. It's good and even wise to have good influences in our lives. In Proverbs 27:17, it says, "Iron sharpens iron, and one man sharpens another." If you don't have someone already, I encourage you to find someone that follows God and uses His Word as a pattern for their life. Maybe it's someone at your church, a minister or spiritual counselor. Secondly, I would urge you to BE a Godly hero for someone else. Remember I Timothy 4:12 that tells us to set an example for others in speech, conduct, love, faith and purity. I pray often that God will send me someone I can guide and influence. That's also my prayer for this book. The main reason I prayed for this book to be published was so that I could share these thoughts and hopefully inspire others to follow God and live as He desires us to live.

Is there someone you know of that needs to find God for the first time? Or maybe they've found that wide path of the world and need to come back to God. Choose to be their hero! We all have heroes like Walt Disney had Abraham Lincoln. Pray that God will give you the courage to be their hero and bring them back into God's flock. After all, that's our purpose while here on Earth, to get ourselves to Heaven and to bring as many as possible with us. How many have you brought? I'm asking myself the same question. Choose good heroes to follow, and choose to be a hero that someone else can follow!

"Sleeping Beauty Castle"

For our next devotional, let's continue down Main Street and what do we see? Well you certainly can't miss that giant castle at the end of the street. Now, if you've been to Disney World, you quickly realize that the castle there is much bigger...nearly 200 feet while this one is only 77 feet high. However, it is still the park's icon and certainly an important part serving as the central hub of all the lands. Therefore, I feel like we need to spend some time today talking about Sleeping Beauty Castle.

Sleeping Beauty Castle opened with the park in 1955, four years before the movie it's based on was even released! Walt Disney was in the process of making the film while he was putting the finishing touches on this park, and it was decided to name the castle after the upcoming film to help promote it. It was originally going to be Snow White's castle. Hong Kong Disneyland also used to have a castle dedicated to Sleeping Beauty but it closed in early 2018 to make way for a new, much larger castle coming in 2020 named "Castle of Magical Dreams." There is also a Sleeping Beauty Castle at Disneyland Paris. Just like Cinderella Castle at Disney World, the castle in Disneyland Park is inspired by Neuschwanstein Castle in Germany. One very interesting fact about this castle is that it actually has a working drawbridge. This drawbridge has only been publicly lowered twice: once during the park's opening and again in 1983 when Fantasyland was rededicated. There is a walk-through attraction inside the castle that changed after 9/11. Guests used to be able to climb into the upper stories of the castle but this was changed presumably for better security, although handicap accessibility is also a theory. Finally, there is at least one time capsule buried beneath the castle to be opened in 2035.

Have you ever seen the movie "Sleeping Beauty?" I had never seen it until about a year ago. I realized that this was one Disney classic that I had never taken the time to watch, so I got it on Netflix. While it wasn't my favorite Disney movie ever, it was certainly a good movie with an interesting story. In a nutshell, the film is about Princess Aurora who is cursed by the evil Maleficent. Because of the curse, Aurora falls into a deep sleep and can only be awakened by true love's kiss. Sounds like a classic Disney plot right there! Maleficent is considered by many to be the most evil of all the Disney villains. She is featured near the end of the great show, Fantasmic seen at both Disneyland and Disney World. For today's thought, I think we can compare what she did to Aurora with what Satan does to us.

There's no doubt that Satan is our most evil villain, and I would argue that he too puts us to sleep sometimes. We fall asleep to the evils of the world. We fall asleep to temptation. We fall asleep to sin. We get way too comfortable in our sleep and fail to see the danger we are in. Just like Princess Aurora, we need to WAKE UP! Did you know that there are several verses in the Bible that tell us to wake up? Read and think about the following:

"Besides this you know the time, that the hour has come for you to wake from sleep. For salvation is nearer to us now than when we first believed. The night is far gone; the day is at hand. So then let us cast off the works of darkness and put on the armor of light." (Romans 13:11-12)

"For you are all children of light, children of the day. We are not of the night or of the darkness. So then let us not sleep, as others do, but let us keep awake and be sober." (I Thessalonians 5:5-6)

"Wake up, and strengthen what remains and is about to die, for I have not found your works complete in the sight of my God. Remember, then, what you received and heard. Keep it, and repent. If you will not wake up, I will come like a thief, and you will not know at what hour I will come against you." (Revelation 3:2-3)

Do you see how all of those verses tell us to wake up? They are all warning us not to be asleep in our spiritual walk with God. The last one from Revelation even cautions that if we don't wake up, we may miss our opportunity with God. It is very easy to get comfortable with this world. We often get caught up in the fun and temptation and forget our life's purpose. Luckily, as expected, the Sleeping Beauty film has a happy ending. Aurora gets her kiss, wakes up and lives happily ever after with her prince. Hopefully we all can have our happy ending and live forever with our Prince...of Peace, Jesus Christ. However, first we need to make sure we are awake to Satan's attacks so that we don't fall asleep and miss out on our happily ever after.

"Indiana Jones Adventure"

We need a thrill ride already, don't we? We've been in this park for five devotionals and haven't really done anything super exciting yet. We need something intense. Something scary. Something adventurous. Well, have I got just the ride! This is the ride that my family runs to first. This is the ride that will undoubtedly have a long line for most of the day. And this is the ride that just happens to be my favorite ride in this park. Today we are going to head over to the Adventureland section of the park and ride Indiana Jones Adventure!

The full name of this ride is technically "Indiana Jones Adventure: Temple of the Forbidden Eye." There is another ride like it in the Tokyo DisneySea Park. This ride opened to the public on March 4, 1995 and was built due to the success of the Indiana Jones Stunt Spectacular show at Hollywood Studios in Florida. It is an enhanced motion vehicle dark ride transporting guests on a wild quest with Indiana Jones as your host. During the ride you are taken on a journey through a dangerous lost temple guarded by mysterious powers. There were several ideas for this ride that never materialized including a jungle cruise style adventure, as well as a mine cart type roller coaster. Instead, Imagineers opted for a unique style dark ride that was later copied at Animal Kingdom in Florida for the Dinosaur ride. (Maybe that's why I like this ride so much as Dinosaur is still my favorite WDW ride!) Harrison Ford was asked to reprise his famous Indiana Jones role for this ride, but for some reason contract negotiations broke down and another actor was brought in that sounds like Ford. Indiana Jones acts as your host but ride planners also realized that guests would want to see their hero so there are several audio-animatronics of Indy throughout the ride. The ending of the ride is randomized as after your narrow escape you'll hear Jones utter one of seven phrases. You can look online to see all seven possibilities. Even the line queue of this ride is fun and fascinating as you'll see several scenes from the films as well as some actual movie props. This ride took seven years to plan and build and cost nearly 100 million dollars.

I've seen all the Indiana Jones films and am excited that there's a fifth one coming in 2020. One of the most famous scenes in all the films happens during the first one *Raiders of the Lost Ark*. In this well-known scene, Indiana Jones is thrown into a pit full of snakes. We have already found out that he hates snakes, and he utters the famous line, "Snakes, why did it have to be snakes?" This scene is replicated in the ride at Disneyland Park in which you enter a room full of snakes (not real of course) as well as a giant audio-animatronic cobra. Remembering that scene got me thinking about snakes in the Bible.

Snakes and serpents are mentioned many times in the Bible. However, there are three instances I want to remind you of that are important to our lesson today. In Exodus chapter 7, God instructs Moses and his brother Aaron to throw down their staffs in front of Pharaoh. When they do, their staffs become snakes. This was to show the power of God. In Acts 28, Paul is gathering firewood and is bitten by a snake. The people think this happens because of his sin and expect him to die. However, when Paul casually shakes the snake off, goes about his business and suffers no effects, the people change their mind and think he is a god. This was to show the power of God. Finally look at Revelation 12:9 which says, "And the great dragon was thrown down, that ancient serpent, who is called the devil and Satan, the deceiver of the whole world—he was thrown down to the earth, and his angels were thrown down with him." This reminds us that Satan who once disguised himself as a serpent or snake was thrown out of Heaven by God down to the Earth because of his sin. Again, this shows the power of God.

Indiana Jones Adventure is a super exciting and thrilling ride, just like the films it's based on. I'm remembering the snake scene today and how God shows us His power using snakes in Scripture. I Corinthians 6:14 says that God will raise us up by his power. Our God is so powerful and he displays this in the Bible often using things like snakes, weather, miracles and so much more. Let us remember today how strong and powerful our God is. He has a plan that will be accomplished. Nothing can stand in His way. Remember to thank Him today for his power and ask Him to continue to use it to raise us up so that we can be with Him one day and continue to resist the power of Satan.

"Tarzan's Treehouse"

Since we are here in Adventureland, we might as well stay in this area and focus on the only other attraction here that is unique to Disneyland Park. We do find the Jungle Cruise here as well as the Tiki Room, but those are also at WDW. So today, we're going to focus on the distinctive Tarzan's Treehouse. Now I realize that there is a treehouse at Disney World that we had a devotional for in the first book. However, it is dedicated to the film *Swiss Family Robinson*. This treehouse in Disneyland was refurbished for the film *Tarzan* which provides some definite differences, so let's start climbing.

Tarzan's Treehouse opened in June of 1999 just as the Disney film opened in theaters. This treehouse had been themed like its sister tree in Florida, but Imagineers decided to refurbish and pattern it after the new film to hopefully capitalize on the hype. The new tree featured 10 more feet of height, 6000 brand new vinyl leaves as well as a new suspension bridge entrance. They did leave behind a couple of acknowledgments to the old Swiss Family tree. You can see a "Mind Thy Head" sign from the old tree, as well as hear the famous "Swisskapolka" playing on a vintage gramophone as a tribute to the old theme. You can now also find a reference to Beauty and the Beast as there is a teapot and cup that look just like Mrs. Potts and Chip in the campsite scene. Tarzan's Treehouse is 80 feet tall and weighs 150 tons. It cost nearly $255,000 to build. There is also a Tarzan's Treehouse at Hong Kong Disneyland.

On our last trip to Disneyland, we decided to climb this treehouse as there was no line, which is typical. I'll be honest and say that I wasn't exactly thrilled to be entering this attraction. I'd done the Swiss Family Robinson Treehouse at WDW a few times, so I figured it would pretty much be the same. Plus, it's a lot of steps which required climbing, and I was already pretty worn out from the day. I almost declined and was about to tell my family I'd wait for them at the end. However ,for some reason at the last second, I decided to follow them up the tree. It was a fine attraction, but as I climbed what seemed like the eternal steps and looked around, it really didn't appear to be anything too special. But then something amazing happened. On one of the many stair landings, I just happened to turn around and was completely blown away by the view I was seeing. Climbing this treehouse allows you to have the best aerial view of Disneyland, with the exception of being in an airplane. I stood there for a minute or two just admiring the beauty of what I was seeing and thanking God that I didn't skip the treehouse. I strongly encourage you to make the climb if you are ever there, just for the view alone. It's pretty impressive!

I'm glad I made the climb because the view turned out to be a hidden treasure, and one I will repeat next time I get to go. It was well worth the effort it took to climb those steps. I think Bible study is a lot like that. It takes effort, time, dedication, motivation and discipline to study the Bible. But it's so important! 2 Timothy 3:16-17 tells us that all scripture is from God and is profitable. It goes on to say that scripture equips us for life. In Acts 17, we hear about the Bereans, a noble group of people, who studied the scriptures daily with eagerness. They were excited to study the Word of God. Do we have that same excitement? Finally, remember Ephesians 6 where we hear about the armor of God. We are told all the valuable pieces we need to complete our suit of armor. And what is our weapon? What should we have in our hand at all times? The answer is our sword, which Ephesians says is the Word of God. You see, the Bible is our most powerful weapon against the evils of the world. It is our most powerful tool to find how to live our lives and what God wants from us. If we get lazy or complacent in our study, we may miss out on important information that the Bible has to offer. When I take the time to really study the Bible and read it for an extended amount of time, I always seem to find something new and valuable to my life.

So don't forget to check out the amazing view from the top of Tarzan's Treehouse! Make the effort! Climb those steps! I think you'll be glad you did. And more importantly, don't forget to make time and take time to study God's Word. You will find something amazing in there too that might just surprise you. It will no doubt be valuable information that is well worth the effort!

"Davy Crockett Explorer Canoes"

Having admired the incredible view from the top of Tarzan's Treehouse, let's head back down the steps and exit Adventureland to find another unique Disneyland attraction. Let's venture into what is called "Critter Country" because there is an attraction here that used to be at Disney World, but is no longer. It is a simple attraction, but a distinctive and fun one as well. It's a ride dedicated to the American folk hero, frontiersman and politician, Davy Crockett, the so called "King of the Wild Frontier." Let's go pick up a paddle and take a ride on the Davy Crockett Explorer Canoes!

These canoes opened in 1956, a year after Disneyland Park opened. They were also in operation at the Magic Kingdom in Disney World when it opened in 1971, but closed there in 1994. They are also currently in operation at the Disney parks in Tokyo and Shanghai. They were also found in Disneyland Paris, but for only two years before they closed. This attraction has the unusual distinction of being the only attraction at Disneyland that is powered by park guests. Up to 20 guests can board a 35 foot canoe and literally paddle their way around the Rivers of America accompanied by two guides. The experience begins with a short lesson on paddling and then riders begin the nearly half mile trek around Tom Sawyer Island. Along the way, the guides point out various sights and points of interest. The ride typically takes around 10 minutes depending on how fast the guests paddle. It is said that sometimes Disneyland employees compete in canoes races early in the morning before the park opens. There are also periodic competitions to see who can paddle around the island the fastest. Apparently the fastest time ever is somewhere around 4 minutes.

As mentioned, this is the only ride that is powered by guests. It's a real team effort which is part of the fun of the experience. There is no track and no motor. If guests don't do the work, well, it's gonna be a long ride! This is just like our spiritual life as well. In our walk with God, we can't just sit back and do nothing. God does a lot and blesses us in many ways, but we have to meet Him halfway. We have to do our part. The Bible is pretty clear on that. When God first created man and woman and placed them in the Garden of Eden, He made it pretty clear what He expected of them. In Genesis 2:15 we read, "The Lord God took the man and put him in the Garden of Eden to work it and keep it." 2 Thessalonians 3:10 even says, "If anyone is not willing to work, let him not eat." We are commanded to have good work ethic and not be lazy in our lives. This is also true in our spiritual life. Hebrews 11:6 says that God rewards those who seek Him. We can't just sit back, do nothing and expect God to find and save us. We have to always be seeking Him and learning more about Him through His Word.

Our family has never been able to do the canoes due to time, weather or other conflicts. However, I do hope to try them one day. They sound like fun, and I've read many good reviews about this attraction. Yes, it takes some work, but I think it would be worth the effort to be part of the team and get to power these boats around Tom Sawyer Island. More importantly, I want to do my part to meet God and make Him proud of my work. Ephesians 2:10 says that we are God's workmanship and we are created in Christ Jesus for good works that God has prepared for us. Check yourself today and make sure you are working hard for God, not just in your job or school work, but in your effort to know Him more. We must daily study His Word to know His plan for our lives so we can work hard to do everything He asks us to do. This will assure that God will indeed meet us and take us home to be with Him one day.

"Mark Twain Riverboat"

Did you know that there are actually three rides in the Rivers of America here? Disneyland Park has really taken advantage of this waterway! There are of course the canoes that we just finished, as well as two large ships that you can experience. So let's hop aboard the first of the two and take another scenic trip around Tom Sawyer Island. This time we don't have to paddle or do any work, so just relax and enjoy a ride on the Mark Twain Riverboat!

Yes, if you read the first book, we took a trip on the Liberty Square Riverboat at Disney World. However, the riverboat here has its own unique history, kind of like the Disneyland railroad, so we are going to give it a devotional all its own. The Mark Twain Riverboat takes park guests on a 12-14 minute scenic journey around the island at a nice leisurely pace. This attraction opened with the park in 1955 and was the first functional riverboat to be built in the United States in 50 years. There are also riverboat rides in Florida of course, as well as Tokyo and Paris. The riverboat travels along a hidden guide rail throughout the journey so the captain serves simply as a lookout for other rides, especially the canoes. Guests can venture to one of three decks available, with the top deck having the best views of the scenery provided. A couple of lucky guests might even get to stand with the captain and help "pilot" the boat. In 1995, a wedding took place on the riverboat as it circled the rivers. This is thought to be the one and only wedding to ever take place on a Disneyland attraction. My son and I got to enjoy a trip on this riverboat as the park was about to close on our last trip. We thoroughly enjoyed it, and I'm glad we decided to give it a try.

There is another story involving this riverboat that I want to focus on today. It involves Lillian Disney, the wife of Walt. Lillian Disney was known for being a very kind and generous woman. She is also credited with naming a very important character. After Walt created his signature mouse, he wanted to name him "Mortimer Mouse." However, Lillian considered that name depressing and suggested "Mickey" instead. The rest is history. The very first voyage that the Mark Twain Riverboat took was four days before the park opened for Walt and Lillian's 30th anniversary. There was a private party planned for the happy couple as well as many of their friends and family. Before the party, Joe Fowler, Disneyland's construction supervisor and a former navy admiral was checking the boat to make sure everything would be ready for the 300 invited guests. Inspecting the boat, he found something unexpected. He came upon Lillian Disney sweeping the decks of debris just before the party was to begin. That selfless act of service leads to our thought today.

Lillian Disney had no obligation to sweep the decks of this huge riverboat. She was the wife of Walt Disney. Certainly, they had people that were expected to do that. Not to mention that it was her 30th anniversary! She had every right to be getting dressed, putting on makeup or just relaxing in anticipation of the celebration honoring her and Walt that night. Instead, on this very special day, she chose to pitch in and serve. From my reading and studying about her life, that was just typical Mrs. Disney...a very caring and giving woman. We can all learn a simple but important lesson from this. In John 13, there's a very familiar story where Jesus gets up from the table and begins washing his disciples' feet. Jesus did this! The Son of God! Washing dirty feet! He did it for a simple reason...to show that it doesn't matter who you are or how important you are, we are all here to humble ourselves and serve. Jesus certainly demonstrated this on many occasions.

Allow me to conclude by reminding you of a few important verses. I Peter 4:10 says that we should use our gifts to serve each other. Acts 20:35 tells us it's more blessed to give than to receive. Galatians 5:13-14 reminds us that we should love our neighbor and that this love means serving one another. Finally, Matthew 20:28 declares that Jesus himself came not to be served but to serve. We can all take a lesson from Lillian Disney and of course from Jesus to look for ways to serve others. Make it a goal each and every day to do one random act of service for someone else, even if it's something small. What a better world this would be if everyone did that!

"Sailing Ship Columbia"

Two down, one to go! On to our third attraction that takes place here in the Rivers of America. I promise we'll get out of this waterway soon, although I think it's great that there are so many attractions to choose from here. The final option we have is called the "Sailing Ship Columbia." This giant vessel is an exact replica of the "Columbia Rediviva" which was the first American ship to ever circumnavigate the globe. This full scale model resembles a giant pirate ship and even plays that very role during performances of Fantasmic. During the day, however, guests can take a ride on this amazing ship, so let's discuss it today.

The Sailing Ship Columbia opened in 1958, three years after the park. It is 110 feet long and can accommodate 300 guests on its 12 minute journey around the island. The ship is powered by a gas engine and follows the same track as the Mark Twain Riverboat. At a certain point during the ride, a cast member will typically fire a couple of shots (blanks of course) from one of the ship's ten cannons. There used to be a cannon on Tom Sawyer Island that would fire back, but this was discontinued a few years ago. There is a small museum below deck that guests can check out during the voyage. Sadly, this attraction doesn't always operate...typically only on the busiest days or when the riverboat is down. Finally, there was an unfortunate accident on this attraction in 1998. On December 24 of that year, one of the cleats used to secure the ship to the dock tore loose striking park guests. Several were injured and one man died a couple days later at the hospital.

As mentioned above, this attraction is an exact replica of a very famous and important ship in history. When Walt Disney decided he wanted another boat in this area, he asked Joe Fowler, mentioned in the last devotional, to replicate a historical sailing vessel for inspiration. Fowler chose the Columbia Rediviva because of its status as the first American ship to sail around the world. However, at that time there was only one known picture of the famous ship so Disney Imagineers had to work really hard to make an exact copy from one lone picture. This gives us an important reminder today. We are also created as a replica. You and I were created and formed from something already in existence as well...not from a picture, but from the image of God Himself.

Remember in Genesis chapter 1 when God created the world and all the things in it, verse 27 says, "So God created man in his own image, in the image of God he created him; male and female he created them." Ephesians 4:24 and Colossians 3:10 remind us of this fact as well. We were all created in the image of God. What does that mean exactly? Good question! I did some research and found one scholar who studied the original language of the Bible. He concluded and stated that we are "a *formal, visible, and understandable representation* of who God is and what He is really like." What an honor! I think we often forget the fact that when God made us, He wanted us to represent Him. Therefore, He created us to be like Him. For that reason alone, we should respect our bodies and each other and try to live as God wants us to.

The Sailing Ship Columbia is an impressive ship. I definitely want to give it a try next time. It also represents a very special and important ship. At the same time, we represent God. We are made in His image. We need to respect that and treat ourselves and others accordingly. Let me finish by reminding you what was said about Jesus in Hebrews 1:3 where it reads, "He is the radiance of the glory of God and the exact imprint of his nature." Jesus was certainly an "exact imprint" of God. As we try to walk in the footsteps of Jesus every day, we need to act as though we are God's image as well, because we are!

"Millennium Falcon: Smuggler's Run"

I don't know about you, but I'm getting a little seasick here. As fun as those three boat rides were, it's time we move on to something different...and our next adventure is definitely that! I'm so excited about where we are heading next because I've not been there...yet! I wanted to talk about these next two attractions in the first book, but as I was writing, they were being built, and I really didn't have enough information about them. But they are now complete and open...well, the first is open and the other is coming very soon. And we already have two trips planned so we can ride them both. So let's spend the next two devotionals in Star Wars: Galaxy's Edge! This is the next land we come to here at Disneyland Park, so it makes logical sense to visit it next. Let's start with the attraction that is actually open currently at Disneyland and WDW. It's time to ride the Millennium Falcon: Smuggler's Run!

As a kid, I liked the Star Wars movies. They weren't my absolute favorite, but I enjoyed them. But Disney has molded me into a much greater Star Wars fan. They have built up so much hype over the last three movies, as well as this new land, and I'm very excited to experience it. I have heard great things about this new ride, and I can't wait to enjoy it on our next trip coming very soon! This Millennium Falcon ride is a simulator of sorts but with new and very advanced technology. It opened here in Disneyland Park at the end of May 2019 and soon after in August at WDW. Guests enter the ride through the life-size Millennium Falcon, the first time fans have ever seen a replica of this size. They are then seated in a 6 person motion simulator patterned after the very famous Millennium Falcon cockpit. The story of the ride is set between the most recent movie *The Last Jedi* and the one coming out soon at the end of 2019, *The Rise of Skywalker*. In preparation for the ride, you are given one of three job assignments. Therefore not only is this a ride, it is an interactive experience where you must participate and fulfill your responsibilities during the course of the action. The three possible jobs are pilot, gunner and engineer. The two pilots must of course steer the ship in and out of danger. The two gunners must fire upon potential threats and enemies. The two engineers must repair any damage to your ship and restore it to full power. Obviously if you sit and do nothing, the ride will continue, but I'm told that you have a much better experience if you actually participate and work hard at your job. I'm also told that you get better each time you ride which, in true Disney fashion, encourages you to come back again and again.

I'm not sure which job I want. I do know one thing...in our spiritual lives, all three of these jobs are important and we have to do them all at the same time! Let's look at those three jobs again related to our own lives with a scripture reference for each:

PILOT: Philippians 2:12 says that we must work out our own salvation with fear and trembling. It goes on to say that God will of course work in us, but scripture makes it clear that we have to constantly work at our spiritual life. As mentioned in a recent prior devotional, we have to meet God halfway. He is not going to do everything for us. We must be a pilot of sorts and steer our lives in the right direction at all times.

GUNNER: Ephesians 6:11-12 reads, "Put on the whole armor of God, that you may be able to stand against the schemes of the devil. For we do not wrestle against flesh and blood, but against the rulers, against the authorities, against the cosmic powers over this present darkness, against the spiritual forces of evil in the heavenly places." Those verses even mention that we wrestle against "cosmic powers!" Talk about a similarity to Star Wars! The whole point of those verses is that we have to fight. We have to put on the armor of God to fight against Satan and his clever schemes. There is constant evil all around us in the form of temptation and sin, and we must be on constant alert and fight off anything getting us off track.

ENGINEER: Acts 3:19 says, "Repent therefore, and turn back, that your sins may be blotted out." Revelation 2:5 reminds us to remember where we fall and to again repent. Repent is an important spiritual word that basically means to feel regret about sin and therefore change. As the engineer of our own lives, we must make constant repairs and change any wrong doings. We have to always fix our lives if they are damaged or heading in the wrong direction.

The Millennium Falcon ride sounds pretty intense. Again, based on what I've heard, all three jobs are significant, and team effort is very important here. The ride provides a better experience if everyone does their part and works hard at their assigned job. Our lives are even more important, and it takes dedicated effort to accomplish the same jobs and keep our spiritual lives right. Pray each day that God will help you pilot your life in the right direction, fight off the evil of Satan and fix any problems that are keeping you from a relationship with Him.

"Star Wars: Rise of the Resistance"

Now that we've had an adventure on the Millennium Falcon, it's time for the other ride here in this galactic land. It's called Star Wars: Rise of the Resistance. I haven't got to do this one either. Actually, nobody has yet as I'm writing this. It's scheduled to open in December 2019 in WDW and January 2020 in Disneyland. My wife and I have a January trip planned to WDW, and hopefully getting to ride this will be one of the highlights of our trip. I debated doing a devotional on this ride since it's not yet opened, but since it will be very soon, I decided to go ahead with it. So let's go check out this exciting new attraction for our devotional thought for today.

From what I've read in anticipation, Star Wars: Rise of the Resistance is being called one of the most immersive and techno-logically advanced experiences Disney has ever created. One writer even stated that this will be the "grandest theme park attraction ever realized!" Wow! Hope it lives up to that review! We are being told we will be shocked, amazed and filled with awe. It appears that guests will begin by entering an old Resistance base where they will get to see many of their favorite characters from several different Star Wars films and TV shows. The riders will then enter a ship of sorts and be transported into space, only to have things go awry when the ship is intercepted by the enemy. After being caught, guests will have to figure a way out of the Star Destroyer and back to the Resistance base. Guests will then board trackless vehicles to search for an escape route. Basically, you will be completely immersed in a massive Star Wars story that will take you way beyond the typical theme park attraction. There will be multiple characters and audio-animatronics as well as life size vehicles, ships and machines from the films. In short, it looks to be an amazing, incredible and breath-taking experience. I wish I could write more about it, but as nobody has officially done it yet, I can only go on projections and interview reports.

As mentioned, it appears that a major part of the experience will be when you are captured by the enemy, called the First Order. You then will apparently have to search the ship to figure out how to escape. Maybe there will be some teamwork, strategy or skill involved, but the fact that you will have to attempt to flee the enemy leads us to our spiritual thought for today. Luckily, like all Disney rides, this experience will all be fantasy. You won't really be captured. You won't really need escape. But consider just a moment if this was real. What if you really were apprehended by your worst enemy and you knew he was going to do terrible things to you? However, you also realized that you had just a few moments to try and escape. How desperate would you be in those few minutes? How hard would you work to get away? Look closely at your life right now. You may indeed be captured and not even know it.

2 Timothy 2:26 reads, "...and they may come to their senses and escape from the snare of the devil, after being captured by him to do his will." Satan is just like the enemy on this Disney attraction. He captures us. He ensnares us. He traps us and tries to get us to do his will. Just like this verse says, we have to escape. Earlier in this chapter in verse 22, we are told to flee from youthful passions and instead pursue righteousness. Sometimes we get caught in sin, maybe a particular sin that we tend to repeat over and over. Is there something like that in your life right now? If so, the fact is it's keeping you from God. You are trapped! The enemy has you! The good news is that God is giving you an escape. I Corinthians 10:13 says, "No temptation has overtaken you that is not common to man. God is faithful, and he will not let you be tempted beyond your ability, but with the temptation he will also provide the way of escape, that you may be able to endure it." See that? God provides our escape. We just have to look for it quickly and act on it before Satan traps us for good.

I can't wait to see what Star Wars: Rise of the Resistance entails. I wouldn't mind a little challenge. It might be fun having to use a little strategy to try and escape the enemy. Take some time today to evaluate your life. Are you trapped? Do you need to escape? Do you need help to do it? Be honest with yourself or even a friend, if you're comfortable. Admit what has got you trapped and begin immediately looking for a way to escape. It's so important to your eternal life with God that you do!

"Goofy's Playhouse"

Ok, it's now time to leave this Star Wars land and take the small path here to the very back of Disneyland Park. We're going to do a complete 180 as far as our surroundings and go from cosmic battles with laser weapons to cartoons in a colorful, wacky land. We are entering the area known as Mickey's Toontown to ride or experience several attractions here that are unique to Disneyland. Let's begin with what may be the silliest of all. Let's enter Goofy's Playhouse!

Goofy's Playhouse is simply just that. It's a playhouse belonging to that lovable character, Goofy that opened in 1993. Kids of all ages can experience this attraction, while their parents sit outside and relax. It's a great way to have kids burn off a little excess energy which matches the goal of several of the attractions in this land. Originally this was called Goofy's Bounce House which was a ball crawl with padded walls, but it was refurbished in 2006. Kids will most likely enjoy this new experience where you get to see all of the crazy items in Goofy's house. There are several interactive things for kids to do as they explore this one of a kind property. For example, the piano makes Goofy noises instead of playing notes.

Goofy's full name is "Goofy Goof," or he's occasionally been given the name "Goofus D. Dawg." He was created in 1932 by Walt Disney and others and first appeared in a cartoon entitled "Mickey's Revue." In that short classic, he was known as "Dippy Dawg" but was later reimagined and given the Goofy name. He is without a doubt one of Disney's most recognizable characters. He is typically shown as clumsy and a little absent-minded, although that is not always the case. Some of the classic cartoons show him as clever, but in his own unique way of course. Within all the information one can read about Goofy and his history, there is always that one eternal question that pops up...What on Earth is he? Is he an animal? Is he a person? Is he somewhere in between? There's always been a little confusion, because he looks most like a dog. But Pluto is a dog. And there can't be two dogs, right? Wrong. Most experts agree that he is indeed an anthropomorphic dog (meaning a dog with human traits and characteristics.) However, I found one entry on snopes.com stating that a lot of people think he is a type of cow. Go figure!

With Goofy being as much of a Disney classic as he is, I find it a little sad that his identity has been questioned for decades. Poor Goofy! I guess the good news is that he's a cartoon so there's no real hurt feeling here. Unfortunately, sometimes real people that do have feelings question their own identity and don't like who they are. I once heard a statistic that seventy-five percent of people don't like what they see when they look in a mirror. Seventy-five percent! That's a lot. It's sad to me that a lot of people are ashamed of who they are. Maybe they don't like their size or their shape or their hair or their personality. There are unfortunately a lot of reasons people don't like themselves, and the sad truth is that a lot of people desperately try to change who they are and what God created. Maybe we need a reminder today of Psalms 139:14 which says we should praise God because we are fearfully and wonderfully made. In addition, I Timothy 4:4 says that everything created by God is good and nothing is to be rejected. Sadly, many people focus too much on the outside and what they see in that mirror and forget the person they really are. I Peter 3:3-4 reminds us, "Do not let your adorning be external, the braiding of hair and the putting on of gold jewelry, or the clothing you wear, but let your adorning be the hidden person of the heart with the imperishable beauty of a gentle and quiet spirit, which in God's sight is very precious." It's not what we wear or what we look like on the outside that's important. It's what in our heart that matters. That's what God looks at. That's what is "very precious" to Him.

I remind you of the old cliché "God don't make no junk." God created you just the way He wanted you. There's no reason to change anything that God made. Unlike old Goofy, we shouldn't have to question what we are, because it's very simple. We are all children of God created by Him in His image. That means you are special. Be proud of who you are today. And if others around you need a reminder, share this message with them.

"Donald's Boat"

We visited one important character's house. Why not another? We'll just start our tour of Toontown by visiting different character residences. We've done Goofy, today Donald and then we've got Mickey, Minnie, Chip and Dale coming up. Donald apparently lives in a very different type of house. In fact, it's not really a house at all. Donald after all is an expert sailor...or at least he thinks he is. So today let's go visit Donald's boat.

Donald's boat is a colorful attraction next door to Goofy's house that is, as expected geared towards kids and burning that energy. Parents can once again rest in the shade. His boat is aptly named the "Miss Daisy" after his longtime girlfriend, Daisy Duck. Donald's boat which is actually shaped like Donald himself, includes several different levels to explore, with the top offering some great views of Mickey's Toontown. Kids can also enjoy the many interactive things to do, including pulling the whistle cord which triggers some water spouts. They can also search for several hidden Mickeys on the boat and maybe even a hidden Goofy!

Donald Fauntleroy Duck was created by Walt Disney in 1934 and first appeared in a cartoon called "The Wise Little Hen." He was voiced by Clarence Nash for over 50 years until his death in 1985. He has since been voiced by Tony Anselmo who continues to this day. Donald began dating Daisy Duck in 1940, and the two have been together ever since. He is one of the most popular cartoon characters ever created. He also happens to be my personal favorite Disney character.

I have always loved Donald Duck. Maybe it's because he makes me laugh. Maybe because I remember watching him a lot as a kid. Or perhaps it's because I got to play him in my first grade play way back in 1982. (Yes I'm that old!) Can I just say that my first grade play was incredible? It knocked grades 2-4 out of the park. It was a tribute to Disney where every one of us got to play a Disney character, and we sang at least 20 classic Disney songs. I know this because my dad videotaped it on one of the first video cameras ever invented. That thing was huge and very heavy! (Shout out to Al. Good job, dad!) Nevertheless, I used to watch that video tape over and over. I only wish I could find it because it's currently lost. ☹ But I'll never forget my first grade teacher asking me if I would be willing to be one of the three main parts which were Mickey, Minnie and Donald. I was going to be Donald Duck, and I was very excited. My mom worked for hours (days? weeks?) making my costume, and I looked pretty good if I do say so myself. (Shout out to Pam. Good job mom!) Wonder if that costume is still around? Anyways, I had a lot of lines and stayed on stage the whole time with my mice counterparts. I'll never forget show night because something very scary happened. Right before the show, my dad challenged me to do something special, but also terrifying. As I was one of the last three to take a bow, he told me I should turn around after my bow and shake my poufy duck tail at the audience. Not sure why dad offered this challenge. I guess he wanted to capture that special moment on his 400 pound camera. I didn't want to do it. I remember being very nervous and turning him down telling him I would not be doing that. However, during the show, I decided I was up for the challenge and did indeed give my rump a little shake after my bow. It was small and subtle, but it was there. I did it! My dad laughed. Not sure anyone else did. At least dad was happy. But I was happy too. I conquered my fear and met the challenge.

We all have fears in life. Life can be very scary after all. We all have to meet challenges, face fears and do things we'd rather not do. Some of these things are very important, whether it's starting a new school, changing careers or dealing with life's plethora of problems. It's ok to be scared, nervous, worried or anxious. However, it's not ok to let those emotions take over your life and affect your relationship with God. Luckily, He is always there to wrap His loving arms around us when we are afraid. Isaiah 41:10 says, "Fear not, for I am with you; be not dismayed, for I am your God; I will strengthen you, I will help you, I will uphold you with my righteous right hand." Isn't that comforting? Also remember that scripture says we can do ALL things with the strength that God freely gives us. (Philippians 4:13)

I realize that my Donald Duck tail shaking wasn't a vital part of my life. If I hadn't done it, the world would've moved on. But I'm glad I did. I was proud of myself. After all, I was really nervous about it, but I made the decision to face my fear and give it a shot. We will all face much bigger challenges that will tug at all of our different emotions. Just remember to lean on God, be in constant prayer with Him about your fears and rest easy in these words from Joshua 1:9. "Be strong and courageous. Do not be frightened, and do not be dismayed, for the Lord your God is with you wherever you go."

"Mickey and Minnie's Houses"

On to some more residences of Toontown, and these are a couple of very important ones! Today we are going to see where Mickey and Minnie live. Technically these are two different attractions which I could've done separately, but I decided to combine them since the two just seem to naturally go together. Both houses opened in 1993 at Disneyland. They had opened five years before that at the Magic Kingdom in WDW but closed there in 2011. Mickey's house is also currently open in Tokyo Disneyland. Mickey's house is a walk-through tour of his various rooms, as well as his backyard, Pluto's doghouse and his movie barn. The barn is a type of studio where guests can watch classic Disney cartoons while awaiting admittance to Mickey's dressing room to meet the honorary mouse himself. Minnie's house is right next door and as one might expect, is geared more in feminine taste as a pink and lavender bungalow. Unfortunately guests don't typically get to meet Minnie here as she is usually found in other areas roaming around the park. Both houses have interactive features that kids will enjoy with many things to look for, including several hidden Mickeys. Minnie's house also has a wishing well out back. Apparently if you make a wish loudly into the well, you might just hear something in return. I'll have to try that next time.

It's interesting that after all these years together, Mickey and Minnie live in separate houses and have never officially married, although Walt Disney said in a 1933 interview that in private life, they are indeed married. Instead, they each have their own unique house geared to their own tastes and personalities. What about your house? Do you like it? I hope so. I hope it's geared to your personality as well, although you may have to share your decorative tastes with someone else. If you are anything like my wonderful wife and me, we have to often work together and compromise on decorating a room or buying something new for the house. Incidentally, if I had my way, I would have a whole Disney room in our house to display all my souvenirs. As it stands, I've been granted a large shelving unit in the corner of my basement, but I'm working on expanding. My wife has pointed out that there are no available extra rooms since our boys need their bedrooms.

I guess I agree. The point is that our houses are special. Most would agree that they like to be in the comfort of their own homes. I certainly do. However, let's remember what the Bible says about our houses.

2 Corinthians 5:1 says, "For we know that if the tent that is our earthly home is destroyed, we have a building from God, a house not made with hands, eternal in the heavens." I used to coach Cross Country, and I would always get to the meets early to set up our large team tent. One particular windy day, I had set up the tent and was sitting in my car waiting for the team to arrive. I was talking to my wife on the phone when I noticed a large tent blowing by tumbling across the field. All it once, it hit me...it was MY large tent blowing by tumbling across the field! I think I spluttered to my wife, "My tent! Gotta go!" before I threw my phone down, jumped out of my car and ran after it. Luckily some others helped to slow it down before it blew into the next county. Unfortunately, the tent took a little damage that day from the adventure. That story reminds me of this very verse. Tents are temporary. Our houses are too, despite how much we love them and how much work we put into them.

I'm sure Mickey and Minnie take pride in their homes and how they are decorated. There's nothing wrong with us having pride in our earthly homes and enjoying being there. We all know the famous phrase "home sweet home." We just have to always remember that our homes, like tents, are temporary. As we work to upkeep our houses, we should also always be preparing for our eternal home. Don't forget that Jesus himself said in John 14 that God's house has many rooms. There are enough for every single person that works hard and follows the Word of God. Jesus also said that He Himself is preparing that eternal home for you and for me. I for one can't wait to see the face of Jesus when I enter the room with my name on it. I hope you will be there too!

"Chip 'n' Dale Treehouse"

It's finally time for our last abode. How's that for a fancy word? I'm having to use the thesaurus here since we've been visiting so many residences. Or dwellings. Or habitations. Ok, that's enough. Today we get to go see where those loveable chipmunks Chip and Dale live, and it's not a house or even a boat. It's a treehouse!

The Chip 'N Dale Treehouse is often overlooked as it's hidden at the back of Toontown and partially hidden by the queue for another attraction. As guests enter the treehouse, they climb a spiral staircase to explore the many personal touches that make this place a unique home for those mischievous creatures. There are no age or height requirements, but some adults might have a hard time fitting into this attraction as it involves some low ceilings and tight spaces. The treehouse used to have a slide and ball pit play area. However, the slide closed presumably due to too many injuries, and the ball pit closed for sanitation reasons.

Chip and Dale were created in 1943. Their names are a play of the word Chippendale which was the last name of a famous 18th century furniture designer. Many folks have a hard time telling the two apart. The best way is to look at their noses. Chip has a black nose while Dale's is brown. They also have very different personalities. Chip tends to be more cautious, attentive and safe while Dale is more relaxed and impulsive with a strong sense of humor. Even in the many cartoons they have been seen in, they tend to be very different. They often argue and disagree, however they have never wavered in their friendship and bond with each other. They are always seen together, even as characters in the parks.

Do you have a best friend? Maybe it's someone you've known for many years. Or maybe it's someone you met recently but feel like you've known forever. It could even be a sibling, spouse or other relative. It's nice to have someone special in your life that you get along with, enjoy talking to and can depend on. The cliché is true in that sometimes opposites attract so your best friend may be quite different from you. Friendship is a wonderful blessing that God gives us. Make sure you thank God often for the friends in your life. Also keep in mind that there are many people out there that need a friend. There's no such thing as too many friends, so look for those in need, reach out and be a friend to them. Scripture reminds us in Ecclesiastes 4:9-10 that "Two are better than one, because they have a good reward for their toil. For if they fall, one will lift up his fellow. But woe to him who is alone when he falls and has not another to lift him up!" I love that passage. It's so encouraging and helps us to remember how important it is to work together and be a friend to others. I'm also reminded of I Thessalonians 5:14-15 where Paul tells us to encourage those who are weak or hurting. He also says that in everything, we should seek to do good to everyone.

Don't forget about Chip 'N Dale's treehouse if you ever find yourself in Toontown. May it remind you of those crazy chipmunks and their special friendship. And may we all be reminded to be a friend to others. Not just those we are already friends with, but others who may need a friend. After all, Jesus was a friend to everyone with no reservations, and we should try our best to do the same.

"Gadget's Go Coaster"

We're finally done with all the houses, but we still have three more attractions here in Mickey's Toontown. And it's really not one of the bigger sections of the park. Obviously, they have crammed a lot of unique Disneyland attractions into this one land. Today, we're going to take a fun ride on the only roller coaster in this area. It's a junior coaster, again mainly geared toward children, as is all of Toontown. So let's hop in line for Gadget's Go Coaster.

This mini-thrill ride opened in 1993 at Disneyland Park and three years later in Tokyo. It is the shortest ride in Disneyland at 44 seconds, only 20 of which you are actually zooming around the track. The rest of the time is leaving the loading area and climbing the first hill. This is the only ride at Disneyland that is based on a Disney afternoon television series. Gadget Hackwrench, a small female mouse, was a major character in the popular series *Chip 'n Dale: Rescue Rangers*. You can see her picture on a postage stamp in the loading area. You can also see her name spelled out with workshop tools as you wait in line. There are a couple of hidden Mickeys to find on this ride as well as a frog that squirts water up and over your ride vehicle as you pass.

As I mentioned, Gadget Hackwrench was an important character in the Rescue Ranger series starring Chip and Dale. She is an intuitive and inventive mouse that is always pitching in to help the Rangers. Gadget is constantly thinking of new and imaginative ways to help. She is creative, mechanically savvy and gets very excited when talking about one of her new inventions. In summary, she is a problem solver, always willing to help with conflicts to make things better. This leads to our devotional thought today. Are you a problem solver or a problem contributor? When it comes to relationships and getting along with others, you are typically either one or the other. It's easy to have conflict with others. It's easy to disagree with someone or just clash your personality with theirs. God made us all very different so it stands to reason that we will not be able to live in peace and harmony with everyone. It's ok to have differences. It's ok to disagree with someone. It's even ok to not like someone. But how you handle those differences and how you treat the person is what matters.

When Jesus was here on Earth, He gave very specific instructions on what to do if someone wrongs you. Read Matthew 18:15-17 which says, "If your brother sins against you, go and tell him his fault, between you and him alone. If he listens to you, you have gained your brother. But if he does not listen, take one or two others along with you, that every charge may be established by the evidence of two or three witnesses. If he refuses to listen to them, tell it to the church. And if he refuses to listen even to the church, let him be to you as a Gentile and a tax collector." According to Scripture, there are steps to follow to solve any problems you may have with someone else. You are going to be wronged by others in your life, probably many times. But we are also told in many verses to forgive others. I realize that's not always easy, but if we want to leave at peace and be a problem solver as we're instructed to do, forgiveness is what we should strive for. Remember these words of Christ in Matthew 6:14-15 when He said, "For if you forgive others their trespasses, your heavenly Father will also forgive you, but if you do not forgive others their trespasses, neither will your Father forgive your trespasses." I think we all want God to forgive any sins we have. I know I do. But I can't expect Him to do that if I can't do it for others as well.

You may not be familiar with Gadget Hackwrench. I can't say that I knew her really well, or maybe at all, before I wrote this. But from what I've read, she was a great one to have around because of her eagerness to help. She worked very hard to solve problems to avoid any conflicts or rough situations. We can learn a lesson from that little mouse. When we have disagreements or even arguments with others, we may end up being angry with that person. But we should avoid holding grudges which solve nothing and instead work hard at reconciling those differences. It should be our goal to treat everyone with respect, even our enemies. In conclusion, I think these words from Romans 12:17-21 say it best. "Repay no one evil for evil, but give thought to do what is honorable in the sight of all. If possible, so far as it depends on you, live peaceably with all. Beloved, never avenge yourselves, but leave it to the wrath of God, for it is written, 'Vengeance is mine, I will repay, says the Lord.' To the contrary, 'if your enemy is hungry, feed him; if he is thirsty, give him something to drink; for by so doing you will heap burning coals on his head.' Do not be overcome by evil, but overcome evil with good."

"Roger Rabbit's Car Toon Spin"

With all the attractions found in Mickey's Toontown, there are really only two that are considered rides. The rest are walk-through attractions, such as the various houses, as well as character meets. I suppose the fact that there is a station here for the Disneyland Railroad makes that a ride here as well, but there are of course other train stations in other lands. That means that technically the coaster we just disembarked and today's topic are the only two rides here. Today's ride is a little scary for me. If you read my first book of devotionals, you know that basically the only ride I can't do at WDW is those spinning tea cups sent by the devil himself! Therefore when I saw the title of today's ride for the first time, I was understandably a little hesitant. But I'm proud to say that just like my Donald Duck, first grade play, shake my poufy tail story, I conquered my fear and gave this one a shot. I'm also happy to say that I made it! I survived! And without spilling my lunch all over the ride! I did it once, and once was enough! I was good to go and didn't need to do it again. But I definitely wanted to give it a try as this ride is based on one of my favorite movies. So let me invite you to come take a "whirl" on Roger Rabbit's Car Toon Spin. Hope your lunch is well digested before you board!

Roger Rabbit's Car Toon Spin is a dark ride that opened at Disneyland Park in 1994 and two years later in Tokyo. Each ride vehicle resembles two connected cabs that will hold 4-6 people. Guests then take a 3 minute 30 second ride through the back alleys of Toontown from the film *Who Framed Roger Rabbit*. As they travel, guests may choose to turn the steering wheel in their vehicle to give themselves a spin, the speed of which is based on how fast they turn the wheel. Trust me when I say that I didn't touch my wheel, although I found that you still spin a little regardless. The line queue for this attraction features several license plates dedicated to other Disney characters. A few examples are 1D N PTR (Wendy and Peter), 1DRLND (Wonderland), and CAP 10 HK (Captain Hook). When this movie first came out in 1988, it was very popular and Roger Rabbit proved to be a lucrative character for Disney. In fact, Hollwoodland, a new land based on him, was planned for Disneyland behind Main Street. There were also at least three rides planned at Hollywood Studios in Florida based on the various characters from the film. Unfortunately, due to the financial troubles of Disneyland Paris, then called Euro-Disney, plans were severely cut back, and just this one ride prevailed.

Have you seen *Who Framed Roger Rabbit*? This movie came out when I was 13, and I loved it. I used to watch it over and over. It's a very clever and funny movie with multiple tributes to classic cartoon characters, even non-Disney ones. If you've never seen it, I encourage you to get a hold of a copy. I need to watch it again myself. The basic premise of the film takes place when Roger Rabbit is accused of a murder. He insists he's innocent and hires a non-cartoon detective to help prove it. The result is a wacky adventure in and out of Toontown to help Roger prove his innocence. If you've never seen it, I won't spoil the ending on whether Roger is found guilty or innocent, but one thing is for sure.... we are guilty! Whether you know it or not, and whether you like it or not, you're guilty. I'm guilty. And there's nothing we can do to prove our innocence. What are we guilty of you might ask? The answer is quite simple. We are guilty of murder.

That might sound harsh and may come as a shock, but it's ultimately true. First of all, we are all guilty of sin. Romans 3:23 says that ALL have sinned. We can't deny it. We've all done it. And then Romans 6:23 says that the wages of sin is death. In other words, the price of our sin is eternal death and punishment. However, because of God's amazing grace and love, thankfully that is not the end of the story. Look at these amazing verses in Colossians 2. Verses 13-14 say, "God... having forgiven us all our trespasses by canceling the record of debt that stood against us with its legal demands. This he set aside, nailing it to the cross." It was our sin that put Jesus up there. We are guilty of His murder, but God forgave all our sins when He allowed His Son to be nailed to that cross as a sacrifice for our sin. Because of that, Romans 8:1 says that "there is no condemnation for those who are in Christ Jesus." Can you believe that? We are guilty, but we have been set free anyways! Do you realize what an incredible gift that is? Have you shared that with others? Have you told anyone that Jesus Christ saved us from eternal punishment with the ultimate sacrifice?

Like Roger Rabbit, we have all been accused of murder. The difference is that Roger adamantly states that he's innocent. He knows he didn't commit the crime. We can't make that same statement. We are guilty, no doubt about it. Our sin is what put Jesus on that cross to die. But we've been shown incredible grace and mercy and have been set free. Praise God today and every day for that!

"Mickey and Minnie's Runaway Railway"

I had every intention of moving on from Mickey's Toontown to the next land. After all, there are no more attractions here. We've done everything there is to do, right? Technically yes, but in a short time that won't be the case. There's a new ride coming to this land! I should skip it since it doesn't exist yet, but I just can't. It's too important. It's coming to Disney World in 2020 and soon after at Disneyland in 2022. And there's already enough information out there about it that warrants a devotional. Not to mention the fact that I'm super excited about it and have a semi-personal connection to it. So today we're discussing Mickey and Minnie's Runaway Railway!

This attraction dedicated to the park's original characters will take the place of The Great Movie Ride in Hollywood Studios in WDW. It is not scheduled to replace anything at Disneyland, but instead will be built at the back of Toontown in what are now storage buildings. This enclosed dark ride will be the first based on Mickey and Minnie. Guests will pass through a simulated movie screen on their way to a wild train adventure with Goofy as your engineer and guide. You will be the star of a classic Mickey Mouse cartoon short where you never know what will happen. In what has been called a "dimensional display of amazingness," the ride will be featured in 2 ½ D which basically means 3D effects without the glasses. It will be an incredible experience with the latest technology, immersive details and visual effects.

I will certainly miss The Great Movie Ride at Hollywood Studios and its creative look at the history of film. At the same time, I am very enthusiastic about this new experience. I can't believe there has never been a ride based on Mickey and Minnie. How is that possible? They are the stars of the show; the most important characters Disney ever created! They deserve at least one ride focused on them, and this one sounds fantastic. I can't wait to ride this and see all it has to offer. I love Disney cartoons, especially the newer ones shown around the clock on Disney resort channels. They are absolutely hilarious and very entertaining. The old, but classic cartoons are great as well.

As mentioned, I have a semi-personal connection to the creation of this ride. We have some close friends whose son (shout out to Davis) worked as a college intern in the engineering department at Disney World. His main focus while he was there was working on this very attraction. He knows what's coming. He knows secrets! I was hoping, as close as we are that he would possibly share some dirt with us. You know, just drop a hint here or there. Innocently pass us some minor details. Accidently leave the blueprints on our doorstep. But no! Apparently he takes his nondisclosure agreements very seriously. He didn't tell us squat! Our friendship is now wavering.

In the first book of devotionals, the very last entry was dedicated to the "Partners" statue in the Magic Kingdom which is the famous sculpture of Walt Disney and Mickey Mouse holding hands. I purposely made that the last devotional, because I love that statue. I love what it represents. I love the history of Mickey's development and what he has become. In short, I am so glad that there will be an attraction dedicated to the famous mouse and his forever girlfriend. They are, in a word, "classic." They are the originals. They are the beginnings in a monumental world of beloved characters. They were first.

This reminds me of another original. Another first. Another beginning. Another classic. This reminds me of God. It is hard for our tiny minds to grasp the concept of forever. We can't comprehend something having no beginning and no end. Mickey and Minnie have a beginning. They will one day have an end. But God doesn't have those things. According to the Bible, He has always been and He will always be. He originated the world. He created everything in it. And one day we will hopefully be with Him forever. There will be no end. Heaven will be forever. It's difficult for us to understand that. Unfortunately, it's a tool that atheists use against those of us who believe. They argue that everything has to have a beginning and an end. But if you believe in the Bible as I do, you have to believe that God is the exception. In Revelation 1:8, God says, "I am the Alpha and the Omega who is and who was and who is to come." As you probably know, those are the first and last letters in the Greek alphabet. God is saying He's the beginning and the end.

Read Psalms 90 today. The first two verses say, "Lord, you have been our dwelling place in all generations. Before the mountains were brought forth, or ever you had formed the earth and the world, from everlasting to everlasting you are God." I'm thrilled Mickey and Minnie are getting an attraction soon. In the world of Disney, they are the originals. But the real original in the true world that we live in is God. And what an awesome, powerful, amazing God He is! Take some time right now to praise His name, talk to Him and thank Him for creating, knowing and loving us in this wonderful world He created. And thank Him that He is forever!

"Fantasyland Theatre"

We are ready to finally move to a new land! We spent a lot of time in Toontown, so it's nice to move to something new. Making our way around the map and layout of Disneyland Park, we naturally come next to Fantasyland, which by far has the most attractions of any land. Like Toontown, we are going to be in this land for quite a while. By my count, there are around ten attractions here that are unique to Disneyland. There are also a few copies that appear in Fantasyland at Disney World such as Small World, Peter Pan, Dumbo and the dreaded Tea Cups (barf). But let's start our focus with a very entertaining and high quality show at the Fantasyland Theatre.

The Fantasyland Theatre opened in 1985 and is a 5000 square foot outdoor amphitheater that functions as a venue for various shows. It can seat up to 1800 people at a time! It was formerly called "Videopolis" and has over time featured many shows, music performances and even television programs. When it first opened, it would feature shows during the day but would be transformed into a dance club with music videos at night. The dance club featured 70 video monitors where guests could watch themselves boogie down. The dance club concept was abandoned in 1989 after several gang related incidents. Yikes! The theater was even featured in a television show called "Videopolis" that aired on the Disney Channel from 1987 to 1989. It featured an array of top 40 bands and singers including Debbie Gibson, Janet Jackson and the New Kids on the Block. There have been nationally televised telethons filmed there as well.

Today, the theatre hosts the show "Mickey and the Magic Map" which has been playing there since 2013. It stars Mickey Mouse as an apprentice to the great sorcerer Yen Sid. Yen Sid is Disney spelled backwards of course and was first featured in the famous Disney film *Fantasia*. The show reveals a giant map which covers the entire length of the theatre stage. The map is a giant LED screen featuring nearly one million pixels. When Mickey attempts to finish painting the one uncovered spot on the map, his adventures begin. Guests then enjoy an array of colors, music, characters and excitement in which several Disney classic songs are featured. The show runs approximately 22 minutes. Over 900 hopefuls tried out for the production that features around 50 performers. There was another Fantasyland Theater (different spelling) that opened soon after the park in 1956. It showed Disney cartoons and also allowed Mickey Mouse Club Mousketeers to feature short films. It was shut down however in 1981 and replaced with Pinocchio's Daring Journey which we will talk about soon.

From reading this brief description of the history of this theatre, it's obvious that it's hosted a huge variety of different shows. Since it first opened, it's introduced at least 15 different shows, not to mention the TV programs, dance clubs and music videos. Some of these shows lasted five or six years while others only a few months. The current show is obviously a hit and has been well received, as it has been one of the longest lasting shows featured here, going on nearly seven years. I'm sure many of the shows here have been greatly enjoyed by audiences while some of the shorter lived ones might not have been quite as popular. I'm glad that Disney changes things up from time to time. If you know anything about Disney, you know that they are constantly refurbishing rides and shows. One important philosophy that Walt Disney himself had was that Disney should always be changing. This is what brings people back. They should be able to see new things every single time they come. While it's hard to see favorites go or change sometimes, I think this concept is important, and I'm glad Disney does this.

In the same way, we should constantly be evaluating and making changes in our lives. Read Hebrews 5:11-14. This passage talks about milk versus solid food. As you know, as babies, we live on milk as our bodies grow and develop. Eventually we move on to solid food. In the same way, this passage suggests we should begin our spiritual lives on milk as we learn the basic principles of how to live our lives. As we mature, the passage states that we move on to solid food and can then distinguish good from evil. I Corinthians 14:20 says, "Brothers, do not be children in your thinking. Be infants in evil, but in your thinking be mature." Hebrews 6:1 reads, "Therefore let us leave the elementary doctrine of Christ and go on to maturity."

I have never seen the current show presented at the Fantasyland Theatre. It sounds wonderful, and I hope it will stick around long enough for me to catch it. However, I have no doubt that one day Disney will replace it with a newer and even better performance. This theatre is evidence of the ever changing Disney. Our lives need to be evidence that we are ever changing as we mature in our spiritual walk. We should daily evaluate ourselves and change bad practices as we strive for perfection. We can never be perfect as Jesus was, but we should always work as hard as we can to be as much like Him as possible. Figure out today what is not perfect in your life, and make changes.

"Mr. Toad's Wild Ride"

You ready for some rides? This devotional starts a slew of eight rides in a row here in Fantasyland. We're starting with a very important one, a definite classic among nostalgic rides. This is one of ten attractions that have been open since day one at Disneyland Park. It also was open day one at Disney World but closed there in 1998 to much controversy. Many Disney regulars love this ride and were very upset to see it close at WDW and replaced by Winnie the Pooh. Some even called themselves "Toad-Ins" and had a website, special postcards and T-shirts. One t-shirt said "Ask me why Mickey is killing Mr. Toad." Wow, talk about dedication! I think they are over it now...hopefully. Luckily, it is still around here in this park. Today let's enjoy a journey on Mr. Toad's Wild Ride.

This is another dark ride that was originally planned to be a roller coaster, but Walt Disney only wanted attractions on opening day that were appropriate for all ages. This ride is based on the Disney adaptation of "The Wind in the Willows," one of two segments of the 1949 Disney film *The Adventures of Ichabod and Mr. Toad*. Guests board multi-colored early 20th cars each named after a character from the film. They are then taken on a wild ride with many twists and turns through several scenes including a library, Toad Hall, the countryside and town square. The final scene riders pass through is a version of Hell, although one cast member noted that they are supposed to call it the Inferno Room and not use the other word because it's considered too negative. This scene is not taken from the film or even the book that inspired it. The room is heated and features many little devils bouncing up and down. Riders then see the courtroom scene from the film, but this one features a demon as judge. Finally, a towering green dragon appears and attempts to burn riders with fiery, breathing flames only to cough and sputter. As expected, riders escape this "close call" and disembark the ride soon after.

Are you surprised about this final scene of the ride? I was. After all, it doesn't seem very "Disney" to have a depiction of Hell in a ride. I even saw a couple of websites that warned parents to take caution as young children may be frightened by this scene. If you've read the first book of devotionals, you may have noticed that several of the entries focus on Heaven. I'm sure several in this book already have and will. Heaven is one of my favorite subjects. As I've said many times, I'm working hard every day to get there, and I want you there too. I want my family there. I already have a son waiting for me there. I love talking about, thinking about and planning for Heaven. On the other hand, Hell is a different story. In writing this entry, I did some research to see if the words Heaven and Hell should be capitalized because I've seen it both ways. Most grammar experts advise that it's up to the writer and can be done either way. I choose to capitalize them, because I strongly believe they are both very real places. I promise you they exist. I also believe that one day every single person will be in one of the two. As strongly as I want you and me to be in Heaven one day, I share the same strength in hoping and praying we don't end up in Hell. Unfortunately, the Bible says that many will which makes me very sad.

Take some time today to read Luke 16:19-30. This is the parable of the rich man and Lazarus, a story Jesus Himself used to describe Heaven vs Hell. In the story, the rich man goes to Hell, and the Bible says he's in torment in the flames and begs for just one drop of water to cool his tongue. Revelation 20:10 says that those in Hell will be tormented day and night forever and ever. In Matthew 25, Jesus describes judgment day and says that those who haven't followed the Word of God will be told to depart into an eternal fire. I realize that sounds terrible and very harsh. Many would ask how a loving God could allow that to happen to anyone. That's a good question. I can only answer and remind you that God loves you very much. He loves everyone very much. The Bible even says in 2 Peter 3:9 that He doesn't want anyone to perish. But due to the sin of man, there has to be a punishment. If there was no punishment, nobody would strive for Heaven. Nobody would help others or do good works. Sin would take over this world, and it would be even scarier than it is. God's plan has it so we have a choice. We can choose to follow his Word and one day be rewarded, or we can choose to ignore it and one day be tormented forever.

Mr. Toad's Wild Ride may depict Hell with a silly, whimsical representation. But I promise you that the real thing is far from silly. It is an awful and scary place. Please choose Heaven over Hell. I promise you that both are very real. And please bring as many with you as possible. I remind you that should be our purpose and goal in life.

"Pinocchio's Daring Journey"

Moving on from the last entry's depressing topic, we make our way to the next ride here in Fantasyland. It is based on Disney's 2nd animated feature released in 1940, which was another classic Disney movie with a great story. This ride replaced the original Fantasyland Theater which later became the Mickey Mouse Club Theater. We're living it up on another dark ride today. Let's go try out Pinocchio's Daring Journey.

This ride actually opened in Tokyo Disneyland first. It then arrived in California about a month later in 1983, and then nine years later in Paris. Guests board vehicles designed to look like wooden carts and travel through Stromboli's theater, Pleasure Island, Pinocchio Village and finally into Geppetto's workshop. There was an early concept drawn for this attraction that would've made it a boat ride instead. Guests would've been sent down the tongue of Monstro, the giant whale from the film, similar to the giant hill on Splash Mountain. This ride is the first in Disneyland to use holographic material. It's on the mirror in the scene where the boys turn into donkeys on Pleasure Island. *Pinocchio* the film was based on an Italian children's novel. The film introduced several beloved characters, including Jiminy Cricket, as well as some timeless songs like "When You Wish Upon a Star."

When is the last time you saw this movie? It's been a while for me, and I need to watch it again. In case you don't know, the story involves a woodworker named Geppetto that creates a wooden puppet of a boy he names Pinocchio. Before going to sleep, he makes a wish that the puppet would become a real boy. His wish comes true thanks to a blue fairy and the rest of the film follows Pinocchio and his outrageous adventures. Jiminy Cricket is given to Pinocchio as his conscience to help him. One of the most well-known parts of the story involves what happens early in the story. Pinocchio discovers that every time he tells a lie, his nose grows longer and longer. He has to learn the hard way that one lie leads to another and eventually can spiral out of control. I think the lesson we can draw from this memorable story is an obvious one.

Have you ever told a lie? That's probably like asking have you ever taken a breath. I would think that most people have told a lie at some point in their life. I wish I could say I was the one exception, but I can't. Even younger children sometimes tend to "bend the truth" to avoid getting into trouble. Unfortunately, it falls into our fallible human nature. We often find it much easier to say something that isn't true hoping it will prevent conflict or uncomfortable situations. Sometimes we even mean well in our lies, telling them to avoid hurting others or prevent a bad situation. As you may guess, however, the Bible is pretty clear on this topic. Did you know that the Bible says that God hates certain things? In Proverbs 6:16-19, we learn the seven things that the Lord hates. One of them is a "lying tongue" and another is a "false witness that breathes out lies." If two of the seven involve lying, it's pretty obvious how God feels about it. Colossians 3:9 makes it pretty clear as well when it says, "Do not lie to one another." Additionally, Proverbs 19:9 states, "A false witness will not go unpunished, and he who breathes out lies will perish." Titus 1:2 even says that God never lies. And Revelation 21:8 talks about the final destination for liars... which happens to match the topic from our last devotional. I think you get the point. The Bible is pretty clear-cut on the topic. It's one of the Ten Commandments...Thou shalt not bear false witness. Read Acts 5:1-11 about Ananias and his wife, Sapphira. They are both caught in a lie, not to man, but to God. See what happens to them because of it.

Do you see a pattern here? Obviously, lying is wrong. Pinocchio certainly learned that as it got him into a lot of trouble. For us, lying not only causes trouble, but it is sin. I think God purposely put this over and over in Scripture because it's one of the most widely practiced sins. Again, it's so easy to do and get away with, and so a lot of people do it without even thinking about it. Work hard to not be one of those people. Don't be in the majority. Work hard to keep yourself from lying, even if you have good intentions. God hates it. I don't know about you, but I don't want to be a part of anything our God hates.

"Snow White's Scary Adventures"

I mentioned in the last devotional that Pinocchio was Disney's second animated feature. Do you know what was number one? Well it just so happens that today's attraction is based on that very film. In 1937, *Snow White and the Seven Dwarfs* became Disney's first ever classic film and they've been making and releasing wonderful movies ever since. Let's go take another dark ride on Snow White's Scary Adventures and learn more about this attraction and the film that influenced it.

Snow White's Scary Adventures opened with the park in 1955. It is also found in Tokyo and Paris. It closed at the Magic Kingdom in Disney World in 2012 to make way for the Fantasyland expansion, which of course included the new Seven Dwarfs Mine Train ride. At Disneyland, this ride was originally called "Snow White and her Adventures." The word "scary" was later added to serve as a warning to parents of young children that they may be frightened, especially by the appearance of the evil witch. This is one of several Fantasyland rides where the earliest versions had the guests as the main character. In other words, Snow White was not seen at all when this ride first opened. The riders were supposed to be playing the role of the princess as she traveled throughout the story. Unfortunately, most riders did not understand this concept and kept asking why Snow White wasn't in her own ride. Therefore, she was later added to one scene near the end. In the scene where the witch offers guests the poison apple, many riders would often reach out and try to take it. Some were successful, and the apple kept disappearing. This was corrected in a 1983 refurbishment when the apple was changed to projected image. Guests that now reached out for the apple found their hand simply passed right through it. Next time you go to Disneyland, watch the window above the entrance to this ride. Every thirty seconds or so, the evil queen will pull back the curtain and peek out.

Think about the Snow White movie and see if you can you guess the lesson for today? Do you remember the story? Did you know that Walt Disney received an honorary Oscar for this film? It was presented to him by Shirley Temple and was a special version of the award. It featured one regular size figure with seven little ones beside it. This film was very successful at the box office. In fact, if you adjust the money it made for inflation, it is the highest grossing animated film in history. If you need a reminder, the story involves a wicked queen who is stepmother to Snow White. The queen always worries that one day Snow White will be more beautiful than she, and so she constantly asks her magic mirror, "mirror mirror on the wall, who's the fairest one of all?" Just as she fears, the mirror eventually tells her that the answer is Snow White. The queen is furious and orders Snow White killed. Luckily, Snow White escapes to live in hiding with the dwarfs. As expected, the queen eventually finds her leading to the powerful and climactic ending. Do you know the lesson now? It's another sin that many struggle with. Today we are focusing on the sin of jealousy.

In this film, the queen was jealous of Snow White's beauty. What else do people get jealous of? You can probably think of several answers such as money, fame, attention and talents. Just like our last devotional on lying, jealousy is another sin that's easy to get caught up in. Again, our human nature causes us to want things. We see what others have and think that our happiness depends on us having it too. Do you remember the story of Cain and Abel, one of the earliest stories in the Bible? God is very pleased with Abel's sacrifice which leads to his older brother's jealousy. It eventually causes Cain to kill his brother because of his wanting the praise that Abel is receiving. Jealousy can do just that...cause us to say, do or think things we shouldn't. James 3:16 says, "For where jealousy and selfish ambition exist, there will be disorder and every vile practice." Just like lying, jealousy is also found in the Ten Commandments. The last commandment says, "thou shalt not covet" which means to want what someone else has. Finally, in the love chapter of 1 Corinthians 13, it says that love does not envy.

Snow White is a classic movie full of humor, adventure, romance and thrill. It also contains a timeless tale of jealousy brought on by the evil queen whose jealousy eventually led to her downfall and demise. The same can happen to us if we're not careful. If we want to follow the laws of God and live at peace with others, we need to be content when others are happy or successful. We also need to be content with what we do have. If we really take some time to count the blessings God has given us, I dare say that most of us would realize we have nothing to be jealous about. If you ever find yourself with feelings of jealousy, work really hard to instead be content. Remember that your life on Earth is not about material possessions, good looks or attention from others. It's about preparing for Heaven and building our relationship with God. If we have that, we have absolutely nothing to be jealous about.

"Alice in Wonderland"

Guess what? It's time for another dark ride here in Fantasyland! Are you shocked and surprised? I doubt it because there seem to be a lot of those around here. This one is again based on a memorable Disney film. However, unlike some of the other rides here, this one is very unique to Disneyland. It's never been in any other Disney park. So come board your caterpillar-shaped vehicle and jump down the rabbit hole, because it's time to ride Alice in Wonderland.

This ride debuted at Disneyland Park in 1958. The film had come out just a few years earlier in 1951. This was originally slated to be a walk-through attraction, but plans were delayed and later changed. This is a dark ride because it takes place mostly inside, but there is an outdoor portion of the track. This ride typically shuts down if there is rain for that very reason. The ride was once shut down for a month because the California Department of Safety and Health pointed out the lack of handrails on that same outdoor portion, and they had to be added. This ride actually takes place mostly on a second story over Mr. Toad's Wild Ride in the same building. The voice of Alice for the film also lent her voice for this ride. In 1983, the Mad Tea Party ride was relocated just outside of this attraction as both are based on the same film.

I can't say for sure if I've ever seen this film. I know I've certainly seen parts of it, but I'm not sure I've ever watched it all the way through. I guess I need to add it to the ever growing list of Disney movies I need to watch. The lesson here may be a little bit harder to figure out. The movie begins with Alice expressing how bored she is and how much she longs for adventure. Talk about foreshadowing! Soon after, she walks to a riverbank and spots a white rabbit who tells her he's late for a very important date. Maybe the talking rabbit should've been clue one that something unusual was going on, but Alice follows him anyways. Once she follows the rabbit into his hole, the adventures begin. Alice shrinks, grows, parties, plays croquet, goes on trial, is sentenced to death, flees and finally realizes it was all a dream. Sorry...should've said spoiler alert. The point is that Alice gets what she asks for...she gets quite an adventure...too much of an adventure as she very quickly regrets her wish and longs for home.

Throughout the film, she is trying to figure out how to get home asking directions from various characters. Basically, Alice finds herself lost in the strange world of Wonderland.

Have you ever been lost? Believe it or not, I remember a time when I was about 3 or 4 years old. I was at a department store with my family and I somehow wandered off and became lost. I don't really remember being worried or scared. I think I was just having a little adventure of my own like Alice. The thing I remember is when my parents found me and how relieved they were. I remember just a few years ago when my own family was at the beach and a child from another family was lost. For several minutes, nobody knew where the child was and his mother was absolutely frantic to say the least. The beach would be a scary place to lose a child. Luckily, the child had again just wandered off and was eventually brought back by a lifeguard.

The Bible talks a lot about being lost, not as much in the physical sense, but spiritually. As I may have mentioned before, my favorite parable is "The Lost Son" found in Luke 15. That story, told by Jesus, is actually similar to Alice in Wonderland in the fact that the boy in Jesus's story also wants adventure. He goes to his father to get his inheritance and then leaves home. He quickly gets caught up in his adventure and spends all his money. He then has to get a job feeding pigs just to survive and longs to just be home again. He feels ashamed but decides to go home to beg to be his father's servant, just so he can be home. I think you probably know the end of Jesus's story. The father not only welcomes him home, but runs to him with open arms. He gives him gifts, holds a feast for him, and celebrates his return with a large event. That's God, and that was Jesus's point. God celebrates when we come home.

Luke 19:10 says that Jesus came to this Earth to seek and save the lost. Sometimes we are the lost. Isaiah 53:6 says that all of us are like sheep that go astray. We all get lost. Sometimes we, like Alice, want adventure so badly, and we totally lose focus and get caught up in this world. Luckily, God is always on that narrow road, waiting with open arms for us to come back. It doesn't matter how lost we become. Let me say that again. It does NOT matter how lost you are or how far off the path you have traveled. You can ALWAYS come back home and God will be there waiting for you. Are you lost? Come back home and have your adventure with God involved. That will be a much more fun and meaningful journey anyways.

"Storybook Land Canal Boats"

The next Fantasyland ride is one that is very special to me. Maybe it's because the first time I went to Disneyland nearly 15 years ago, I remember riding it with my sons. They were 5 and 2 at the time, but I remember them really enjoying this ride and being fascinated at all the scenery. I also remember when we went to Disneyland just six months ago. I was very eager to ride this once again. It had started raining while we were in the long line to board, but the ride was still running. We waited probably 20 -25 minutes and were next in line when they shut the ride down. Talk about disappointment! We never got a chance to go back and ride which made me a little sad. This ride just has some great memories for me not to mention it's very unique and clever. I'll just have to go back soon and ride now won't I? Let me tell you about the Storybook Land Canal Boats today!

This ride opened with the park and is an outdoor boat ride. Passengers travel with a guide on motorized boats leisurely through a winding waterway while viewing various scenes from classic Disney films. Each film is displayed in miniature buildings and decorations. When the ride first opened, it did not have these scenes and was just a simple boat ride called "Canal Boats of the World." The original intention was for it to have miniatures, but of various landmarks around the globe. Time and money prevented this, and it was opened anyways unfinished. That first year was plagued with several other problems. The boat motors were prone to overheating often forcing the boats to be pulled by hand. The ride also opened with very little landscaping so the banks around the ride would often be muddy earning it the nickname "The Mud Bank Ride." The ride was subsequently shut down soon after opening for several months to allow for landscaping and for the miniatures to be added. In addition, the giant whale, Monstro, which "swallows" your boat soon after launch, was added. That idea was taken from a "Monstro the Whale" ride that was planned but never materialized. There are currently at least eleven different miniature scenes on the ride, although Disney often adds or replaces as new films are released. The canal for this ride contains 465,000 gallons of water which flows via pipes to the moat around Sleeping Beauty Castle, the Jungle Cruise and the Rivers of America where it is then pumped back to this attraction. There is also a version of this attraction in Paris although the boats are guided by an underwater wire and there is no guide.

Can you imagine being pulled around this ride by hand today? I don't think Disney would ever let that happen today. That would've been very interesting to see, though, as well as all the other problems this ride faced when it first opened. It sounds like this ride wasn't the most attractive thing in the world those first few months, hence the muddy nickname. Luckily, Disney Imagineers took action, as they always do and worked their magic to change it into the special and beautiful ride that exists today. In other words, they took something that was unpleasant and unattractive and changed it into something lovely and appealing. Did you know that God does the exact same thing?

One of my favorite men of faith from Scripture is Paul. He has an amazing story, particularly in the book of Acts. He certainly doesn't start out a hero...in fact quite the opposite. When we first meet Paul in Acts 8, he is standing by allowing men of God to be tortured and killed. He actually approved God's people to be executed. Fortunately, in Acts 9, he is converted when Jesus Himself speaks to Paul on the road to Damascus. Paul ends up becoming a great man of faith. Read Acts 22:19-21. In these verses, Paul is recounting his story, and he remembers what a horrible person he once was. But he also knows that God chose him and changed him. Paul is the ultimate example of how God can take something ugly and broken and transform it into something amazing and wonderful. Psalms 51:10 says, "Create in me a clean heart, O God, and renew a right spirit within me." God does just that. He can make anyone new again, no matter how old and dirty they might be. What a loving, forgiving and caring God we serve. Never forget that.

The Storybook Land Canal Boats are a fun ride, and it's so interesting to see the detail of all the little scenes along the way. I'm very glad Disney cleaned up this ride from all its opening issues and turned it into a beautiful and memorable attraction. In conclusion, look at Ezekiel 36:26 describing how God can the same thing. It reads, "And I will give you a new heart, and a new spirit I will put within you. And I will remove the heart of stone from your flesh and give you a heart of flesh." If you are feeling lost in sin and "dirty" before God, give Him control and allow Him to change you. He will turn you into something amazing...a servant of His that can help change the world one person at a time.

"Casey Jr. Circus Train"

Did you know there's another way to see the miniature scenes from our last ride? Maybe I should've remembered that on the day we got rained out of the boats. We've already discussed how much Walt Disney loved trains so not only did his park have a big train on opening day, it also had a small one for kids as well. This is found just above the canal boats on the hill overlooking Fantasyland. So all aboard for another train ride on the Casey Jr. Circus Train!

There is also a Casey Jr. at Disneyland Paris, but it is a roller coaster. This train at Disneyland is a much more peaceful, nearly four minute ride. As mentioned, riders get to see many of the same miniature displays seen on the canal boats taken from various Disney films. This train was briefly operational on the park's opening day in 1955, but closed the next day for safety testing. It didn't reopen for two weeks. Some of the cars on this train used to be a part of King Arthur's Carrousel which we'll talk about very soon. When that ride refurbished and switched to all horses, they moved the sleighs to this ride instead. While the first car of the train may look like a locomotive, it doesn't house the engine. The engine is actually in the second section called the calliope car. The monkey cage car is generally the most popular and a lot of guests wait specifically to sit there. If you know your Disney history, you know that this ride is based on the opening scene of the film *Dumbo*. Therefore it is one of two rides in this land based on that film. If you listen very carefully while riding this train, you can hear Casey Jr. saying, "I think I can. I think I can," as he climbs the small hill.

You may wonder why he is saying that. Most likely it's because he says the same thing in the *Dumbo* film. That phrase is based on the American fairytale "The Little Engine That Could" that was published around 1930, although the phrase itself was first seen as early as 1902. In the film, the Casey Jr. train is carrying all of the zoo animals and comes to a large hill. As it struggles to climb, it repeats "I think I can" over and over again as you see the strain and struggle on its face. (Yes, the train has a face. It's Disney for crying out loud!) When he finally makes it over the hill, he repeats "I thought I could. I thought I could," as he flies down the hill with a smile on his face. That leads to our thought for today.

Has there ever been anything in your life that you really wanted to accomplish but maybe you had hesitation or doubt about actually getting it done? Maybe there is something like that in your life right now. Maybe it's a new position in your job, an athletic team or club officer at your school. Maybe it's a personal hobby or a physical challenge. Or maybe it's a spiritual goal of talking to someone else about God or making your own life right with Him. It's great to have goals, especially spiritual ones. It's also a good idea to write them down and put them somewhere where you'll see them every day. The best way to accomplish those goals is to focus and set your mind to them as well as plan time in your schedule to work on them. Go read Luke 14:28-33. In this passage, Jesus basically talks about a goal of building a tower. He makes it clear that you have to focus, plan and prepare before beginning or you won't be able to complete the project. This is true of any goal. I Peter 1:13 says, "Therefore, preparing your minds for action and being sober-minded, set your hope fully on the grace that will be brought to you at the revelation of Jesus Christ." You see, we must prepare and focus our minds for any task set before us. Particularly with spiritual goals, we need to set our minds on God and allow Him to be a part of our planning and preparation. Colossians 3:2 reminds us to set our minds on things above and not on things of this world. Finally look at Proverbs 21:5 which reads, "The plans of the diligent lead surely to abundance, but everyone who is hasty comes only to poverty." We can't be hasty and rush in trying to accomplish goals or it won't work. We have to instead be diligent in our planning and invite God to be a part of each step of the process.

Watching Casey Jr. climb that hill, you can see the determination on his face. You can see his focus, hard work and tireless drive. He even speaks his effort out loud saying, "I think I can" over and over. Once he accomplishes his goal, you can see joy, satisfaction and pride in the fact that he made it and finished the task. Don't forget what Paul said in Philippians 3:13-14 that he was forgetting what was behind, straining forward to what lies ahead, and pressing on towards his goals. If we do the same and keep our minds and focus on our Heavenly Father, we can accomplish any aspiration we might have. Do you have goals that you aren't sure you can accomplish? Well "I think you can" if you approach them correctly. Just focus on God and you'll soon be saying, "I thought I could!"

"Matterhorn Bobsleds"

It's been a while since we've done anything too thrilling, hasn't it? We've been stuck on boats, trains and dark rides for several entries here. Maybe it's time we mix it up a bit here in Fantasyland! Today we are going on one of my favorite rides at Disneyland Park. Indiana Jones is probably still my top choice, but this is a close second. If you want some adventure, excitement and maybe a little bit of fear, this is the ride for you! Buckle up as we zoom on the Matterhorn Bobsleds today!

The Bobsleds are a pair of intertwined roller coasters housed in a mountain made to look like the Matterhorn, a famous peak in the Alps on the border of Switzerland and Italy. When Disneyland was being built, a large dirt pile was formed after digging the moat around Sleeping Beauty Castle. This large dirt hill was present on opening day and was branded with various nicknames such as "Holiday Hill" and "Lookout Mountain." When the Disneyland Skyway, which no longer exists, opened in 1956, it gave Walt Disney the idea of a toboggan style ride with real snow on the mountain. However, Disney executives quickly pointed out to Walt that the logistics wouldn't work. Instead, the giant hill was being used for guest picnics during the day and a type of "lovers' lane" at night. Walt didn't like this at all and wanted to put something better there. Executives then got the idea to build a toboggan themed roller coaster on an artificial mountain. Soon after, Walt was vacationing in Switzerland while filming a movie and sent his chief architect, Vic Greene, a postcard of the Matterhorn. On the back of the card, he wrote simply, "Vic. Build this. Walt."

The Matterhorn Bobsleds became the first steel tubular roller coaster in the world. Guests board bobsleds and are taken on a thrilling journey in and out of the mountain through multiple twists and turns. Riders also come face to face with the Abominable Snowman or Yeti with his sharp teeth, growl and flashing red eyes. Apparently his name is Harold. When the mountain was first built, it not only served to house the ride, but also to hide a large column for the Skyway which passed right through the mountain. Guests on the Skyway could actually look down from their buckets in the sky and see the inner workings of the Matterhorn ride. The mountain is exactly 100 times shorter than the real thing. During busy times in the past, climbers have been hired to scale the mountain to entertain guests. Mickey Mouse himself has even climbed the mountain. You may have heard what I think is the most amazing fact about this ride in the fact that there is a basketball court inside the mountain. This half-court was originally placed there for the climbers to enjoy between climbs. Over the years, it has grown smaller, but according to many cast members, you can still find a backboard and hoop somewhere up there.

There are a lot of fun facts about the Matterhorn Bobsleds; many more I could've shared, but I simply don't have the room. The one I want to focus on is the fact that the Disneyland Skyway was built first. Then, when they built this ride, they didn't move the Skyway. They didn't make it go around or over the mountain. Instead, they simply cut holes through the mountain and let the Skyway travel right through. That interesting fact is going to lead into our thought for today.

We all have mountains in our lives. That is to say, we all face challenges at certain points of our life. Some of these challenges we get through easily, and some are pretty difficult, like a steep, snow-covered mountain. In James chapter 1, we read that we should be joyful when we have to face trials. Easier said than done, I know. But the point James is trying to make is that trials make us stronger and increase and fortify our faith. In addition, read 2 Corinthians 12:1-10. In verse 7, Paul begins talking about his "thorn in the flesh." We are not really sure exactly what this was, but it was some sort of challenge, trial or "mountain" that Paul had to deal with. In verse 8, he says that he begged God to get rid of it. In verses 9-10, Paul realizes that this trial, whatever it was, made him stronger. Look at what he says in verse 10. It reads, "For the sake of Christ, then, I am content with weaknesses, insults, hardships, persecutions, and calamities. For when I am weak, then I am strong." You will face trials in life. You probably already have. Like Paul, we need to remember that trials are important and they only make us stronger in our walk with God. Whenever we face something difficult, we simply have to find a way to deal with it. We have to lean on God first and others around us and put our hearts and minds into overcoming any trial that the world throws at us. Just like that Skyway found a way through the giant mountain built in its path, we must find a way to deal with sufferings. They are an important part of our spiritual faith.

The Matterhorn Bobsleds is a fantastic ride. I think you'll really enjoy it and want to ride it several times. See if you can see the holes where the Skyway used to pass through. They've been covered up, but you may catch a glimpse of where they used to be. Use that visual as a reminder to work hard when you face troubles in life. If the world puts a mountain in your path, find a way to get by, even if you have to go through it.

"King Arthur Carrousel"

Ok, now that we've gotten our heart rate up riding something as thrilling as the Bobsleds, it's time to calm back down. Let's choose a much more peaceful and relaxing ride next. How about King Arthur Carrousel? You may wonder why we are talking about this one as we did Prince Charming's Carousel at WDW in the first book. Yes, they are similar, but in the same way we did a repeat on the train and the riverboat, we're going to devote an entry to this ride because of its uniqueness and interesting history. So choose your horse, and come with me on a very special and very old Disney classic.

King Arthur Carrousel opened with the park in 1955, but this ride is actually much older than that. This carousel, which is actually spelled with two "R's" after the original French spelling, was built in 1922! That makes it nearly 100 years old! It first operated at Sunnyside Beach Park in Toronto, Canada. That park eventually shut down, and the carousel was relocated and refurbished for inclusion at Disneyland. The original ride had several chariot type benches that guests could choose, but as previously mentioned, these were relocated to the Casey Jr. train because Walt Disney wanted all horses on this carousel. There are currently 68 horses to choose from as well as one chariot bench added in 2003 for handicap compliance. There used to just be one horse that was painted white, but guests would always run and fight for that particular horse. Because of this, all the horses have been painted white since 1975. All 68 of the horses have names, and this list of names is said to be kept at City Hall on Main Street. The lead horse is named Jingles and is said to have been Walt's favorite. Jingles was ceremoniously dedicated to Mary Poppins herself, actress Julie Andrews, in 2008 and a honorary plaque was placed beneath the horse. Maintenance crews touch up the paint on all the horses daily, and every horse undergoes a yearly total refurbishment. Although each is mostly white, it takes more than thirty different colors to paint all the detail on each horse, and no two are painted exactly the same. Walt Disney insisted that all the horses be leaping or galloping, and therefore some had to be reconfigured to a new pose. The carousel revolves a total of eight times exactly per ride as guests end up at the same spot they began.

As you can probably see, this ride was very special to Walt Disney. Most historians agree that he got the idea for Disneyland while watching his two daughters ride a carousel at Griffith Park in Los Angeles. Therefore, he definitely wanted a special carousel at his own park. Though Walt is not around anymore, I think he would be pleased at the care and attention to detail that is given to this ride still today after nearly 65 years in the park. The fact that each horse is touched up every single day. The fact that each one is yearly refurbished and hand painted with 30 different colors. The fact that each has a name, a unique pose and decorations. Every aspect of this ride and its parts are thoroughly considered and properly cared for.

Did you know that God does the same with you? In a way, we are the horses on His giant carousel, but there's a lot more than 68 of us. As of September 2019, there were approximately 7.7 billion people in the world. This doesn't count of course all the people that have passed on. Nobody knows for sure of course, but some estimates put the number of people that have ever lived on Earth somewhere over 100 billion! That's a lot of people! If those people were indeed carousel horses, that would be quite the ride! The point is that God knows every single one of those billions of people. He created them all! Please take some time today to read Psalms 139. I wish I had the space to include the entire psalm here. This beautiful work of David talks extensively about how well God knows each and every one of us. Romans 8:29-30 says that God even knew us before we were born. The verse goes on to say that he predestined us to be his called, chosen children. In John 10:14, Jesus said, "I am the good shepherd. I know my own and my own know me." Jesus knows us just like a shepherd knows his sheep, because we are His sheep and He watches over and cares for us. I love I Corinthians 8:3 which simply says that if anyone loves God, that person is known by God.

Do you love God? I hope so. We certainly have many reasons to love God, just one of which is the fact that He knows each of us by name. We've already talked about how God created each of us in His own image and the image of His Son. Therefore, we are special. We are His sheep. We are His children. No matter what you do, how far you stray or even how much you might disappoint Him, He always knows you and loves you. Isn't it an honor to be one of the horses on God's carousel? Isn't it a blessing that He knows you and every detail about you? Isn't it wonderful that He pays careful attention to you and is always there listening when you call? Be proud of your place as a chosen child of God. Work hard to give that position the honor and respect it deserves. Make God proud as He watches over you on this carousel of life, and one day you will "gallop" your way right into Heaven.

"Fantasy Faire"

It's finally time! We are now ready for our last attraction of Fantasyland! It's definitely been a fun ride (pun intended). This last devotional however, is not about a ride at all. It's more of an interactive section of Fantasyland that includes character meets as well as entertaining shows. If you're into princesses, you'll love this attraction. If you're not, well, you still might find something interesting here. Let's go visit Fantasy Faire!

Fantasy Faire actually includes two main structures that are both found just to the left of Sleeping Beauty Castle as you approach from Main Street. They are Royal Hall and Royal Theatre. This attraction is fairly new, opening back in 2013. Prior to that, this area was known as the Carnations Gardens Plaza and it held various musical experiences, including dancing events mostly at night. Today, Royal Hall includes several princess character greets where kids of all ages can get their picture taken as they "hold court with royalty." The Royal Theatre is an outdoor stage and 300 person seating area where various shows are held based on classic Disney stories with a comic twist. Typically the shows are based on *Beauty and the Beast* or *Tangled*. Each show lasts about 20 minutes. The architecture of these two buildings as well as the surrounding areas resemble a European fantasy village so that guests feel as if they have been transported there as they prepare to meet their favorites. Guests can explore around for many hidden sights such as Figaro the cat from Pinocchio, the Hunchback of Notre Dame and Rapunzel peeking out from the top of her tower. There is also a shop here called Fairy Tale Treasures as well as a food cart called Maurice's Treats.

This is one attraction that many kids genuinely love. The Bibbidi Bobbidi Boutique nearby even offers a special package where after you are made up with exquisite detail to look like a princess, you can be escorted down to meet your favorite princess with all the royal fanfare expected. Most of the time you will see many smiling faces at this attraction as kids get very excited to meet their heroes and heroines. After all, they've read about them and seen them in movies and on TV, but now they are finally getting to meet them in person. It's another one of those things that makes Disney so magical. So think about this, what if Disney magic was so powerful that it produced a similar attraction where you could meet your heroes...and it could be anyone you wanted. Who would that attraction be for you?

Who are your heroes? And I'm talking real life here, not superheroes or princesses. Maybe you are thinking of a great athlete from the past or a movie star. Maybe it's a former mentor of yours, a teacher or minister. Or maybe it's somebody from your family, a grandparent or great grandparent that has possibly passed on. Wouldn't that be a wonderful attraction? I've already mentioned the fact that I was asked recently on a podcast who I would choose to have lunch with if I could pick anyone. I chose Walt Disney as I consider him one of my heroes, and I would've loved to have met him. Unfortunately, Disney magic isn't quite that powerful. But the good news is that one day you will be able to meet some of your former heroes. Just part of the greatness of Heaven is going to be reunions with those who have gone before us. It's not clear in what capacity we will be reunited, but I do believe we will know them. And it won't be just family members. I believe we'll get to meet some of our Biblical heroes as well. Can you imagine getting to speak with Abraham, Moses, Noah or David? Would you enjoy speaking with them? I know I would. I only have about a million questions. The greatest part of Heaven, however is that we'll get to meet God and His amazing Son, Jesus Christ. Matthew 5:8 says, "Blessed are the pure in heart, for they shall see God." Go read Revelation 21 today as John describes what Heaven will be like. Verses 3 and 4 say, "And I heard a loud voice from the throne saying, "Behold, the dwelling place of God is with man. He will dwell with them, and they will be His people, and God Himself will be with them as their God. He will wipe away every tear from their eyes, and death shall be no more, neither shall there be mourning, nor crying, nor pain anymore, for the former things have passed away." Isn't that incredible? Those verses give me such hope and joy. It literally says there that God will dwell with us, that He Himself will be with us. The second verse is wonderful too describing how happy it will be there with no tears, sorrow or pain.

Fantasy Faire is a fun place to visit with many interactive things to do. It is a place of happiness bringing smiles to many faces young and old. Heaven will be like that in such a greater capacity as we are reunited with heroes from the past, get a chance to meet heroes we've only read about, and finally get to meet our loving Father and His Son. As you continue your day today, find hope in this verse..."Beloved, we are God's children now, and what we will be has not yet appeared; but we know that when He appears we shall be like Him, because we shall see him as He is." (I John 3:2)

"Disneyland Monorail"

We're finally leaving Fantasyland today and moving on to the future. In other words, we are walking next door to Tomorrowland. There are many attractions here of course, but only two that are essentially unique to Disneyland. Actually, you might even argue with me about the first one here. When you saw today's title, you might have wondered why this is even a devotional entry at all. I know, I know…we already did the monorail in the first book. But once again, this monorail has too much history and too many unique facts to just pass it by. For one thing, it was intended to be an actual ride here in Tomorrowland. As you know, at Disney World, you can only enter and exit the monorail outside the parks, but not here. Walt Disney built this to be a ride and not just transportation, and so that's how we're going to treat it. So please stand clear of the doors! "Por favor manténgase alejado de las puertas!" I love that recording! Actually right now, I can't remember if the Disneyland Monorail says that or not. I hope so. Anyways, let's hop on the monorail.

The Disneyland Monorail opened in June of 1959 just four years after the park and was the first daily operating monorail in the entire Western Hemisphere. Today there are 3 monorail trains, red, blue and orange, that each holds 120 people. The top speed of 30 mph is perfect for your leisurely tour around Disneyland Park, Disney's California Adventure Park (where we're going very soon) and Disney Springs. When this monorail first opened, it was indeed intended as simply a ride and sightseeing attraction. There was only one station, here in Tomorrowland. The second station was added two years later in 1961 as a convenience to Disneyland Hotel guests so they could travel back and forth. Today, the second station is in the same place, but it has been expanded and lies in the middle of Disney Springs, still near the Disneyland Hotel. When the 2nd station opened, riders would actually set a dial in their particular car showing if they were riding round trip, going to the park, or if there was a mixture of destination choice inside. Ride attendants would then open the appropriate doors at the Tomorrowland station depending on if guests were getting out or not. Today, riders must have park admission to ride as there's no round trip available from Disney Springs. Guests must disembark at the park.

Due to crowd levels, you are typically not allowed to stay on and ride continuously like at WDW. This monorail passes right through the Grand Californian Hotel, similar to the Contemporary at WDW. You also get to pass through Disneyland's other park, Disney California Adventure and see some behind the scenes areas there. A final fun fact about this ride is that then Vice-President Richard Nixon once visited Disneyland and Walt Disney was anxious to take him on a monorail ride. Apparently, he was a little too excited and pulled Nixon onto the ride before Secret Service had a chance to get on. Essentially, Walt Disney kidnapped Richard Nixon!

So what's the lesson we can take from the Disneyland Monorail? Don't kidnap government officials? Sure, that's a good one. But we'll try something else. As I mentioned, this attraction was originally intended to just be a ride...a nice, calm, relaxing sight-seeing tour. My guess is that today, most don't see it that way. They instead see it as a mechanism of travel...a way to get from one place to another. The monorails at Disney World are the same way. People use them to get from the Magic Kingdom to the resorts or to Epcot. There's nothing wrong with that. They are a great and efficient way of travel. However, that wasn't the original intention of this particular monorail. Walt wanted folks to ride it and enjoy the views, see the sights and get to rest and relax on a leisurely tour of the park and surrounding areas. Sometimes in life, we also need to just relax and enjoy the ride. We get so busy in our normal, everyday lives and sometimes forget to just stop, take a breath, and appreciate our surroundings. Like the current monorail system, our goal is often to just get from one place to another and go, go, go. We always have things to do, deadlines to meet and tasks we have to get done right now.

Don't forget that after God created the Earth and everything in it in six days, even He rested! Exodus 31:17 even says the He rested and was refreshed. He took the 7th day off to relax, recharge and enjoy what He had done. Psalms 46:10 says, "Be still and know that I am God." When is the last time you took some real time to just be still? It's important that you do. If you have trouble finding the time or are too caught up in life's business, remember Matthew 11:28 where Jesus said, "Come to me, all who labor and are heavy laden, and I will give you rest."

I really enjoyed the Disneyland Monorail on our recent trip. It was indeed a pleasant and peaceful ride as we took the round trip. We enjoyed looking out the windows and seeing several backstage areas and other remarkable sights. Even I need a reminder to do the same in my life. God has blessed us so much with beautiful surroundings, and we need to honor Him by taking a break from life to take the time to enjoy it. "Let us therefore strive to enter that rest." (Hebrews 4:11)

"Finding Nemo Submarine Voyage"

Believe it or not, it's time for our final ride in Disneyland Park. I want to assure you that there are of course other attractions here. Keep in mind that we only talked about ones that are not copied at WDW and are special to Disneyland. And if there ever was a ride that was unique and special, this is the one. Hope you've got that claustrophobia in check my friend, because today we're heading, as Sebastian would say, "Under the Sea!" Let's go take a submarine voyage.

The Finding Nemo Submarine Voyage opened in 1959 but of course had nothing to do with the Nemo film at that time. It was called "Submarine Voyage" from 1959 until 1998. During the summers of 1965-1967, female cast members were paid to dress in mermaid costumes. They would sun-bathe and perform synchronized swimming and underwater stunts to entertain the crowds on a bank near the ride. Disney ended this feature after several of the "mermaids" reports health issues related to the fumes of the subs as well as the highly chlorinated water. In addition, guests watching and taking pictures often blocked the way, and there were even reports that some guests tried to jump in and swim to the mermaids. Disney World had a nearly identical ride called "20,000 Leagues Under the Sea" based on the film of the same name. It opened with the Magic Kingdom but shut down in 1994. This original Disneyland ride was loosely based on the USS Nautilus, the first nuclear-powered submarine and its journey to the North Pole. In 1959, Soviet Primier Nikita Khrushchev was denied permission to go to Disneyland during his US visit. Walt Disney was reportedly disappointed to hear it as he wanted to introduce Khruschev to his submarines. Walt was proud of his fleet of eight subs and used to boast that he owned the "eighth largest submarine fleet in the world."

The ride shut down in 1998 with promise it would be back with a new theme, only to remain closed for nearly a decade. During that time, Imagineers went through several ideas, but debated permanent closure due to high maintenance costs and slow loading times. Thankfully, it came back in 2007 with the Finding Nemo theme after the huge popularity of the film. Each sub holds 40 guests who are seated in two rows back to back, each with a porthole type window. As the sub dives (it actually doesn't fully submerge, but uses special effects to appear that way), riders get to see animated figures, artificial foliage and 23,000 pieces of artificial coral in a 6.3 million gallon tank. In 2001, when Imagineers were trying to figure out whether to keep or shut down the ride, a navel engineering firm inspected the subs and reported they each had 40 to 50 years of life left in them. That ultimately aided in convincing them to keep the ride open...hopefully for years to come!

Have you ever taken a submarine ride? My guess is that unless you've been to Disney, the answer is probably no. Submarine rides just don't seem to come as often as say a boat, train or plane ride. Disney certainly accounts for the only times I've ever been on a submarine. It's an unusual experience, and for that, I am grateful to Disney. This is why I hope they decide to keep this ride for many years. It provides a unique opportunity that many would not receive otherwise. This leads me to another question...do you know someone that needs to hear about God? I'm sure you do. So how else are they going to hear it unless you tell them?

Just like Disneyland is the only place you will likely get to ride a submarine, YOU may be the only place where someone gets to hear about God. You may think that there are plenty of others out there that can share the Gospel and Word of God. But what if everyone thinks that way? What if you are the only way that person will know about God and His plan for their life? It is up to you to give them that information. I Peter 2:9 reads, "But you are a chosen race, a royal priesthood, a holy nation, a people for his own possession, that you may proclaim the excellencies of Him who called you out of darkness into His marvelous light." You see in that verse that we have been chosen to proclaim the good news about Christ. In I Corinthians 11:1, Paul tells the people to imitate Christ. Pair that with Luke 8:1 which says that Jesus went through cities and villages proclaiming and bringing the good news of the kingdom of God. Therefore, if we really are working hard to be just like Christ, we need to do as He did. And all He did during his adult years was to go out and spread the Word.

Where else but Disney can you ride on an authentic submarine? And where else but from you will others hear about God? You can't depend on anyone else to tell them. Talk to others. Share. Tell them what God has done for you. Tell them what He will do for them. Remember Romans 1:16 which says, "For I am not ashamed of the gospel, for it is the power of God for salvation to everyone who believes, to the Jew first and also to the Greek." Hopefully you aren't ashamed of the Gospel, so why not tell others? It is so powerful and essential to our salvation. Don't be the reason that someone misses out on their chance!

"Main Street Electrical Parade"

I've enjoyed so much being here in Disneyland Park and talking about all the attractions. Before we leave, there is one more we can't ignore. I said that the submarine entry was the last ride, and that's true. This is instead an experience you will not forget if you are lucky enough to catch it. Today we are talking about a parade that currently takes place at this park each night. At least it was at the time of this writing. Unfortunately, it is on a limited run so it may not be available when you are reading this, but I'm hoping it will come back soon. It tends to come and go from time to time, but I wish it wouldn't go at all. It's probably my favorite parade that Disney has ever done. It's time to watch the amazing and visually stunning Main Street Electrical Parade.

This nightly parade debuted in June of 1972 at Disneyland with 12 floats covered in lights. It was inspired by another parade of sorts at Disney World, the Electrical Water Pageant that has been floating around the Seven Seas Lagoon there for almost 50 years. This parade started in Disneyland, but at times has spread to WDW as well as Tokyo, Paris, and even the park across the street, Disney California Adventure. Today, the parade has 22 floats that are completely enveloped in 600,000 electronically controlled LED lights along with a synchronized soundtrack. When this parade began, this sound system was the first of its kind with speakers triggered along the way by radio control instead of the music coming directly from the floats. Of course, this is how Disney does all its parades now. The iconic song for this parade was not actually written for the parade but was an already existing piece of music called "Baroque Hoedown" released in 1967. The first rehearsal of this parade was apparently a disaster when one of the floats crashed into a building on Main Street as well as some of the performers' costumes emitting sparks. Despite this rusty start, the parade debuted on schedule successfully with all the kinks worked out. If you've seen this parade, you might think that the Elliott the dragon float from *Pete's Dragon* is the tallest at 16 feet, but actually Cinderella's clock tower grabs that distinction at 18 feet tall!

Did I mention I love this parade? Maybe it's because it does give a nod to *Pete's Dragon* which is my absolute favorite Disney movie.

Maybe it's because it is so visually spectacular. Maybe it's because I do love that theme song. If you've never seen it, you can check it out on YouTube. It won't be the same as being there, but it's better than nothing. As I mentioned, I wish the parade was a permanent fixture. It's too good to go away. Maybe Disney has it come and go to make it more appealing and make us anticipate it more. It works! We never know when it's going to return so that makes us look forward to it and long to see it again. This reminds me of something very important.

Like that parade, there is something else that will return one day, but we don't know when. That of course is Jesus Christ. Before he ascended into Heaven after His resurrection, He assured us that He would return one day. Matthew 24:36 says, "But concerning that day and hour no one knows, not even the angels of heaven, nor the Son, but the Father only." Only God knows when Christ will return. Jesus doesn't even know! Read I Thessalonians 5:1-4. It tells us that Jesus will return like a thief in the night. In other words, it will surprise most people and they won't be expecting it at all. I realize that thieves are typically unwelcome and scary. But Jesus will be the one and only time we welcome a "thief in the night." Bring on the thief! As Christians, we should be ready at all times to see Him again. Also read Matthew 25:1-13 today. It's one of Jesus' most important parables about the Ten Virgins. Make sure you are like the five who are ready for His return.

I really want to see the Main Street Electrical Parade again. I love that thing and I long for its return. But I would much rather see Jesus returning through the clouds. I long for His return in a much greater way, as we all should. What a glorious day that will be when His return marks the beginning of our great reunion in Heaven with our loved ones and our Father!

"Disney California Adventure Park"

Today is a special day! We are scanning our ticket into a new park! Let's enter Disney California Adventure! This is a fairly new and wonderful park, full of great rides, shows and attractions. There are a few copycats here also found at WDW, but most are unique to Disneyland which means we'll be here for several devotionals. As usual, let's begin by talking about this park in general before we get to any specific attractions.

Disney California Adventure (DCA) opened on February 8, 2001 making it the newest Disney park in the United States. DCA is 72 acres in size and themed to present the history and culture of California. In 2018, DCA entertained almost 10 million guests making it the 12th most visited theme park in the world. (9 of the top 12 were Disney parks!) When DCA opened, it had 4 sections with 22 attractions and 15 restaurants. Today, it has 7 sections, 30 attractions and over 35 places to eat. This area of land served as a Disneyland parking lot for over 40 years. DCA took three years to build and was accompanied with the building of Downtown Disney and Disney's Grand Californian Hotel which is essentially inside the park with an entrance directly from the hotel. When this park first opened, attendance was much less than expected due to several negative reviews. Some of the complaints during that first year were lack of attractions for children, too many stores and restaurants compared with the number of attractions, lack of focus in certain areas as well as a redundant theme being that the park is already in California. Guests also complained that there was no perimeter barriers as in most Disney parks as you are able to see power lines, radio towers, and surrounding buildings from the neighborhood. Due to the low attendance and complaints, Disney did a complete over-haul of this park starting in 2007 adding several lands and attractions to the tune of 1.1 billion dollars! This is the main reason the Electrical Parade mentioned in the last devotional came over to DCA for a while.

Did you know that originally this new park was going to be called WestCOT and be a remake of Epcot at WDW? WestCOT would have included hotels inside the park as well as a 300 foot tall golden replica of the "giant ball" Spaceship Earth (the one at Epcot is 180 feet tall). There would also have been a giant white spire at the center of Future World. However, very soon after Disney announced plans for WestCOT, they got several complaints from surrounding neighbors. Most complaints were due to the sheer size of the park and subsequent landmarks, light pollution at night, and skyrocketing property costs due to the announcement. Disney was planning to spend approximately 3 billion on this WestCOT Park! Due to the complaints, the WestCOT idea was scrapped in 1995 and Imagineers went back to the drawing board to figure out what to do. DCA was what they eventually came up with.

A 300 foot golden sphere! A giant white spire! A three billion dollar park! While that would've been impressive, it sounds like Disney over-stepped their bounds a little bit. They went too big, too fast and scared the neighbors. When they backed off a bit and returned with DCA, the complaints were minimal and the park was built. This leads to our thought for today as we consider telling others about God.

Have you ever opened up to anyone and talked to them about your spiritual life? Have you ever asked someone about their spiritual life and relationship with God? I know it's not an easy thing and can take us way out of our comfort zone. One thing that might make it easier and an important point to remember is to take it slow. Start out small and gradually build the conversation over a period of time. Go read I Corinthians 9:19-23 where Paul discusses his approach to talking with others. He makes it clear that he meets people where they are. He says to the Jews, he became a Jew, and to the weak, he became weak, etc. In verse 22 he says, "I have become all things to all people, that by all means I might save some." Paul knew to get on their level. He didn't come at them heavy about their sin and what they are doing wrong. That would be a terrible approach. Instead, he became what they were and met them there to open the conversation. Also read Matthew 9:9-13 where Jesus called Matthew, the tax collector. He told Matthew to follow him and then went to eat at his house. When he was criticized by the Pharisees for eating with a sinner, Jesus replied in verse 12, "Those who are well have no need of a physician, but those who are sick...For I came not to call the righteous, but sinners." Jesus also met people where they were. He often ate, talked and associated with sinners so he could first get on their level and then slowly change them into disciples.

Disney California Adventure is a great park. But the plans for this area didn't start out so great. Disney planned too much too quickly and crossed the line just a bit. Remember to not do the same when talking to others about God. Start small, casual and comfortable. Give it time so you can build the conversation and relationship. Paul and Jesus knew this was the best approach, and it will work for us too!

"Red Car Trolley"

Well, here we go! Another park with another set of fun attractions. And Disney California Adventure certainly has its fair share of great rides, shows and other enjoyable things to do. So let's get started. If we were really entering this park, we would probably want to strategically make our way to Cars Land first. But we'll talk more about that later. Instead, we're just going to pretend we have this park all to ourselves and can do everything at our leisure. Wouldn't that be nice! Therefore, let's just go around the park in a nice circle and catch each attraction as we come to it. The first one we see here at the entrance to DCA is a very unusual but creative ride. Today we are taking a trip on the Red Car Trolley.

The Red Car Trolley opened in 2012 as part of the rededication of this park. It was one of four new rides that opened at virtually the same time to revitalize and bring new life to the park. The other three were all in the brand new Cars Land. As part of this attraction, riders board replicas of the Pacific Electric Railway "Red Cars" that once were a vital part of Southern California travel. There are two trolleys that each hold up to 21 passengers. They both travel along a path from the park's main entrance to the Guardians of the Galaxy ride in Hollywood Land. There are four total stops along that way where guests can get on or off. The trolleys run every 8 minutes from the stops all during park hours except when there is a parade. There is a guide wire above the trolleys just like originals used for power. However, at DCA, these wires are just for show. These trolleys actually run off a battery that is recharged each night. The numbers on the two trolleys are 623 and 717. The 23 refers to the year that Walt Disney first came to California (1923). 717 refers to the opening date of Disneyland Park (7/17/1955). At certain points, you might catch the newsboys from the musical and Disney film *Newsies* performing from the trolleys. You might also see your favorite mouse riding along.

As I mentioned, these trolleys are inspired by the historic trolleys of Los Angeles that ran in the 1920's and 30's. They are a tribute to the time period when Walt Disney first arrived in California and began what would become the Disney empire. This is something else that Disney typically does very well. They incorporate several things throughout all their parks to honor the past and remember where it all came from. I like the fact that even though Walt Disney died more than 50 years ago, he is still remembered and honored in several ways. After all, it was his hard work and vision that led to all of this, and that's too important to forget. In the same way, we need to remember our past. We tend to focus on the future and concern ourselves more often with what's coming and what we need to do. However, it's also important to remember our roots and where we came from. There are so many verses about this in Scripture. Allow me to just highlight a few. I Corinthians 11:2 shows Paul reminding us to maintain traditions. Proverbs 22:6 tells us to train up a child properly so he'll remember it when he's older. Isaiah 46:9 says to remember the former things of old. Lastly, Romans 15:4 reminds us to remember ancient words such as the Old Testament because those were written for our instruction and to bring us hope.

Yes, it's important and Biblical to look to the future. That is what you should be preparing for. It's important to set goals and work hard for them. At the same time, our past is important, and we can't simply forget it. We can learn from it and honor the valuable training we've received. I'm glad that Disney has the trolleys and other attractions that pay tribute to the past and remember the time when Walt was beginning his notable career. I also hope we will all honor our own past and not forget important moments that made us who we are. Say a prayer tonight and thank God for your past and all those individuals who trained and aided you in your growth. Finally, remember these words from Deuteronomy 32:7. "Remember the days of old; consider the years of many generations; ask your father, and he will show you."

DEVOTIONAL #35

"Frozen—Live at the Hyperion"

We're now going to walk (or trolley) from the entrance down the street in Hollywood Land. At the end of the street, you'll find what I think is the best show in all of Disneyland. It's actually strong competition for my favorite show at any Disney park. I still give that nod to the Finding Nemo show at Animal Kingdom, but this one is strong competition. I'll just give as evidence the fact that I liked it so much on our recent trip, that I went back the next day to watch it again. It is a fantastic show full of incredible special effects and stunning visual images. The acting and singing is pretty great too. Today, we are watching the Frozen show!

Frozen—Live at the Hyperion is the technical name of this show. It opened in May of 2016 replacing the wonderful Aladdin show that had been there for 13 years. We saw that one a while back too, and I remember it being fantastic. There is also a version of this Frozen show on the Disney cruise ship "Wonder," but on a slightly smaller scale. The Frozen show here was written and is directed by Tony nominated artists. When this show was first announced, 3500 performers tried out and only around 100 were selected to perform in five daily shows. There are four different casts that rotate days. The show runs 55 minutes in the Hyperion Theater that seats around 2000. More than 1000 costumes have been created for the show, and all vocals are performed live. For the "Let it Go" sequence, Elsa stands on top of a huge and exquisite set of crystal stairs that rotate out over the crowd. The special effects also include 36 ice spikes built into the stage as well as an enormous chandelier that drops from the ceiling. It is made up of 60 individual shards and has more than 500 points of light.

This show was superb! I think I said something to that effect, but I want to reemphasize. I already liked the *Frozen* movie, but I think this show was maybe even better. You absolutely have to check it out if you haven't seen it. Of course the highlight as in the movie is the song that the movie made famous, "Let it Go." During this song, there are several special effects as Elsa builds her ice palace. These are done with concealed ice spikes, a colossal staircase, the beautiful chandelier and a huge LED screen on stage. If you've never seen the movie or heard the song, I'm guessing you have been living the life of a hermit the last several years. In the song, Elsa is finally allowing herself to use her special powers after trying to hide and conceal them for so many years. I think we can also apply "Let it Go" to our spiritual lives as well.

As we've talked about previously, we all sin. The Bible says it, but we all know it's true. We all mess up from time to time. Sometimes our guilt causes us to hold on to these sins. Even though we've asked for forgiveness and even though time has passed, we still dwell on the sin and feel bad about it. I think sometimes our human minds have a hard time grasping the fact that when God forgives our sins, they are really forgiven and forgotten. Let me remind you of a few verses. Hebrews 8:12 says that God shows us mercy and remembers our sins no more. Hebrews 10:17 repeats that. I John 1:9 says, "If we confess our sins, he is faithful and just to forgive us our sins and to cleanse us from all unrighteousness." As long as we are honest about our mistakes, confess them to God and are genuine in seeking forgiveness, those sins are gone! We are completely cleansed according to that verse. Not only are we clean, but Romans 8:1 says we won't be condemned because of our relationship with Jesus.

Like Elsa, we sometimes need to just let it go. Don't hold on to mistakes of the past. If you have been honest in your confession and asking for forgiveness, you have to believe that God has given you just that. Not only has he forgiven you, he's forgotten it! It won't be brought up again, even on judgment day. And why is that true? Because of our Savior's death on the cross that took the place of all of our sin. Look at Colossians 2:13-14 that reaffirms that. "And you, who were dead in your trespasses and the uncircumcision of your flesh, God made alive together with him, having forgiven us all our trespasses, by canceling the record of debt that stood against us with its legal demands. This he set aside, nailing it to the cross." Thank God today for the amazing gift of his mercy, grace and forgiveness. Ask Him to help you overcome any guilt you may have from past sins. Continue living for God and don't dwell on the past. Just let it go!

"Guardians of the Galaxy— Mission: BREAKOUT!"

Continuing down the street here in Hollywood Land, we come to a ride that is old and new at the same time. You may wonder how that's possible. In book one, we had a devotional about the Tower of Terror at Hollywood Studios and DCA park has had that same ride since 2004. However, in 2017, it was closed for five months while an extensive refurbishment took place. This was met with some criticism and skepticism, even from yours truly here. I was sad to see them changing a classic ride like Tower of Terror. However, after riding it recently, I guess I'll have to give my stamp of approval. The changes are actually pretty cool, and it warrants a brand new devotional about this new edition which is now called Guardians of the Galaxy—Mission: BREAKOUT!

As you probably know, there have been two *Guardians of the Galaxy* movies with another in the works. This ride opened with its brand new theme just two days after the second movie was released. Both films have been extremely popular and box office gold. Disney of course wanted to capitalize on that franchise, and so they decided to re-theme this ride around the hype and fame that these Guardians have produced. The ride is basically the same as far as your ride vehicle and the fact that you are in an elevator that drops repeatedly. However, you now have a mission. At the beginning of the ride, the popular character Rocket Raccoon lets you know that you are being recruited to help free the rest of the Guardians who are being held captive. This is the first Disney attraction to open based on the MCU—Marvel Cinematic Universe. However, because there is still some contract negotiations going on with Universal, Disney can't use the Marvel logo in the title or in any advertising for this ride. To be honest, I don't really understand how it all works. Disney bought Marvel, but Universal apparently still owns the rights to Marvel attractions, especially in Florida where it is a huge part of their parks there. You can read all about it online. I honestly tried, but it's all very confusing to me. Why can't they just all get along? Actually, Disney is in the process of building a whole Marvel Land at DCA right now scheduled to open in 2020. There are not a whole lot of details as of this writing, so I can't tell you much about that. But back to this ride...there are six different versions of the ride, each with its own song, visuals and drop sequence. The Guardians cast all came back to film several sequences for the attraction. This ride is 183 feet tall and guests get to drop 130 of those feet at a speed of 39 mph.

We really enjoyed this ride on our recent trip. I already liked Tower of Terror. This new version just adds some fantastic new visuals and creative elements. The drop still gets to my stomach a little, so I can't ride it more than a couple of times without needing a break. I'll also say that I've enjoyed the Guardians movies. They are pretty entertaining, funny and action-packed. The general premise of the films, as you might guess is that these characters are indeed guardians trying to protect the galaxy from the forces of evil. This leads me to our thought for today.

If you think about it, we are also guardians of the galaxy in a way. Part of our job as children of God is to protect others around us from the forces of evil...particularly the evils of Satan. 2 Peter 2:1 warns us that we will experience many false teachers claiming to be from God. It says they will come in secretly and bring destruction on those who aren't careful. I Timothy 4:1 says that some of those false teachers will succeed. It reads, "Now the Spirit expressly says that in later times some will depart from the faith by devoting themselves to deceitful spirits and teachings of demons." That's a pretty scary fact that a lot of people will fall victim to these false teachers and depart from their faith. It is our job as God's warriors to fight Satan and protect as many of our fellow Christians as we can. There's a constant battle going on in the "galaxy" between God and Satan. We know that in the end God will win, but for now, Satan is trying to bring as many to his side as he can. We have to fight first to keep ourselves on God's side and then try to win as many others to join our ranks as well.

Take some time today to read Matthew 24. Jesus talks about this very thing. He foretells about the end times and how many will fall away and be led astray. I think we may be living through some of this right now. As wonderful as this world can be, there are many forces of evil out there trying to lead people off the path to Heaven. Our whole purpose in life is to get ourselves and as many others as possible home to God's kingdom. In that sense, we are the guardians of the galaxy and must serve God by fighting for Him. Watch out for your own soul and assist others in fighting temptation that may take them away from God. Take your job seriously as a guardian of the galaxy!

"Monsters, Inc. Mike and Sully to the Rescue"

Stepping off of the Guardians ride, you may feel a little wobbly, so find your balance and follow me over to our next ride. This one is also here in Hollywood Land, although a lot of people seem to overlook this one. We've had more than one family tell us that they didn't see this ride or even know it existed. Therefore, this attraction is sort of like a hidden treasure in the fact is that it's a great ride, especially if you love the movie Monsters, Inc., which I certainly do. Let's go try out Monsters, Inc. Mike and Sully to the Rescue.

That's a long name! We'll just call this the Monsters ride if you don't mind. Opening in 2006, this is a dark ride, which is fairly rare at this park. This ride is semi-hidden behind the backlot stage, so a lot of people pass it by, meaning typically shorter wait times. During this ride, guests board taxi cabs with Mike and Sully to try and find Boo before Randall or the CDA (Child Detection Agency) does. Again, if you've seen the movie, you know what all those things are. When the ride begins, you hear an announcement that a human child is loose in Monstropolis, and the chase is on. You then find yourself winding around through various scenes from the movie. In each scene, you should be able to spot the hiding little girl, Boo. Each vehicle has a video monitor that shows random news clips shown throughout the journey. The ride also has some neat special effects such as the smell of ginger as you pass the restaurant. It also uses the "Peppers Ghost" trick made famous in the Haunted Mansion, to make Randall appear and disappear. There is also a large speaking audio-animatronic of Roz who apparently will interact with you if for instance you take a picture of her. This ride follows the same track and layout of the ride that was previously in this building called Superstar Limos. In that ride, you boarded a limo and were taken on a tour of Los Angeles.

One of the best parts of the Monsters ride is the door scene. If you remember the film, near the end, Mike and Sully enter a room full of thousands of doors. They are trying to find Boo's door so they can rescue her. That scene is recreated on this ride using mirrors so it looks like you are among the numerous doors. If you look close enough, you can spot Boo's special door with the flowers on it. That door is very important in the film as it's the only way that Mike and Sully can interact with the child. They search desperately for that door so they can find her and help her to get home. Did you know that there's also a door in your life that's very important?

Revelation 3:20 says, " Behold, I stand at the door and knock. If anyone hears my voice and opens the door, I will come in to him and eat with him, and he with me." That is Jesus speaking to all of us. Jesus is always at the door of our heart waiting for us to open it and let Him in. This is especially important for those who don't know Jesus or don't have a relationship with Him. He's right there! You just have to open the door! In a similar way, Matthew 7:7 is Jesus reminding us that all we have to do is knock on the door and it will be opened for us. Finally in John 10:9, Jesus says He IS the door to salvation. In other words, if we want to enter Heaven one day, we have to go through Jesus. We have to believe in Him and know Him.

Do you know Jesus? Do you have a relationship with Him? Do you read and study about His life often? Do you know someone who doesn't know Jesus? Just like Boo's special and important door, there is a door in everyone's life with Jesus standing patiently on the other side. All we have to do is knock or open it, and we can make that connection with our Lord and Savior Jesus Christ. Open that door! Encourage others to do the same! If we want to see Him one day, that special door has to be found and opened!

"Animation Academy"

We're done with the rides and shows here in Hollywood Land, but there are still a couple of important opportunities here we can't skip over. If you enter the building across the street from Monsters, Inc. you'll actually find four attractions in one. Upon entering and arriving inside what is called the Animation Courtyard, you find yourself staring at several large projection screens playing clips from your favorite Disney films. At that point, you are invited to choose your animation adventure as there are four possible ways you can go. One of the doors leads to a character greet with Anna and Elsa from Frozen, a very popular choice that typically has quite the line. Another door leads to Turtle Talk with Crush, an attraction we discussed in the first book. The other two doors lead to attractions unique to Disneyland so we are going to discuss them today and next time. We'll start today with what is called the Animation Academy.

The Animation Academy opened with the park in 2001 and at times has also been present at WDW's Hollywood Studios and DisneyQuest, as well as Tokyo and Paris. It is currently open in Hong Kong and Shanghai, although in the latter it is dedicated to Marvel heroes instead of classic Disney characters. It was recently announced to be making its way to Epcot in 2021. Just outside the attraction at the beginning of the queue, you can see a schedule of classic Disney characters listed every 30 minutes. This way you know which character will be presented at a certain time. Upon entering the Academy, you are seated in a small auditorium with stair-step rows of seats. Everyone is given a large drawing pad as well as a pencil. A Disney cast member will then enter and demonstrate step-by-step how to draw a Disney character on your blank piece of paper. The cast member draws along with you and projects his or her drawing up on a screen. The class usually lasts around 15 minutes and you get to take your drawing home with you. The stage where the cast member sits to draw is decorated like an art studio, but if you look really close, you might just spot some hidden Disney characters such as Mushu, Winnie the Pooh, Donald Duck, Sully and Baymax.

My family really enjoyed this attraction on our trip. We honestly had no idea what to expect when we walked in, but it was so much fun that we ended up going back at least twice more. This is an experience for all ages and all levels of skill. I'll be honest and say that I am not the best artist in the world and neither are any members of my family. However, if someone shows me one step at a time how to draw something, I can usually create a decent drawing. This is exactly what happened to us. Each member of my family was able to decently draw each character and take home something we were proud of. This leads us to our spiritual thought for today.

When we walked in that drawing studio, we began with nothing except an old pencil and a blank piece of paper. 15 minutes later, we walked out with a beautiful drawing that we took pride in. Basically, we took nothing and made it into greatness. God can do exactly the same thing with us. He did it several times in Scripture using Jesus. Let's briefly look at the life of Peter. When Jesus first met Peter, his name wasn't even Peter. It was Simon, and he was just a lowly fisherman. He was nothing special. He probably didn't expect to be anything great. He just expected to try and get by, living the life of a fisherman. However, that all changed when Jesus told Simon and eleven others to follow Him. After meeting and getting to know Simon, look at what Jesus said to him in Matthew 16:18. Christ said, "And I tell you, you are Peter, and on this rock I will build my church, and the gates of hell shall not prevail against it." Jesus changed his name! He called him Peter which means "rock," and said upon this rock I will build my church. In other words, He chose Peter to start the church after His death, and that's exactly what Peter did. In Acts 2 on the day of Pentecost, Peter began the church and baptized over 3000 people. Even though he made mistakes from time to time, such as denying Christ before His death in Luke 22, Peter was still destined by God to be and do something great. Through Jesus, God took an unknown fisherman and changed him into a great leader of the church that will always be remembered.

Make sure you try out the Animation Academy. I promise you'll enjoy it, even if you aren't artistic at all. It is still a fun experience, and I'm pretty sure you'll exit with something in your hand you are proud of. Keep in mind that God does the same with all of us. If you seek Him and ask, He will change you into something wonderful. He will use you to change others. He will take you and turn you into greatness, if you'll only allow Him to.

"Sorcerer's Workshop"

The final area you might want to check out here in the Animation Courtyard is called the Sorcerer's Workshop. This is another experience that my family really enjoyed and visited at least twice during our last visit. It is a walk-through attraction that you can enjoy at your own pace. It has several clever elements to it that we'll discuss today.

The Sorcerer's Workshop also opened in 2001 with the park and was designed to allow guests to discover the secrets of animation. Originally this attraction was divided up into three different rooms. The first room is a demonstration of early animation and how it works. Guests are invited to draw a figure or character several times in succession on a long strip of paper. There are examples on how to do this that you can copy or trace. You are basically drawing a shape or figure several times having it move slightly each time. You then place your long strip drawing in a circular spinning device and give it a whirl. You then get to see your drawing come to life. It reminds me of those animation books where you flip the pages real fast to make a figure move. There are several different devices in this room all used as animation machines. They are called phenakistascope, praxinoscope, thaumatrope and zoetrope. And yes, I used copy and paste on those names! I don't even know how to say those names. And I certainly don't know what they do! Luckily, there are descriptions of each, and you can play with and figure out how to use them.

The second room is called the Beast's library and is patterned after the famous room from the *Beauty and the Beast* film. Above the mantle in the room is a portrait of the Beast before he was transformed. If you watch the portrait carefully, you can see it slowly change as he did. You can also find the magic rose in the room which is slowly losing its petals as in the film. In addition, you will find several machines in this room where you can sit down and answer a series of questions about yourself. Once you have given some information, it will tell you which Disney character you are most like. This was a really neat aspect that we enjoyed and each family member wanted to try. As I mentioned, there used to be a third room off the library called Ursula's Grotto where guests could record and insert themselves into a video clip. However, this room was closed on our recent trip and apparently has been for some time. There's no word on whether it will open again someday.

We really enjoyed this attraction and spent a considerable amount of time here. Our favorite part was probably finding out which Disney character we are most like. I know you're going to hate me, but I cannot remember which character I was. I've been sitting here racking my brain to no avail. Sorry about that. I guess I'll just have to take another trip back so I can do it again. But here's the point I want to make. It's fun to sit there, answer questions and wait with anticipation to see which character matches your personality. It's kind of like those numerous online quizzes and tests that reveal some magical information about you. There's nothing wrong with having fun with that. However, in reality, there's only one character we should really want to be like.

In John 13:15, Jesus said, "For I have given you an example, that you also should do just as I have done to you." I can't say it any better than that. This is probably a repeat lesson that I've mentioned several times, but that's only because it's so important. We should be striving every day to be more and more like Jesus. We should be studying His life every chance we get so we can live as He did. In I Corinthians 11:1 Paul even said, "Be imitators of me as I am of Christ." Paul also knew that was his first priority...to pattern his life after that of Jesus. If you are having trouble figuring out how to do this, start with John 13:34. Jesus said, "A new commandment I give to you, that you love one another: just as I have loved you, you also are to love one another." So start by just loving each other. Treat each other with respect despite any differences you may have. This is what Jesus demonstrated, and we should follow in His footsteps and work hard to love our neighbor.

If you find yourself in the Sorcerer's Workshop, go ahead and find out which character you most resemble. It's a lot of fun. Just make sure you are working hard each and every day to most resemble Jesus in your attitude, example, and love for others. Do as He did. Speak like He spoke. Live like He lived. Love like He loved.

"Radiator Springs Racers"

Today is another special day! We are moving out of Hollywood Land and making our way to the next area of DCA. We're going to Cars Land! Now, in real life we would've gone here first. In fact, let me advise you right now for your next trip,...get there before park opening and GO TO CARS LAND FIRST!! Depending on the time of year, this land will get very crowded very fast, and so unless you have a fastpass, you'll be waiting a long time for this next ride. We're doing the racers today! This ride is phenomenal. It is my favorite in the park, and in all of Disneyland. My entire family would agree. So get your game face on! You ready for a little competition? It's time for a race!

The Radiator Spring Racers opened in 2012 as part of the 1.1 billion dollar expansion of DCA. This ride alone accounted for 18% of that cost! That's right, this ride cost 200 million dollars to build making it one of the most expensive theme park attractions in the world. Only Test Track at Epcot was more expensive at 300 million. This ride is actually very similar to Test Track and uses the same technology. In the same way, you are placed in a six person convertible and you make your way around Radiator Springs, the fictional town from the *Cars* movies. At the end of the ride, you are side by side with another guest-filled car to participate in a randomized race to the finish line. The top speed is 40 mph, but it feels much faster. This is of course the best part of the ride. However, the first part is pretty incredible also. The scenery is gorgeous with the rock formations and waterfall all set to music in your vehicle. At one point during your visit through the town, the track splits. If your car goes left, you receive a tire change. If you make the right split, you receive a fresh coat of paint. They are both neat to watch making it necessary to try and ride multiple times. You'll want to anyways...trust me!

I've had the pleasure of riding this five or six times, and every time has been great. Again, I would advise you to get there early, grab a fast pass for the ride, and then quickly get in line so you can at least do it twice. Otherwise, the typical wait is around 90-120 minutes on any given day. As I mentioned, the best part is the race at the end. After your car is fixed up and ready, you see your competition pull up beside you and then the race is on! It's a fun competition, and the winner is completely random each time. It doesn't matter which side of the track you are on. In all the times I've ridden, I've won about half the time. One thing I noticed every time I rode was the smiles on everyone's faces, regardless of who was declared the winner. Do you want to win? Of course! But it's a fun competition, and I've never seen anyone, even kids, get upset when losing. Everyone is having too much fun to care about winning and losing. This is how it should be...on the ride and in life!

Throughout our lives, we are constantly involved in competition, and I'm not just talking about sports. Even adults will sometimes make a competition out of job promotions, large purchases or posts on social media. Our human nature has us trying to better one another and boast about our accomplishments. Don't get me wrong, there's nothing wrong with working hard, setting goals and being proud of your achievements. But we should do it out of self-motivation and not trying to better anyone else. We also should be proud of others when they succeed at something. We shouldn't get upset if someone legitimately does something better than us. There is nothing beneficial about being a sore loser.

Philippians 2:3 says, "Do nothing from selfish ambition or conceit, but in humility count others more significant than yourselves." Proverbs 25:17 tells us it's not glorious to seek our own glory. Being humble is very important. Jesus demonstrated this very well. He could've boasted all over the place about His power and the fact that He was the Son of God. Instead, He definitely put others first and did not seek His own glory by any means. Proverbs 24:17 says, "Do not rejoice when your enemy falls, and let not your heart be glad when he stumbles." This reminds me of when I used to coach middle school cross country. I had two brothers on the team, one being two years younger. He was always trying to beat his older brother in our races and kept gradually getting closer throughout the season. In our very last meet, he passed his older brother about a minute from the finish line only to hear his brother trip and fall behind him. Instead of racing on to a long awaited defeat, he turned around and helped his brother up so they could cross the line together. That's what competition should be...celebrating others' victories as we celebrate our own.

You're going to love the racers! It's worth a trip to California just to experience this ride. Yes, it's that good. You really feel like you are in Radiator Springs as this ride fully immerses you with sounds, audio-animatronics, scenery and special effects. The race is a lot of fun too! Go ahead and root for your car. Cheer loud if you win. Congratulate the others car if you lose. Do the same in life. Don't ever be a sore loser! Instead, be humble in your victories and commend others in theirs. That's the way a true race should always end.

"Luigi's Rollickin' Roadsters"

Exiting the racers, we're now standing in the middle of Radiator Springs, so what do we want to do now? I know! Another ride on the racers! We could probably enjoy riding those all day, but there are a couple more attractions here, so I suppose we should give them a shot too. We'll start with the one right next door to the racers called Luigi's Rollickin' Roadsters.

When this ride first opened with Cars Land back in 2012, it was called Luigi's Flying Tires. Guests boarded a giant inflatable tire that would fill with air and essentially hover. Riders could then move the tire around an enclosed space by leaning their bodies. The goal was to ride around and bump into other tires similar to bumper cars. We actually rode those a couple of years after they came out. The problem we found, and apparently many others did too, was that they were very hard to move. You had to lean just right, and if you went too far, your tire would get stuck on the pavement. Needless to say, the first ride in this spot was met with a lot of complaints and issues, and so the ride was changed just three years after it opened. This new version opened in 2016 and has guests placed into a car to experience a trackless, dancing car ride set to music. You have no control and don't know where your car will go as this is the first trackless ride at any U.S. Disney park. The premise is that Luigi, the Italian roadster from *Cars* who runs the tire shop, has invited 20 of his cousins to participate in a dance festival behind his shop. You can tell that exactly half the vehicles are male based on the mustaches on their front grill. Once everyone is seated, the Italian music begins and the cars will dance and spin in their own unique way. Near the end, the cars instead move in synchronous harmony dancing together to the lively music. If you are lucky early in the ride, you may even get pulled to the middle while the other cars dance around you, but there's no way to know which car might experience this. There are 20 cars each holding 2 guests so 40 is the capacity during this 90 second ride. This attraction is fun to ride of course, but it's also fun to watch one round and see all the cars move simultaneously at the end.

As mentioned, this is the first ride in the United States to use a trackless ride system. The cars are free to move about as they please and are controlled by wireless location technology. Luckily the technology is advanced enough to keep the cars from running into each other. This won't always be the only trackless ride in the U.S. as the Ratatouille ride coming to the France pavilion at Epcot will also be trackless. There are additional trackless rides in other Disney parks around the world. The trackless approach apparently leads to much more creative and smoother rides. While trackless may be the ride of the future and the way to go, it is the exact opposite of how our life ride should be. We have a definite path we have to follow, and it's very dangerous if we decide to go "trackless."

Psalms 37:23 says that the steps of a man are established by the Lord. In Job 23:11, Job said, "My foot has held fast to his steps; I have kept his way and have not turned aside." Psalms 32:8 says that God will teach us the way we should go. The point is that there is a definite path we are to take in our spiritual life. When we get off and go trackless on our own, we put ourselves in danger of falling away. The best way to stay on this path is to study the Bible. Psalms 119:105 even says that the Word of God is a lamp to our feet and a light to our path. The Bible provides the way we should go. One of my favorite passages, Proverbs 3:5-6 tells us to just trust in God and He will make our paths straight. In other words, if we just let God have control and trust in Him, he will lead and guide us in the right way. And don't forget in John 14:6 when Jesus said that He is the way. Anytime we get off track, we just have to turn back to Jesus and follow in His footsteps. That will always direct us in the way we should go.

Luigi's Rollickin' Roadsters is a fun little ride. It's worth a try to experience the unique movements and dance of your vehicle. It's also neat to have the opportunity to enjoy a trackless ride. Just make sure you don't go trackless in your walk with God. Let God guide your steps. Remember that the path to Heaven is narrow and we can't afford to get off of it. Stay on track!

"Mater's Junkyard Jamboree"

We've done some racin' and some synchronized dancin' here in Cars Land. Now it's time for some spinnin'! Today we move to our last ride in this land. There are of course other wonderful things to do here such as fantastic places to eat, character greets and shopping. This land really is a fun and creative place to spend some time. The Imagineers that put it all together really outdid themselves and produced quite the immersive experience. Today we get to hop aboard some miniature tractors created just for this attraction. Come join me on Mater's Junkyard Jamboree!

This is an outdoor type of whip ride themed to Mater's junkyard. Mater is of course the infamous tow truck from the *Cars* films. He hosts this ride and even sings one of seven songs in a square dance style. While he entertains you with his less than perfect vocals, your tractor vehicle whips around and spins on a circular track. It always appears as if you're going to whip right into another vehicle, but of course that won't happen. This is the same style of ride as the Alien Swirling Saucers at Hollywood Studios in Florida. Supposedly once every hour, an eighth song will play that was put together using outtakes from the recording session. That would be fun to hear, although I'm not sure I'd want to sit there for an hour waiting for it. There are 22 possible tractors you can board each holding 2 riders. Be prepared to crash into your partner as you spin around as the centrifugal force will grab a hold of you. Before or after you board, you'll also want to check out Mater's junkyard jukebox nearby, a contraption worthy of your attention.

Have you seen the *Cars* movies? I've seen all three and they are all very entertaining. Like many of you I'm sure, Mater is one of my favorite characters. He provides much comic relief with his unusual mannerisms and phrases. He is of course voiced by Larry the Cable Guy, a well-known comedian. Mater is portrayed as an old, beat-up tow truck that is basically, well, a piece of junk. He's kind of outdated and rusty looking, unlike his shiny pal Lightning McQueen. If you've seen the films, you know that Mater always seems to get into trouble, and say or do something kind of dumb. Sometimes he even makes mistakes that get others into trouble. At the same time, he also tends to end up being the hero and saving the day on several occasions. He sometimes ends up being the friend that Lightning McQueen and others need in times of trouble. So he may look junky and archaic, but he's definitely a worthy friend to have around.

Awhile back I referred to the phrase "God don't make no junk." While that may be grammatically incorrect, it's a very true statement. Take some time today to read Judges chapter 6 and the story of Gideon. Notice in verse 14 God calls Gideon to go and save the Israelites from oppression. Gideon's first reaction is to question God in verse 15. He says, "How can I save Israel? My clan is the weakest, and I am the least in my father's house." In a sense, Gideon considers himself to be junk calling himself lowly and weak. God then tells Gideon that He will be with him. Gideon ends up asking for a sign which God complies with. Continue reading to find out that Gideon does end up being a great judge and leader for the Israelites, saving them from an army much bigger than his. There are many stories in Scripture with a similar premise. You see, everything and everyone that God has made is valuable. God gives all of us different talents and abilities and we need to look for the good in others before we judge them to be junk. Matthew 7:12 is the well-known "golden rule" telling us to treat others the way we want to be treated. Luke 10:27 reminds us to love our neighbors as we do ourselves. Romans 12:3 says that we ought not to think of ourselves as higher than anyone else. The point is that we should not go around judging others based on what we see on the outside.

Mater doesn't look like much on the outside, but he ends up being very useful and vital on several occasions. As you ride these spinning tractors and hear Mater's voice, keep in mind that God doesn't make junk. Everyone has value and is important and should be treated as such. Even Gideon, who was from a lowly tribe and family, ended up being a significant Biblical hero that saved many of God's people. If you find someone is different from you, look for their strengths and potential instead of judging their weaknesses. Find their talents, highlight them, and work with them to glorify God.

"Grizzly River Run"

Now it's time to leave Cars Land. It doesn't seem like we've been here very long. Maybe that's because we haven't. Three rides. That's about it. Now don't get me wrong...it's a great section of the park, and you'll want to spend a lot of time there. That land is just more about quality and not quantity. We'll get to some of the quantity sections later. For today, we are heading to another land that doesn't have a lot of attractions...three again as a matter of fact. Let's head to Grizzly Peak and ride the Grizzly River Run.

Grizzly Peak is another section here at DCA that includes Soarin' Around the World, which we talked about in the first book...love that ride!! It also includes today's attraction and one more we'll discuss next time. Grizzly River Run, as you can probably imagine, is a water raft ride. It's similar to Kali River Rapids at Animal Kingdom but distinctive in the fact that the raft you are in is designed to spin as it descends several chutes. This ride opened with the park and takes you on a 7 ½ minute ride with several twists and turns through turbulent waters. During the ride, you make your way around Grizzly Peak, the 110 foot bear-shaped mountain. The beginning of the ride takes you up higher so that you can experience a 21 foot drop near the end, the highest in the world for this type of attraction. Make no mistake you will get wet on this ride and most likely soaked. However, depending on the time of year, the amount of splashing is controllable by cast members. In other words, in colder months, they can lessen the amount you get splashed. I may have to special request that next time.

When my family went to Disneyland several years ago, it was nighttime and pretty cool outside by the time we approached this ride. I'll be honest and tell you that I chickened out. If there's one thing I'm not fond of, it's getting wet when I'm cold or vice-versa. My brave wife and one of my sons decided to accept the challenge and board the raft. They looked like they had a lot of fun despite the slight shivering afterwards. Because of their positive reviews, I was all ready to ride on our most recent trip as it was quite warm outside. However, the ride was being refurbished and closed, much to my disappointment. I enjoy water rides when it's the right temperature outside. Rides like Splash

Mountain, Kali River Rapids and this one are great when it's nice and warm. They can even feel refreshing when it's hot outside and you are worn out from all the walking. That's the blessing of water. Have you ever been really hot and had the opportunity to jump into a swimming pool? It can be very invigorating and instantly change how you feel.

The Bible talks about how water can be refreshing in a different way. Read John chapter 4 today about Jesus and the Samaritan woman. In that story, Jesus finds a woman drawing water at a well and asks for a drink. She's surprised He's even talking to her as Jews normally didn't associate with Samaritans. He then goes on to tell her about living water, a water so special that if you drink of it, you'll never thirst again. She is intrigued and asks for some of this "special" water. Jesus is of course talking about eternal life in Heaven. Take some time to also read Revelation 21 and 22 as it describes what Heaven will look like. It describes a spring of life there for all those who are thirsty. It also mentions the river of life several times saying all those who are thirsty will be able to drink of it. I believe this is the water that Jesus was offering the Samaritan woman. He was trying to teach her about Heaven and how she needed to change her life of sin and follow Him instead.

I hope to ride Grizzly River Run next time. I was saddened that it was closed on our recent trip. Sometimes a good water ride can be refreshing and help rejuvenate us when needed. We have been offered an even better type of water. The river of life in Heaven is waiting for all of us. It's available for you and me, and I'm planning to see and drink of it one day. Isaiah 44:3 says, "For I will pour water on the thirsty land, and streams on the dry ground; I will pour my Spirit upon your offspring, and my blessing on your descendants." God is offering you this special water right now. He is showing you through His Word how to live your life in preparation for Heaven, so one day you can drink of this living water and never thirst again. Won't that be wonderful? Talk about refreshing!

"Redwood Creek Challenge Trail"

There's only one other attraction here in Grizzly Peak, and it's not a ride or show. It's another experience, and one that kids especially will love. The Redwood Creek Challenge Trail is a forest themed play area geared for children, but adults can certainly enjoy it as well. It features a system of trails that simulate a journey through a redwood forest, as well as a network of stairs, rope bridges, slides, a zip-line, rock climbing wall and an amphitheater. This area first opened with the park in 2001. In 2003, it was re-themed after the Disney film *Brother Bear*. In 2011, it changed once again to its current state, being themed after the movie *Up*. In that film, Russell is trying to become a Wilderness Explorer, which is exactly what kids in this area try to achieve. Kids can burn a lot of excess energy as they climb, jump, zip and swing around trying to complete six tasks. They can find these tasks by picking up a map as they enter. Upon completion, they are presented with a badge for each as well as a Senior Wilderness Explorer sticker. During their quest, they can also enter the "Spirit Cave" to find out what spirit animal represents them best. The choices are bear, wolf, eagle, moose, salmon and skunk. Wait, what? Skunk? I'm sure that would be mine. Be sure to have them climb the ranger station or even climb it with them. Apparently it provides a great view of the Grizzly Peak Mountain. Also check out the Millennium Tree which is a real cross-section of a tree that fell in a 1937 storm. At certain times, you might even find some characters here like Chip and Dale. Even Santa sometimes makes an appearance in this area around Christmas time.

While we didn't do this attraction on our recent trip, I remember vividly doing it when our boys were younger, and they absolutely loved it. We spent a lot of time at this forest playground. The boys loved completing the tasks and getting their badges. They took pride in those stickers and worked hard to finish each challenge. Do you like a challenge? I do. If someone gives me a task or a job to complete, I usually want to get it done quickly. I especially like when it is a little difficult, or I have to figure out the process of how to complete it. Have you ever done an escape room? I've had the pleasure of doing this twice thanks to my awesome sister-in-law (shout out to Beth) who always likes to treat us to this fun activity when she comes in town. They are so much fun as your group works together to figure out very clever puzzles and challenges to escape from a room. We have succeeded both times and escaped. It's been a blast and to me, the challenge is the best part about it. So I'd like to issue you a challenge today. I'll actually challenge myself as well. I'd love for you to take it on full force and work hard to complete it. It won't be easy because it will take hard work the rest of your life. I challenge you to develop a strong, daily relationship with God.

Maybe you already spend time with God daily. That's great! But we can always make it better, myself included. Remember the story of Daniel? What a great example of someone who had a strong relationship with God! In Daniel 6:10, we read that he got down on his knees three times daily and prayed. He had a routine and he stuck with it every day, even when his life was threatened. Do you pray three times daily? Do you get down on your knees? In Matthew 6:6 we are told that when we pray (not "if"), we are to go into our room and pray in secret and we will be rewarded by God. Even Jesus had a daily relationship with God. In Mark 1:35, we learn that he would talk to God early in the morning, finding a desolate place to be alone. I challenge you not only to develop a good prayer relationship with God, but also a daily time to study His Word. Acts 17:11 tells us about the Bereans who studied the Scriptures daily, and Paul commends them for it. A good relationship with God involves listening to Him just as much as talking.

Give the Redwood Creek Challenge Trail a try. You may enjoy it whether or not you are a young'un. Take on the challenges and see if you can earn your badges and sticker. But more importantly, please take seriously and consider the challenge I issued today. Will you please take on the task of developing a stronger, healthier and more consistent connection with our Father in Heaven? I promise it will benefit you both now and forever.

"The Bakery Tour"

Today we are moving on to another of the seven lands at DCA. This section is called Pacific Wharf and really only has one attraction. It does contain a walk-through preview center where you can see upcoming attractions and renovations, as well as ten different places to eat or drink. However, the only real attraction in this land is a tour and probably also my biggest regret. We didn't take advantage of this tour on any of our trips, and I'm not exactly sure why. I think we just got so busy with other rides and shows and simply forgot about this. I know I would've really enjoyed it, at least the smell and the taste! Hope you're hungry because today we're touring a bakery!

The Bakery Tour is hosted by Boudin Bakery and is free to all guests. It opened with the park in 2001 and is basically a self-guided tour that shows how sourdough bread is made. The tour does include preliminary video screens that give information about the bread and bakery. There is also an optional touchscreen trivia game. The best part of the tour happens before the tour even begins. Upon entering the building, all guests receive two pieces of sourdough bread to enjoy during the experience. The video is hosted by Rosie O'Donnell and Colin Mochrie as each provides some humor as they discuss the history of the bread. After this video, guests are free to walk through the hallways at their own pace to look through glass windows and see the sourdough bread being made. Through the various windows, you can watch the special dough be mixed, proofed, formed into loaves and baked. The only ingredients in the bread are flour, water, salt and a portion of the mother dough. The "mother dough" recipe was created and developed by French baker, Isidore Boudin back in 1849. The bacteria in this special dough is unique to San Francisco.

This bakery tour will be a definite must-do on our next Disneyland trip. I absolutely love the smell of fresh bread being baked. And the fact that each person is provided with free samples of delicious bread is just icing on the cake. As you know, Disney doesn't give away much for free, so this is one tasty experience to definitely take advantage of. Speaking of bread, can you think of a time when bread is mentioned in the Bible? There are many! You may think of the Old Testament as bread is mentioned in all but nine of the 39 Old Testament books. Maybe you remember the Passover feast early in Exodus that involved bread. Or maybe you think of a few chapters later when God had manna, a type of bread, rain down from the sky for the Israelites. Perhaps a New Testament story comes to mind such as Jesus feeding the 5000 with five loaves of bread and two fish. We could talk all day about the significance of bread in the Bible. Instead, let me just highlight three times when Jesus himself talked about bread.

The first occurred in Matthew 4 when Jesus was tempted in the wilderness by Satan himself. Jesus hadn't eaten in 40 days and the first attempt the Devil makes is to tempt Him with food. He tells Jesus to turn stones into bread which Jesus definitely could have done with God's power. Instead in verse 4, Jesus quotes Scripture and says, "Man shall not live by bread alone, but by every word that comes from the mouth of God." Jesus was telling Satan that physical food wasn't important, but instead, feeding on God's Word was what mattered. In John 6, Jesus is talking with his Apostles after the feeding of the 5000 and talks extensively about bread. He mentions Moses and the bread of the Old Testament. He then tells them several times, "I am the bread of life." He says that whoever comes to Him will not hunger or thirst. This is similar to His discussion with the Samaritan woman that we talked about recently. Again, Jesus is talking about Heaven and how one day there will be no hunger, thirst, sadness or suffering. The final passage about bread takes place just before Jesus' death on the cross. In Matthew 26:26, He once again speaks privately with His Apostles and has them share bread. He tells them the bread is His body and that they should take of it regularly to remember Him. This was the beginning and institution of the Lord's Supper which is a regular remembrance of Jesus that all Christians should participate in.

Bread is very important. Is it one of our basic foods and if you're like me, you are glad we have it. We use it in so many ways to make many different types of delicious food. Bread is also an important part of the life of Jesus. He used it to resist temptation. He used it to describe Heaven. He used it to set up a remembrance and tribute to Himself. Focus today on these important ways Jesus used bread. They are an encouragement and help to us all. We too have to resist temptation. We too need to strive for Heaven so we can receive the bread of life. And we too need to constantly remember Jesus, His life and His sacrifice on the cross. Let me close by reminding you of the Lord's Prayer in Matthew 6:9-13 when Jesus showed us how to pray. Part of that very special prayer is "give us this day our daily bread." Maybe this means more than just food. Maybe this means a daily remembrance of Jesus and how important He is to our lives.

"Golden Zephyr"

It's time for the last two lands of Disney California Adventure, and unlike recent lands, these two are full of attractions. One land has six attractions, five of which we'll discuss. The other also has six attractions and we'll talk about four. These are the quantity over quality lands as they really pack in the attractions all around Paradise Bay, the large body of water found at this park. Don't get me wrong...there are some great attractions around the Bay, but some are pretty simple and mimic your basic carnival type rides. We could go either way around the water. I've chosen to go counter-clockwise heading to the right first as we approach the water. The first unique ride we come to traveling that way is the Golden Zephyr, so we'll start there.

The Golden Zephyr is found in the Paradise Gardens Park section of DCA. The word "zephyr" may be strange and unfamiliar to you, but it means soft, gentle breeze which is exactly what this ride provides. Towering 85 feet high, this is a spinning ride that raises you up and swings you out over the water. This ride opened with the park and has guests boarding 90 foot long, 1940's sci-fi style rocket ships. These shiny vehicles are the type that were found in the old Buck Rogers and Flash Gordon comic series. Each of the six rockets holds up to 12 people. As the ride begins, your rocket spins around the giant center column gradually gaining speed. As speed increases, centripetal motion carries your rocket out further and further over the water to the point where you feel like you might fall in. This ride is similar to other swinging rides at Disney, however in this ride, guests have no control over the vehicle. When designing this ride, engineers visited England to examine a similar but much larger ride called the Captive Flying Machines that has been operating there since 1904. This ride is one of the very few that has no Disney theming whatsoever. It also can't operate in constant wind speeds over 10 mph or wind gusts of 15 mph. I'm told this ride is much better at night, so that may be a better strategy.

As mentioned, this ride is similar to other swinging attractions found at other Disney parks such as Dumbo, Astro Orbiter or Aladdin's Magic Carpets. However, in all those rides, guests have control of how high they go. I know when our boys were younger, they would always want to be the one controlling the height. I know on the carpets, the back seat riders get to control the tilt, but that was definitely the less desirable position. The height was the way to go. That was the fun control. For that reason, some on this ride might not enjoy the fact that they have no control at all. When they look down and find themselves swinging way out over the water, they may long for that control to bring them safely back down and closer to the ground.

In Galatians 5:22, we learn the fruits of the Spirit which are qualities we all want to strive for. The last one mentioned is self-control. This is a characteristic that is very important in our spiritual life. In Titus 1 when describing the qualifications for Elders in the church, self-control is mentioned as well. Proverbs 25:28 says, "A man without self-control is like a city broken into and left without walls." It might be thrilling to some on the Golden Zephyr to have no control...to just let things go and see what happens. But in life, that's a very dangerous practice. I Peter 4:7 reads, "The end of all things is at hand; therefore be self-controlled and sober-minded for the sake of your prayers." It's a dangerous world out there with lots of distractions, temptations and obstacles that get in the way of our spiritual focus. When we let our guard down and lose control, Satan sees an opportunity and is always ready to pounce. We must instead set limits and always strongly manage our words, actions and practices. That's not always easy to do, but the good news is that God will give us self-control if we ask for it. 2 Timothy 1:7 says, "for God gave us a spirit not of fear but of power and love and self-control." God will provide us with the power to control our lives. He will give you rule over your life and the strength and courage to stand firm, so ask Him for that, whether you think you need it or not.

The Golden Zephyr is a simple but quality ride. It provides some neat views and an exciting swing over the water. But be warned that you won't have any control of your rocket, so you will be at the mercy of the ride for 90 seconds. But don't worry. You'll be fine and safe on the ride. However, you may not be fine if you lose control of your life, even for 90 seconds. Satan doesn't need much time to sway you his way. Don't give him the satisfaction. Always keep self-control and be in charge of your life!

"Goofy's Sky School"

Continuing around the circle here in the Paradise Gardens Park section, we come to another ride way over in the corner of the park. If you've been to Disney World, this ride may look familiar as it's very similar to Primeval Whirl that you'll find at Animal Kingdom. However, once again this is a ride that may look and feel similar but has a very different theme and history so we're going to discuss it today. It's called Goofy's Sky School and you can't miss it. It is a fairly large structure and makes a lot of noise as you approach the area. This is another one that might get your stomach, so make sure your food is digested a little bit, and prepare for our flight with Goofy.

Goofy's Sky School is a steel, wild mouse type roller coaster. I don't think I had ever heard that term "wild mouse," but that just means a roller coaster with single cars that takes tight and flat but fast turns. When this ride first opened with the park, it was called Mulholland Madness and was dedicated to the famed Mulholland Drive in Los Angeles. This is the road we took on our recent trip to check out the famous "Hollywood" sign. Within the first month of this ride opening back in 2001, there were at least three accidents where guests got injured so the ride had to be shut down and refurbished rather quickly. At that time, the ride vehicles were themed to the many cars that you'll find on the Southern California freeway. In 2011, this ride was refurbished and reopened as Goofy's Sky School. You now board a plane themed vehicle to navigate a crash course on how to fly taught by Goofy himself. Throughout the ride, you'll see various signs and billboards with Goofy giving you the steps to fly a plane. You'll probably miss these signs if you aren't watching for them because of the thrill and G-forces experienced. There are many sharp turns, steep drops and sudden stops and you'll wonder if you're "plane" is even going to stay on the track. You'll definitely want to hold on as part of the scare factor of this ride includes the uncertainty of being able to remain in your vehicle. Rest assured that you are safety secured inside. This ride's theme is based on the short film called "Goofy's Glider" released in 1940. The cartoon is about Goofy's attempt to learn to fly by reading to "How to Fly" book.

I would love to be able to fly a plane. I think I would've really enjoyed being a pilot, and I kind of regret not looking into it more. This is one of the areas that my oldest son is thinking about as he is currently making college plans. We're traveling to Auburn University very soon to check out their aviation program. (War Eagle!—sorry, had to throw that in.) If I were to learn to fly, I think I might look into an actual training program instead of letting Goofy teach me. I'm not sure his training is quite enough! Teaching someone to fly or training someone in any area is important, but none as important as instruction in the Word of God.

I used to be a school history teacher, and while I'm glad I switched careers to become a paramedic, there are times that I miss being able to teach. The best part for me was seeing that look on the kids' faces when they understood something or enjoyed a story I told. Luckily, I still get to teach occasionally at the church where I attend, and it's a blessing. I actually work in a training program that teaches teenagers how to be Bible class teachers. This is something I wish I had growing up. One of the things we discuss is why we teach. The most important reason is that we are commanded to in Scripture. One of many verses with this command is Colossians 3:16 which says, "Let the Word of Christ dwell in you richly, teaching and admonishing one another..." We also talk about James 3:1 which says, "Not many of you should become teachers, my brothers, for you know that we who teach will be judged with greater strictness." That verse makes it sound like we shouldn't teach, but what it is really saying is that teaching is so important, that we need to take it very seriously. We need to teach others from the Bible and not lead them astray with false teaching.

I want to strongly encourage you to teach others about God whether in a formal Bible class setting or simply a private one-on-one session. How else will others know about God, His plan and His Son unless someone teaches them? We understand training is important in school when learning the basic subjects or in college when learning a career. Why should spiritual training be any different? In 2 Timothy 2:2, Paul says, "and what you have heard from me in the presence of many witnesses entrust to faithful men, who will be able to teach others also." Paul is encouraging Timothy and others to be teachers, to take what he's said and pass it on. We have to keep the cycle of good spiritual training going. Take a lesson from Goofy's Sky School today and become a teacher. I'm sure you can do it much better than Goofy. As long as you are teaching from the Bible, you can't do it wrong regardless of how well you teach. Any training in God's Word is important, so find a way to do your part and spread the Word!

"Jumpin' Jellyfish"

If we cross back over the path to the edge of the water, we find a couple of basic rides here. Neither one is too intense or really that thrilling to be honest, but they aren't intended to be. They are geared more towards children, which is important and needed to balance things out. The first one we'll talk about today is called Jumpin' Jellyfish. You'll be able to easily spot this one as it looks like, well, a bunch of jellyfish jumpin' up and down.

Jumpin' Jellyfish is a paratower type ride which means parachute jump-style. Imagine beautiful and colorful cartoon jellyfish floating up and down in a pretend sea and that's what this ride looks like. It opened with the park and is also available at Disneyland in Tokyo. There are also similar attractions in Paris and Hong Kong, however those are themed after the parachuting toy soldiers from *Toy Story*. The one in Hong Kong is 80 feet high. This one here at DCA is only 40 feet high and again is geared more towards younger children, so it's not too extreme. There are two towers here each with six jellyfish. Each jellyfish holds two guests and gently rises and falls for around 90 seconds or so. Is it me or do a lot of the rides here last 90 seconds? That must be a standard of some kind. Anyways, at first thought I assumed the name of this ride came from *Finding Nemo* with its jellyfish scene, but that's incorrect. Can you guess where the name comes from? It's another well-known Disney film. I'll give you the answer at the end of this devotional. There used to be another ride near this one called Mailboomer that opened with the park as well. It was way more thrilling and intense. It was 185 feet high and launched guests from the bottom up in the air. Unfortunately, that ride didn't survive the 2011 expansion.

As I mentioned, this is a parachute jump type ride. You are gently raised into the air and then float back to the ground with your jellyfish shaped parachute. Did you know that the parachute was invented way back in 1783? What's even more amazing is that famous painter and inventor, Leonardo DaVinci made sketches for a parachute back in the late 1400's! I don't know if I'll ever do it, but skydiving is on my bucket list. I'd have to get past my wife first. Oh don't get me wrong, I'd be scared to death (not of my wife...I meant skydiving), but I would do it. The thrill of falling to Earth and essentially flying followed by (hopefully) floating gently with a parachute would be the ultimate in adventure and excitement. I'll admit I'm not a big fan of heights. The fear of falling makes my knees wobble and my heart skip a beat. I don't even like putting Christmas lights on the roof anymore. Just like falling physically, we can also fall spiritually, and we do all the time. We fall spiritually by sinning against God and straying from the path to Heaven. The good news is that just like a parachute, God is there to soften and cushion our fall as well as pick us right back up.

Look at Psalms 37:23-24 with me. It reads, "The LORD makes firm the steps of the one who delights in him; though he may stumble, he will not fall, for the LORD upholds him with his hand." Another Psalm echoes this sentiment when it says, "The LORD upholds all who are falling and raises up all who are bowed down" (Psalms 145:14). Isn't it nice to know that God is always watching us, always protecting us, and always there to catch us when we fall? The Bible says God won't let us be tempted beyond what we can bear (I Cor. 10:13). It also says God provides us with safety so we can sleep in peace (Psalms 4). And it also says God comforts us when we suffer (2 Cor. 1:4). God has a solution for every problem we may have. He is always there for us to lean on, talk to, cry to, yell at, and fall into. His arms are big enough to gather us all unto Him. He is also always there for us to love, praise, respect, thank, and worship. He deserves all of that for what He has done and continues to do for us. Micah 7:8 reads, "Rejoice not over me, O my enemy; when I fall, I shall rise; when I sit in darkness, the LORD will be a light to me."

If you ride Jumpin' Jellyfish, you will fall. But it will be a nice, relaxing fall while enjoying a great view of the park. In your spiritual life, you also will fall. And it probably won't be quite as peaceful and enjoyable. But never forget that God is there to catch you. Look to him and He will show you the way to get up. Like that verse in Micah says, when you fall, you shall rise again, thanks to God. By the way, the name of this ride comes from a line in *The Little Mermaid*. When the fireworks first blast from Prince Eric's ship, Sebastian gets startled and yells, "Jumpin' Jellyfish!"

"Silly Symphony Swings"

The last ride we'll discuss in this area of the park is another simple ride. It's one you can ride at most generic theme parks, but still one I typically enjoy. If you look carefully as you approach this ride, you can see the one and only Mickey Mouse standing atop conducting to the music. You might also recognize the music as the well-known "William Tell Overture," made famous in "The Lone Ranger" films and TV shows. Today we're trying out the Silly Symphony Swings.

Yes, this is your classic swing ride where guests can board one of 48 possible swings for a (you guessed it) 90 second ride. This ride opened in 2010 and took the place The Orange Stinger which was literally a giant orange surrounding the swings to honor the famous orange fields of California. At one time there was even an orange scent pumped in to that ride, but the smell attracted bees and had to be shut off. That was also a swinging ride, but riders were enclosed inside the orange with views of the park through the peel. The ride was heavily refurbished after closing in 2009 and these new swings have much better views of the surroundings. The Silly Symphony Swings are now themed around "The Band Concert" which was a 1935 Disney short film starring Mickey and Donald. This renowned cartoon was the first Mickey Mouse animation produced in color, and its story is what we will focus on today.

I don't know if you've ever seen this legendary Mickey cartoon, but it is one of the most highly acclaimed Disney shorts in history. You can definitely see clips of it on YouTube, and possibly the entire nine minute cartoon. The story centers around Mickey trying to conduct his band in a park concert. They are of course playing the same song the ride plays, the "William Tell Overture." Throughout the concert, the music keeps getting interrupted by various distractions, namely Donald Duck who keeps playing his flute. This confuses the band and they begin playing with him instead of Mickey. There are several other disturbances and near the end of the cartoon, a tornado hits and begins to suck up everything in its path, band and all. The band is so used to the distractions by now that they just continue to play. Mickey, of course gets continually frustrated and conducts feverishly to try and keep his band together. There is of course a lot more to the story, but that's the general plot which leads to our lesson today.

In a way, we are like the members of that band, constantly faced with distractions. God is our conductor and He works tirelessly to keep us on track and in tune with Him. Now I love Donald Duck, but in this comparison, he is similar to Satan who is always trying to distract us and convince us to follow him instead. Look at Proverbs 4:25-27 which has some great advice for this scenario. It reads, "Let your eyes look directly forward, and your gaze be straight before you. Ponder the path of your feet; then all your ways will be sure. Do not swerve to the right or to the left; turn your foot away from evil." I definitely don't like giving him compliments, but there's no denying that Satan is good at what he does. He knows what distracts you most and what "tune you will follow," and so he plays it at just the right moment to pique your interest. Sometimes, like the band in this cartoon, we are so used to the distractions that we don't even realize who we're following. We just keep playing along. Colossians 3:2 reminds us to set our minds on things of above and not of those on Earth. It is up to us to be able to tell the difference in what is right and wrong. We should be able to distinguish what we should and should not be following. The easiest way to do this is to keep our focus on the proper conductor. Hebrews 12:2 tells us to keep our eyes always fixed on Jesus who is the founder, the author and the perfecter of our faith. God, through His Son, Jesus, is always standing in front of us patiently and diligently conducting us through life. All we have to do is keep our focus on Him and look to Him for our example and guidance.

If you happen to ride the Silly Symphony Swings, I hope you enjoy the peaceful ride as you feel the breeze and float out over the water. I hope you'll notice conductor Mickey standing on top directing the music during your adventure. I also hope it will remind you that God is our eternal conductor. If we want to keep playing beautiful music with Him and ignore the distractions that Satan brings all around us, we have to keep our eyes on our conductor. Always keep your eyes fixed on Jesus, and don't lose focus! Follow His direction!

"Incredicoaster"

Today is another special day because we are moving to our very last land at DCA. This land is not only our final land in all of Disneyland, but it's also a brand-new themed land called Pixar Pier. There are 5 attractions in this land plus a gaming area and several eateries. All of the attractions here are, as the name implies, geared towards well-known Pixar films. Four of them are unique to Disneyland rides so this is where we'll be for a little while. And we're going to start with a bang! I've already said that the Radiator Springs Racers is the best ride at this park, but this ride is a very close second. Get ready for an extreme thrill and an absolute must do on your next trip! Today we're enjoying an incredible adventure on the Incredicoaster.

The Incredicoaster used to be known as California Screamin' when the park first opened, but is now themed to the very popular Pixar film, *The Incredibles*. This is a steel roller coaster disguised as a wooden one that tops out at 55 mph, the fastest for a ride at Disneyland. It is the only ride at Disneyland with an inversion, and is in fact the longest inverting roller coaster in the world at 6072 feet. It is also a 2½ minute ride! Hooray—we broke free from the 90 second streak! As you zoom around on this high speed coaster, you rocket through several tubes, some of which are open on one side. These tubes serve two purposes. First, they host different scenes coinciding with the theme of the ride. The tubes also help to stifle the inevitable screams of those riding. You see, this park is in the middle of Orange County, California and there are residential houses all around. Consequently, there are noise ordinances, and Disney has to be very careful about the volume of the noises they produce. Some of these tubes are open-faced toward the pier so park guests can see the riders, but the screams will still be quieted with the barrier on the non-park side. There have been a few incidents on this ride, but only when it was California Screamin' and not since 2016. Most of the incidents were caused by park guests. Twice the ride shut down when a rider's belongings fell on the track, a purse and a backpack. A selfie stick also caused a closure.

We absolutely loved this ride and the re-theming on our recent trip. My boys loved it so much that they rode it several times, even going back to the park by themselves to ride it again. I think I rode it three times which is a lot for even me. It's an absolute thrill, clever concept and terrific story from the Incredibles characters. The premise is that baby Jack-Jack has gotten away and is hiding from his family, using his superpowers to escape their grasp. Each tube on the ride contains a different character trying to get Jack-Jack back. Dash uses his super speed at the beginning of the ride, creating quite the water effect. Elastigirl is seen stretching through one of the tunnels trying to grab her son. Mr. Incredible uses his super strength to smash through a wall and offer Jack-Jack his favorite cookie. You actually smell cookies going through that tunnel...one of my favorite parts. The fleeing baby then uses his powers to set fire to the third tunnel, but luckily Violet uses her invisible force field to protect us all. Finally, Jack-Jack multiplies himself and riders begin to see baby Jack-Jacks all over the place, 19 in all throughout the ride. Luckily, in the end, Jack-Jack is reunited with his family and returned safely, with the help of a cookie of course.

So what could be our lesson today? Hold on to your bags and purses? A little cookie goes a long way? Watch out for babies with superpowers? All good lessons, but let's try another. This ride involves a couple of instances of hiding. The tubes serve the purpose of hiding the screams that you will no doubt hear coming from this ride. In addition, baby Jack-Jack does a great job hiding from his family and using his powers to escape when they find him. I assume everyone reading this has had fun playing Hide-and-Seek. It may be fun to hide from others, and you may find a great spot where nobody will ever find you. However, one thing is for certain...you can't hide from God.

In Genesis chapter 3, you may remember that Adam and Eve tried to hide from God after their sin. He easily "found them" of course and questioned them about what they did. There are many verses that talk about the fact that we can't hide from God. Hebrews 4:13 says no creature is hidden from His sight. Luke 8:17 tells us that nothing is hidden or secret from God, and all will come out eventually. Finally, look at Jeremiah 23:24 where God says, "Who can hide in secret places so that I cannot see them? Do not I fill heaven and earth?" If you try hard enough, you can hide things from your friends, your church and even your family. But there's absolutely nothing you can hide from God. He is all knowing and all seeing. Just because we can't see Him doesn't mean He isn't always watching us. He does that not to spy on us like an overbearing parent, but to protect us. He does it to keep us on the path to be with Him one day. Jack-Jack may have succeeded in hiding for a while with his superpowers, but eventually even he was found. Don't try to hide from God. It won't work. Instead, be grateful that He's always there to help you resist temptation and pick you back up when you fall.

"Inside Out Emotional Whirlwind"

Coming off the Incredicoaster, you'll no doubt be on an emotional high with the adrenaline pumpin'. We probably should move on to something a little more peaceful to calm ourselves down from the emotional whirlwind we just went through. Well, have I got just the ride! You see what I did there? This ride is called the Inside Out Emotional Whirlwind! It's brand new as of this writing as it just opened in June of 2019. Therefore, I actually haven't ridden this one. We actually saw it being built on our recent trip. No, it won't be quite the thrill you just received on the coaster, but it's still a neat looking ride. I personally love the fact that they based a ride on the *Inside Out* film. Let's give it a try today.

Inside Out Emotional Whirlwind is similar to a ride at Tokyo DisneySea called Blowfish Balloon Race. This ride has you board a stylized "memory mover" vehicle that is reminiscent of a hot air balloon, each having room for four guests. Each of the eight possible balloons is a different color and represents a different emotion or character from the film. The balloons then spin around Dumbo style as you pass shelves packed with glowing orbs symbolizing memories. If you've seen the movie, you remember that part of the film as well. If you've been to Disneyland before, the ride vehicles on this ride may look familiar to you. That's because they are recycled from the old attraction called Flik's Flyers that used to be in Bug's Land, now closed to make room for the upcoming Marvel Land. This ride features five possible music tracks, one for each of the film's emotions, each written by Academy Award-winning composer Michael Giacchino. This is the same composer which Disney collaborated with for the music of the Incredicoaster.

This is another simple and basic ride, most likely geared towards children. However, I'm looking forward to giving it a "spin" on our next trip. As I mentioned, I'm glad Disney gave a nod to this film with a ride. I thought the *Inside Out* movie was a creative story, and I enjoyed it thoroughly. If you haven't seen the movie, it's about a little girl, Riley and what's going on inside her head as her family moves and makes some drastic life changes. Inside her head, we get to meet the five emotions that are controlling her decisions and feelings. They are joy, anger, disgust, fear and sadness. All five of these are discussed in the Bible as well, so I thought we'd take a look at how Scripture describes these emotions.

JOY—is listed as one of the fruits of the Spirit in Galatians 5:22 naming qualities we should all strive for. Proverbs 17:22 also says that a joyful heart is good medicine. Having joy in life does our heart and our health good. We should strive to be joyful and spread it to others. If they see that our spiritual walk makes us happy and joyful, they are more likely to be influenced to follow God as we do.

ANGER—Ephesians 4:26 says, "Be angry and do not sin; do not let the sun go down on your anger." We are allowed to be angry. There's nothing wrong with that. We just can't let our anger consume us and change who we are. We also need to settle any anger we have with others quickly and not hold grudges.

DISGUST—Psalms 119:158 says, "I look at the faithless with disgust, because they do not keep your commands." We should also be disgusted by those who don't follow the commands of God, especially those who deliberately go against Him. We should then use our disgust to try and help others turn their lives around. It has to be done gradually and with patience to be successful. But we shouldn't just let sinful ways go unspoken, especially with our family and friends.

FEAR—A familiar verse, Isaiah 41:10 reads, "fear not, for I am with you; be not dismayed, for I am your God; I will strengthen you, I will help you, I will uphold you with my righteous right hand." With God on our side, we have no reason to fear. He is there to guide us, protect us and save us from any evil that may come our way.

SADNESS—Sadness is addressed in the famous Beatitudes of Matthew 5 when in verse 4 Jesus says, "Blessed are those who mourn, for they will be comforted." Revelation 21:4 adds, "He will wipe away every tear from their eyes, and death shall be no more, neither shall there be mourning, nor crying, nor pain anymore, for the former things have passed away." There will be sad days on this Earth, no doubt about that. But if we stay close to God and follow His ways, eventually we will be in a place where sadness won't exist. And God is always there, even right now, to comfort us in our sorrow.

Isn't it neat that the five emotions from this film are addressed in the Bible? And there are many other verses on each that we didn't even list. God has an answer for any emotion you may feel. He's there to celebrate with you in your highest highs and pick you up during your lowest lows. We have such an amazing God that can help us out with any "emotional whirlwind" we might happen to face. Aren't you glad He's there?

"Jessie's Critter Carousel"

Still here by the water at Pixar Pier, we come to another simple ride dedicated to a Pixar film. It's probably the most loved Pixar film as it has two rides here in this land. You'll find Toy Story Midway Mania here, which we discussed in the first book. However, you'll also find today's attraction also based on *Toy Story*, a new ride having just opened in April of 2019. Come on! Pick your favorite critter and hop aboard Jessie's Critter Carousel.

This ride is just what you might expect from the title, a simple carousel like the one at Disneyland Park or the Magic Kingdom of WDW. You might be thinking 'another carousel? Really?' But hey, kids love carousels! And you probably do too if you're being honest. This two minute carousel ride contains 56 whimsical, desert-type animals from the "Woody's Roundup" cartoon. The cowgirl herself, Jessie from the *Toy Story* films, hosts you as you spin around to the playful music. As you slowly spin around, you will pass scenery from a western town, eventually leading you past Sheriff Woody too! If you look carefully, you'll also see a cartoon goat holding a stick of dynamite in his mouth. This is a nod to the authentic replica of a dynamite-eating-goat you'll see riding Big Thunder Mountain Railroad. This attraction took the place of King Triton's Carousel of the Sea that opened with the park in 2001. That ride featured displays of the various boardwalks and piers around California's coastline. It closed in 2018 for refurbishment and reopened with this new Pixar theme.

As I mentioned, you have quite a choice of critters when boarding this ride. There are snakes, armadillos, turtles, rabbits, buzzards, owls and more. There are also a couple of critters that look a little different. The two skunks in this ride are both facing backwards. So if you want to ride that little stinker, you'll be looking at his tail the entire time during your leisurely spin. The fact that the smelly and typically unpopular animal is the one facing backwards got me thinking about our lesson for today.

As we've discussed many times before, we are all walking a path right now. It is a narrow path, heading towards Heaven that I'm always praying you and I can stay on. Sometimes we get knocked off or choose to step off ourselves, but the goal is always to get right back on. Luckily, we have God's help of course through His Word to encourage us and give us instruction on how to live. God has also blessed us with family and friends to walk the path with us and support us. This is represented by all the other critters going the same way on Jessie's carousel here. However, in life, you're always going to find a stinker that is purposely going the wrong way. There is always going to be someone that thinks it's fun to go against what's right and push the boundaries. This typically happens more with kids and teenagers in the form of peer pressure. But all of us are easily influenced by someone doing something different and new, especially when it looks enticing and enjoyable. Proverbs 13:20 says, "Whoever walks with the wise becomes wise, but the companion of fools will suffer harm." In Galatians 1:10, Paul says, "For am I now seeking the approval of man, or of God? Or am I trying to please man? If I were still trying to please man, I would not be a servant of Christ." We can only go one direction in our spiritual lives. We are either moving towards God in Heaven or we aren't. We can either please God and seek His approval or please others around us and seek favor with the world. Matthew 6:24 says we can't serve two masters.

Just like that skunk who is smiling as he makes going backwards look fun, there are going to be people in our lives that make sin look fun. They will go against what God says, maybe in a small way, but they will make it look attractive and pleasurable. And it stinks just like the skunk! It stinks because some will unfortunately be persuaded and will step off the path, turn around, and join in the backwards fun. The saddest part is that some will never return to the path. They'll never go the right way again because they enjoy the fun of the world too much. I Corinthians 15:33 tells us not to be deceived and that bad company ruins good morals. Romans 12:2 reminds us not to be conformed to this world. Please take that command seriously and don't be easily influenced by bad company! No matter how fun someone makes it look to go against God and do something you know is wrong, don't join in. It may seem enjoyable for a while, but in the end, when it really counts, you will have taken the road to the wrong place. And that will really stink!

"Pixar Pal-A-Round"

Today we are discussing our final ride at DCA which is therefore our last ride at Disneyland. Don't worry. We've still got a lot of great places to go and interesting things to see. But our last ride here is a giant! If you've been to Disneyland, you can't miss this huge attraction looming over the water. I could say it's just your simple, basic Ferris wheel, but that would be a slight understatement. You'll see that when approaching this wheel in the fact that some of the ride vehicles on the wheel are moving in a strange way. You may have to conquer a fear of heights to ride this, but you absolutely have to at least try it once. I'll give you a gentle push if needed because I'm riding too. It's our last ride for crying out loud! Here we go on the Pixar Pal-A-Round.

This enormous Ferris wheel is 160 feet high with a giant Mickey face in the center. When it was first built, it was called the Sun Wheel and had a giant sun in the middle. From 2009 until just recently, it was known as Mickey's Fun Wheel and Mickey's face was moved from the Incredicoaster to the Ferris wheel at that time. As expected here on Pixar Pier, this ride was recently re-themed and renamed to represent the Pixar films. Each of the 24 gondolas has Pixar characters on this side representing films like *Inside Out, The Incredibles, Coco, Wall-E* and *Up*. Some great movies right there! Each gondola holds up to 8 people meaning capacity for this ride is 192. This ride was modeled after the Wonder Wheel, a Ferris wheel from Coney Island, New York that opened there in 1920. It is still in operation there and moves in the same way the wheel here does. What I mean is that it doesn't just spin around peacefully with all the gondolas on the outside like most Ferris wheels. Both the Wonder Wheel and the Pixar Pal-A-Round have 16 of the 24 gondolas that slide on a track inward and outward depending on where you are on the wheel. This gives you a slight falling sensation and causes your gondola to swing back and forth. I am proud to say that I was brave and gave this a shot on our trip several years ago. I'm also proud to say that it was definitely one and done! Never again! Let's just say that there are vomit bags in those gondolas for a reason. I almost needed one. Thankfully, 8 of the 24 gondolas on both wheels are stable, fixed to the outside and don't move at all. Those I can do and enjoy. Even my two boys, who are typically daredevils, thought the swinging was a little much on our recent trip. I think they may be joining me in a secure gondola next time.

The lesson today is quite simple, and you can probably figure it out. We all need to be firm, stable and secure in our spiritual lives as well. If we're not, and live life without much effort and care, our lives may swing out of control. It may also cause us to get spiritually sick and need that vomit bag. If you aren't firm in your relationship with God, you will slowly veer off course and the further you go, the harder it is to come back. Jesus talked about this very thing in Matthew 7:24-27. Go read that passage today. There's even a song about it! Jesus tells about a wise man and foolish man. The wise man builds his house on rocks where the ground is stable and firm. His house stays where it is. The foolish man builds his house on sand which is moveable and unsteady. When a storm comes along, that house won't last. The wind, rain and floods will wash that house away easily because it has no firm foundation. So where do you want to live? In a house that's stable and not going anywhere? Or in a house that will wash away and be gone when the next storm hits?

The point is that we must be stable in our faith, beliefs and actions. We must have a firm foundation, rooted in Jesus Christ, so that no storm will knock us off track. We must take up residence in one of the 8 stable gondolas that won't slide or swing anywhere. We don't want to risk getting spiritually sick which may lead to totally washing away our relationship with God for good. In Psalms 16:8, King David reassures his sturdy relationship with God when he says, "I have set the LORD always before me; because he is at my right hand, I shall not be shaken." Paul gives advice about this in I Corinthians 15:58 when he preaches, "Therefore, my beloved brothers, be steadfast, immovable, always abounding in the work of the Lord, knowing that in the Lord your labor is not in vain." We must be steadfast. We must be immovable. We must be firm in our faith so that nothing knocks us off track. We get that stability by having a strong relationship with God and His Son. We also get it by studying His Word and learning every day how God wants us to live.

I hope you'll give the Pixar Pal-A-Round a shot, even if you don't like heights. You won't fall out, I promise. However, you do have a choice, just as you do in life. You can choose a moving and swinging gondola or a firm and steady one. On the wheel, it's up to you. However, in life, there's only one right choice, so please choose to be firmly rooted with a strong foundation in Jesus Christ. That's the only way to have a nice stable ride that's always moving towards Heaven.

"World of Color"

Before we leave this park for good, there is one more thing we need to experience here. Yes, we're out of rides and shows as I mentioned, but there's something very special that happens here nearly every night. It's the night time show presented at Disney California Adventure. It is an amazing spectacle, and we definitely need to talk about it. As you probably know, most of Disney's night time shows are great, and this one is no exception. If you haven't seen it, you've gotta catch it at least once. Prepare to be enthralled with the World of Color!

The World of Color takes place on Paradise Bay right here next to Pixar Pier and Paradise Gardens Park where we've been for the last several devotionals. It is a 30 minute show filled with 1200 musical water fountains, lights, lasers, fog and projections. The fountains are capable of sending water up to 200 feet into the air. Keep in mind that the giant Ferris wheel, Pixar Pal-A-Round is 40 feet shorter than that! Similar to the Fantasmic show, this show also projects video of favorite Disney scenes on screens of mist over the water. This show was inspired by Walt Disney's "Wonderful World of Color" TV series and even uses its theme song written by the Sherman brothers. In 2008, Disney drained Paradise Bay in preparation for this new show. It took 15 months to completely install and test the show at a cost of 75 million dollars! Disney did work with the Orange County Water District to conserve and store the water from the Bay instead of just wasting it. Guests are able to get a fastpass to get better seating for this show, but if you get there early enough, you should be able to find a decent spot somewhere around the Bay. Guests can also purchase special Mickey ears that light up in sync with the show. The Ferris wheel and Incredicoaster also have multiple lights on them that illuminate during the show. My favorite fact about this show is that at the very end, during the post-show after all the fountains turn off, there is one little orange fountain that remains on for just a couple seconds. Then it slowly turns off as a bow to the audience still watching. This fountain was meant as a nod to Walt Disney's spirit and all he did to make all of this possible.

This show is called the World of Color for a reason. It is filled with many different colors of lights, lasers, and projections. It makes for a very beautiful display that nearly takes your breath away. Aren't you glad we have colors? I genuinely feel bad for those that have trouble seeing colors. They make the world such a beautiful place. Have you ever seen the Wizard of Oz? The first part of that movie is in black and white and then changes to color when Dorothy finally enters the land of Oz. It's amazing to see the difference and contrast between the two. God of course invented all the colors and has done some amazing things with them. Just look at creation for starters. If you go through each day and compare all the things He made, you can imagine the different colors just coming alive. From the blue of the sky, to the yellow of the sun to the green trees and brown dirt, you can just picture the creation as very colorful and beautiful. He also created different colors of people which we should be thankful for and celebrate. As I've said many times, it would be a much more boring world if we were all the same, so I for one am grateful for the many different looks, features and personalities of others. He also created our eyes of course which have the ability to see so many different colors. Did you know that fish can actually see more colors than we can with their special eyes? Additionally, in Genesis 9 we read about how God created the rainbow with all its colors to represent the covenant He made with Noah. Every time we see a rainbow, it should remind us of that covenant and the fact that God keeps His promises. That was its original purpose and intention.

Revelation 21 describes what Heaven will look like. Read that passage today and try to imagine it as you read. It seems to me from that passage that Heaven will also be very colorful. Revelation 7:9-10 says, "After this I looked, and behold, a great multitude that no one could number, from every nation, from all tribes and peoples and languages, standing before the throne and before the Lamb, clothed in white robes, with palm branches in their hands, and crying out with a loud voice, 'Salvation belongs to our God who sits on the throne, and to the Lamb!'" According to these verses, Heaven will also be colorful with many different people from every nation, tribe and language. Won't that be wonderful when all the colors can become one, and together, as one people, we can worship God with our voices forever?

I'm so grateful to God for the beauty of colors. They make for an amazing show here at DCA with the World of Color show. They also make for many amazing scenes in this world which remind us of our loving God. Take a minute today to thank God for colors and the blessing they bring to us. Also ask Him to help you remain steady in your faith so one day you can experience Heaven and the amazing world of colors that will undoubtedly be there.

"Paradise Pier"

Ok, show's over! Park's closed. It's time to leave DCA. I know, I know. You don't want to, and I don't either. We've had so much fun in these two Disneyland parks...54 devotionals worth of fun, education and spiritual knowledge. But there's nothing else. We've exhausted all the rides, shows, attractions and experiences inside the parks. Sorry, but we have to leave. "So get out!" Now that's Disney security talking, not me. Hey, I'd be glad to try and stay longer, even sleep inside the park, but I'm pretty sure Disney frowns on that. So does that mean that this book is over now too? What else is there to talk about? It could be over I guess. I could stop right here and have a decent sized book all about Disneyland. But I can't do it. I can't stop with 54 devotionals. That number is not round enough. And I like things neat and uniform. So we're going to stick with this 100 devotional formula that seemed to work in the first book. That means I've got 46 devotionals to go, right? So what can I talk about for 46 whole devotionals? I gave it a lot of thought, and as I mentioned in the introduction, I've chosen next to go to all the Disney resorts both here at Disneyland and at WDW. That will get us pretty close to 100. And while that idea may not exactly excite you, there's actually a lot to learn at the resorts, and we can apply Biblical lessons just as easy. So just keep reading. At least give them a shot. You may just learn a few interesting facts. I know you'll get some important Biblical knowledge. We'll start with the three Disney-owned resorts here in Disneyland, and today we're booking a room at the Paradise Pier.

The Paradise Pier, generally the cheapest of the three Disneyland resorts, opened in 1984. It was originally called the Emerald of Anaheim and wasn't even built or owned by Disney. Disney later purchased the property in 1995 for 36 million dollars! At first, they renamed it the Disneyland Pacific Hotel. It was then rebranded and refurbished in 2000 to what it is today. Guests of this property originally had an exclusive entrance to DCA park, but it was closed in 2004 due to low use. Today the resort boasts 481 rooms which include 25 suites. It also has several restaurants, a gift shop, video arcade, multiple meeting rooms, a ballroom and a rooftop swimming pool. Several of the rooms here overlook DCA and the Paradise Bay area. Guests in these rooms can watch World of Color each night from their room with the synchronized music playing through their room TV. The theme of the hotel is casual beach with the décor and colors evoking thoughts of ocean breezes and sandy beaches.

My family stayed on property at Disneyland for the first time in 2013. We had been to Disneyland once before that but didn't stay on property. For spring break 2013, we decided that Paradise Pier was going to be our first Disneyland resort. Being on a budget, we paid for the cheapest room there which of course included no park view. I think we were scheduled to view a parking lot. Upon arrival, we were saddened to hear that the rooftop pool was closed for refurbishment. We heard this while waiting in line to check-in and my wonderful wife immediately got an idea. When it was our turn to check in, and were then told about the pool, she asked if we might could be upgraded in room as a compensation for no pool. To our amazement and surprise, they complied. We got a park view room for our first ever stay! Talk about paradise! I'll never forget seeing that view for the first time.

When Jesus was on the cross, there were two criminals crucified beside Him. One of them criticized Jesus and demanded He save them. But the other rebuked the first because he knew of Jesus' innocence and importance. He simply asked Jesus to remember him. Jesus told this 2nd criminal the famous line, "Today, you shall be with me in paradise." In Revelation 2:7, Jesus spoke to all of us and said, "To the one who conquers I will grant to eat of the tree of life, which is in the paradise of God." Just like the criminal on the cross, Jesus has promised us paradise in which we can eat of the tree of life. This means we will have eternal life with God forever. This is the paradise that was lost by Adam and Eve in Genesis 3 when they sinned, but has now been regained because of the blood and sacrifice of Jesus on the cross. This paradise is available to all of us if we follow the Word of God and live our lives for Him.

My family had a wonderful trip in 2013 at the Paradise Pier, especially with our surprise park view room. When we first walked in our room, we stood at that window for several minutes just staring and admiring what we could see. The whole experience there including the remarkable view was wonderful, but it was absolutely nothing compared to the view we'll have in Heaven when we reach the true paradise. Don't you want to see that?

"Disneyland Hotel"

Let's step out of the Paradise Pier and walk a short distance to our next Disney resort hotel. It's next door but there's a considerable jump in price to stay there. Disney has three levels of resorts: value, moderate and deluxe. At Disneyland, Paradise Pier is considered the value resort even though it is usually more expensive than some moderates at WDW due to the high cost of living in California. Obviously, the three Disney resorts here at Disneyland are pricey. But there are some definite perks to staying at a Disney resort such as proximity, early entrance to parks and theming. Today's resort is considered the moderate of Disneyland and tomorrow we'll talk about the deluxe. Ok, in the time it's taken to read this paragraph, we probably could've walked to our next resort, so let's go inside. Today we're staying at the Disneyland Hotel.

Found at the end of the Downtown Disney District, the Disneyland Hotel is in close proximity to both parks. It has 990 rooms including some special suites dedicated to Big Thunder Mountain Railroad, Pirates of the Caribbean, Adventureland and more. There is even a special suite called the Mickey Mouse penthouse. This property was the first hotel to bear the Disney name. It opened October 5, 1955, less than 3 months after Disneyland. When it first opened, rooms were $15 per night. Today the cheapest room is over $400 per night depending on time of year. This resort may have had the Disney name first, but it was not the first hotel owned by Disney. It was owned by a man named Jack Wrather who agreed to fund and build the hotel with the Disney name as long as he could maintain ownership. Disney tried to buy the hotel back on several occasions, but Wrather always refused to sell. Disney had to wait until 1988 when Wrather and his wife died before they could finally purchase the property.

There's an interesting story of what happened even before Walt Disney agreed to terms with Mr. Wrather. When Walt Disney made plans to build Disneyland, he knew he wanted to build an adjacent hotel as well. He wanted families to be able to come, stay there and make a vacation out of it. Unfortunately, after funding the park, he lacked the money for a hotel and knew he needed help. He first approached the Sheraton and Hilton companies, but they declined because of the unfamiliarity of Anaheim at that time. Walt then approached his good friend, Art

Linkletter. You may not know, but Art Linkletter was a very successful radio and TV host. He is probably best known for a segment on his show called "Kids Say the Darndest Things" where he would interview kids often with very funny responses. Knowing of Linkletter's success, Walt actually approached him before the park was built. He took Linkletter to Anaheim, showed him around and told him of his plans. He strongly encouraged Linkletter to buy up property around Anaheim telling him it would be a great investment. Linkletter later said that he was worried for Walt. He didn't think the park would make it, especially in this unknown city. Therefore when Walt approached him to buy property, and especially to fund a hotel next to Disneyland, Linkletter turned him down. He later said he was worried about how the park would do and didn't want to take the chance. His regret was obvious when later after the hotel was built, he was found walking in front of it and with every step saying "There's another million I missed out on."

My family had the pleasure of staying at the Disneyland Hotel on our most recent trip in March of 2019. While we didn't have as favorable of a view this time, we greatly enjoyed our stay, especially the close proximity to Downtown Disney. The grounds, decorations and scenery were beautiful. When I think about how impressive that property is today, I can't help but understand the regret of Mr. Linkletter after he saw the success of the hotel. If he had only taken a chance on Walt Disney, he could've made millions. Sometimes we too need to take a chance, not for millions of dollars, but for something even more valuable, a human soul. Every day we have the opportunity to tell someone about God, to introduce them to the Bible or share our faith. This is not always an easy thing to do and often takes us out of our comfort zone. But if we take the chance, we may just be the reason that another person gets to enter Heaven one day. James 4:14 says, "yet you do not know what tomorrow will bring. What is your life? For you are a mist that appears for a little time and then vanishes." Our time on this Earth is short. We have to make the most of every opportunity we have to tell others about God. Ephesians 5:16 says we need to make the best use of our time because the days are evil. I know it can be scary and make you nervous to talk to others, but remember that Romans 8:31 says, "If God is for us, who can be against us?" Most likely your fear stems from rejection or failure. But keep in mind that God is on your side. If you try, you might just succeed. But if you don't even try, you will fail.

Art Linkletter always had regret that he didn't work with Disney to build the Disneyland Hotel. Don't suffer the same regret with someone's life. Don't look back and wish you had talked to someone about their faith. Talk to them now. Take a chance. Their soul is worth more than all the Disney properties combined. And you have the power to help save it!

"Grand Californian"

Today we move to what is definitely considered the deluxe resort here at Disneyland. The first two resorts have prices that fluctuate so much that sometimes they are comparable. This one, however, is always the most expensive. By the way, there are many other hotels around Disneyland. The fact that Disney only owns three doesn't mean that's all there is. The others around the property are generally known as "good neighbor hotels." They are called this because although Disney doesn't own them, they typically cooperate with Disney, and you can even book them through the Disney website. Most of them are considerably less expensive, but you may not get some of the perks of staying on site. One of the perks my youngest son and I enjoyed on our recent trip staying at the Disneyland Hotel was getting to walk a 5K in DCA before the park even opened. Our guide and ultimate power-walker gave us a ton of fun facts as we powered through the park, arms a-pumpin'. We wouldn't have gotten this perk staying at a good neighbor hotel. Anyways, back to today's property. This one has the ultimate in perks! Let me tell you what I mean here at the Grand Californian Resort and Spa.

That is technically the full name, although most just call it the Grand Californian. This luxury resort offers 948 rooms, 44 of which are suites. It has 3 pools, 2 hot tubs, 1 ninety foot water slide (and a partridge in a pair tree). This hotel was built as part of the major expansion of 2001. This is the only Disneyland hotel to be operated by Disney since its opening. Its name is based on its sister resort at WDW, the Grand Floridian which is one of the deluxe resorts there. Similar to the Contemporary Resort at WDW, the Grand Californian also has a monorail that travels right through the hotel. However, it doesn't stop inside the hotel here like it does at the Contemporary. At 3am on December 28, 2005, a Christmas tree inside the main lobby caught fire due to an electrical issue with one of the lights. All 2300 guests were evacuated within four minutes, and the fire was contained by the hotel's sprinkler system.

As I mentioned, this resort has the ultimate in perks! You ready to hear what it is? It is the only Disney resort built inside a theme park!

That's right! Technically, this resort was built to be a part of Disney California Adventure Park. This resort has a door that leads right into the park! You can literally step out the door and into a park. How cool is that? I wish Disney would do this more often. They may be planning the same in Florida with the new Star Wars Resort that is said to possibly open up into Hollywood Studios. To me, that is the supreme bonus...to be able to simply walk through a door and step foot into your theme park adventure. What a special door that is! We also have access to a very special door. We are told in Scripture that the door into Heaven is ready and waiting for us.

In John 14:2, Jesus himself says that He is preparing a room for us in God's house. Did you hear that? We have a door of our own right in God's house! And as long as we follow God's Word and stay true to Him throughout our lives, this door is a guarantee. We don't have to wonder if we'll be given that special perk. We can know. I John 5:13 says, "I write these things to you who believe in the name of the Son of God, that you may know that you have eternal life." John says we can know that we have eternal life. It doesn't say we might have it or we can hope we have it. We can rest assured in the fact that it's ours. In James 1:12, it says that all those who love God are promised the crown of life. Do you love God? It's easy to say yes, but do you show that love by following His commands? Do you show that love by telling others about your love of God and sharing your faith? Let me remind you of God's love in the very familiar John 3:16 which says, "For God so loved the world, that he gave his only Son, that whoever believes in him should not perish but have eternal life." As long as we believe in God, believe in Jesus, proclaim that to others and follow in the footsteps of Jesus including His baptism, we are promised the door to eternal life with God forever.

I have never had the pleasure of staying at the Grand Californian. I've been in there several times to look around and dream. It's an absolute beautifully crafted resort, the ultimate in architecture, décor and luxury. Maybe one day I'll bite the bullet, work some overtime, sell a kidney and be able to reside there for a night or two. If I ever get that chance, I will definitely cherish the fact that I have access to a door straight into the park. I will also keep in mind that I've already been given a greater gift at no cost to me. Oh, it cost something! It cost the blood of my Lord and Savior Jesus Christ on the cross. But He gave that to us all. Through His death, we've been given access to the door of Heaven. It's guaranteed as long as we know Him, believe in Him, follow Him, love Him and share Him. I cannot wait to go through that door and see what's on the other side. Talk about the ultimate in perks!

"All-Star Sports"

It's finally time! Time for what you say? It's finally time to book a flight back across the country. Time to fly from Orange County to Orange County. Did you know that both Disneyland and Disney World are in Orange County? Fun fact! Anyways, we're going back to Disney World! Yahoo! Don't get me wrong. I love Disneyland. It is the original park that Walt built and walked in, and the history there is incredible. But Disney World is my personal favorite. It's the first Disney I ever went to as a kid. It's where my wife and I went on our honeymoon. It's where we introduced Disney to our two boys. Disney World is home. And since we've exhausted all the Disneyland attractions and resorts, it's time to go home. We're going to spend the next several devotionals talking about the Disney Resorts at Disney World in Orlando. There are a lot of them, nearly 30, with more on the way. We'll start where my family started. When we first took our boys to WDW, we always stayed at the All-Star Sports Resort.

I mentioned that there are a lot of resorts at Disney World which means a lot of rooms. In fact, if you were to stay in all of the gues-trooms available at WDW at a rate of one per night, it would take you more than 68 years to stay in all of them! Can you believe that? We're going to start with the value resorts and go up. There are five resorts at Disney World that are considered value, and the All-Star Sports is one of them. This one is special to us because as mentioned, this is where we stayed on our first few trips as a family of four. We chose this one for a few reasons. First of all, it was cheap...less than $100 per night at that time. You can still book it today for between $100 and $200 per night. Secondly, my boys liked sports. Finally, we considered this the best of the three All-Stars because the bus always came here first, which it still does. The All-Star Sports Resort opened in 1994 and was the first value resort built at WDW. The other All-Stars would soon follow. This resort has 1920 rooms in 10 buildings. There are five different sections of rooms each based on a different sport. They are surfing, basketball, football, tennis and baseball. As with all the value resorts, each building features larger than life icons as decorations. The football buildings feature large helmets and footballs. A football player would have to be 200 feet tall to wear those helmets. The tennis section features giant tennis balls and tennis ball cans. Each of those cans could hold over 9.4 million tennis balls! The baseball portion has large bats, baseballs, scoreboards and cups of Coca-Cola. It would take more than 20 million, 12-ounce cans of Coke to fill just one of those containers. The surfing building features enormous surf boards and lifeguard stands. Finally, the basketball portion has big whistles, megaphones and a court with super elevated goals.

We've stayed at the Sports many times, probably in every section. Our boys used to love to run on the giant football field or play pretend games on the massive tennis or basketball courts. Actually, they have always been into sports. Between our two sons, we've experienced football, basketball, baseball, bowling, cross country, track, tennis, and soccer. As parents, we've always encouraged them to be a part of an athletic team. Luckily, they've always enjoyed it, for the most part. Athletics are an important part of life. They teach teamwork, cooperation, discipline, competition, hard work, goal setting and practice. One lesson we also tried to stress with the boys on whatever team they participated is sportsmanship. Athletics can be fun and there's nothing wrong with a little competition. However, it's always important to remember whether you win or lose, to be a good sport, a good teammate and a good opponent.

The Bible actually talks about sports and competition on several occasions. I Corinthians 9:24-25 says that every athlete should compete but also practice self-control in all things. 2 Timothy 2:5 reads, "An athlete is not crowned unless he competes according to the rules." It can be fun to compete and even more fun to win. However, we must always compete according to the rules with fairness and a good attitude. I never played football, but the football coach where I attended high school always had a verse as his team motto. It was I Peter 2:17, and it says, "Honor everyone. Love the brotherhood. Fear God. Honor the king." He was a great coach and always encouraged his players to respect God first, and then teammates and opponents. Consider these verses the next time you are involved in athletics. Even as adults we sometimes find ourselves in friendly competitions. We need to make sure that we always have good sportsmanship, compete fairly, show respect and keep a good attitude. Above all, we need to be certain that we are honoring God in all we do and making Him proud. Win or lose!

"All-Star Music"

There are three value All-Star Resorts at WDW, all within walking distance of each other. They are very similar in price so there are not a lot of differences, besides the obvious theming. A few years ago, we set a goal to try and stay at every Disney resort for at least one night. We are slowly making our way through them having done all the values and all but one moderate. We're now also working our way through the deluxe resorts which is taking a little longer simply because, well, they ain't cheap! The values were pretty easy to knock out, and we actually enjoyed trying and comparing them all. Next door to the Sports is the All-Star Music Resort, a hotel dedicated to the history of music high-lighting several well-known music genres. We've stayed here at least twice and enjoyed both times, so let's try it out today.

The All-Star Music Resort also opened in 1994 just after Sports. This resort has 1604 rooms, which is less than Sports due to the fact that some of the rooms here have been converted into family suites. This is the only one of the three All-Star Resorts where families bigger than four people can stay. They have 192 family suites that will each sleep up to six people plus a crib. There are five sections of rooms here each dedicated to a different type of music. They are Broadway, Calypso, Country, Jazz and Rock. Once again, each section features giant icons on each end of the building as well as in the central courtyards. Broadway features top hats and canes as well as a marquee from *Beauty and the Beast*. The Calypso section has conga drums, maracas and a large, colorful xylophone. The Country Fair is dedicated to country music with giant cowboy boots, fiddles, banjoes and harmonicas. Jazz Inn has a large drum set as well as saxophones and clarinets. Finally, at Rock Inn, you'll find a huge jukebox as well as electric guitars and microphones. There are two pools at this resort, the smaller of which is shaped like a piano. The main pool is the largest at all the All-Star Resorts and is shaped like a guitar. It features the three Caballeros in the middle shooting water into the pool.

I've enjoyed staying here. Maybe it's because I love music and always have. I enjoy listening to, singing and playing music. Now I don't claim to be a great singer by any means, but I love leading singing at my church or just singing harmony with those around me. I was in chorus in high school and loved it. I'm thrilled that both my boys are now involved in chorus with the same director I had. When I was 8 years old, my parents got me started taking piano lessons, and that has also been a great blessing. I took for 8 years and still play to this day. Again, I'm not great, but I can play along with most songs, and it's an absolute stress reliever for me. I have also taken guitar lessons and even played the trumpet in band for 3 or 4 years. But there's nothing as great as being alone in the car, finding that perfect song on the radio, and belting it out! Come on, you know you all do it! Or am I the only weirdo? I don't care. I love it. It can almost be like a music high when you're feeling good, driving down the road, and that perfect song starts playing.

Did you know that music of some form is mentioned over 1000 times in the Bible? God certainly blessed us with music, and I'm guessing He's pleased when it makes us happy. There's nothing wrong with enjoying music and even rockin' out in your car. However, I hope we also remember to give that gift of music right back to God. After all, He also created music for us to use in praise to Him. We are commanded multiple times in Scripture to sing to God. Psalms 105:2 tells us to sing praise to God. James 5:13 says that if we are cheerful, we should sing to God. God is pleased when he hears us use the voices He gave us to worship Him. Colossians 3:16 says, "Let the word of Christ dwell in you richly, teaching and admonishing one another in all wisdom, singing psalms and hymns and spiritual songs, with thankfulness in your hearts to God." Ephesians 5:19 says, "...addressing one another in psalms and hymns and spiritual songs, singing and making melody to the Lord with your heart." Notice that both verses mention our hearts. The first one says that with singing we show thankfulness in our hearts to God. The second verse says we actually sing with our hearts. I think both are stating the importance of focusing on the words we sing and being genuine in our praise to God.

I'm very grateful we have music in our lives. There are so many wonderful things that can be done with it. It can cheer you up, make you feel good and provide great entertainment. At the same time, it is one of the primary ways that we can show God gratitude for all He's done for us. Take the time to sing praise to God, whether alone, with a small group or in church with many others. Be genuine in your singing. Focus on the words. Sing them directly to God. Maybe even try closing your eyes when you sing so you aren't distracted. Keep in mind that God doesn't care how you sound or how good your voice is. What matters is that we use the voice He blessed us with and give it right back to Him as praise and worship. He certainly deserves it, doesn't He?

"All-Star Movies"

On down the road we go to the last of the three All-Star Resorts. I really do encourage you to try staying at each to compare and pick your favorite. If you can't do that, at least choose one All-Star and during your stay, take a walk to the others. They are not that far apart, and it is really neat to see all the huge icons and decorations at each. Today we are staying at the All-Star Movies Resort giving homage to some wonderful Disney classic films of the past.

The All-Star Movies Resort opened in 1999, nearly five years after the first two. Just like Sports, this one also has 1920 rooms with no suites. Once again, like all the All-Stars, there are 10 buildings with a different theme for each pair. The five movies represented are *101 Dalmatians, Fantasia, The Mighty Ducks, Herbie: The Love Bug* and *Toy Story.* How many of those have you seen? Most of those have been around for a while, but they are all considered landmark movies that Disney produced. As expected, there are enormous icons at each set of buildings. The *101 Dalmatians* section has a statue of Pongo from the film that is 30 feet tall and weighs 17,000 pounds. Toy Story has a 47 foot tall Buzz Lightyear! There are two pools here, the largest of which is dedicated to Fantasia. It features an oversized Sorcerer Mickey shooting water in several directions into the pool.

I love movies. I wish I could visit the theater more often, but time and cost don't allow it. There's something special about going to the theater and watching the big screen. And now with those recliners? That's quite the treat! I just have to make sure I'm not too sleepy when I go, or I may miss the movie altogether. Believe it or not, I actually remember at five years old, when my mom surprised my sister and me and took us to see *Mary Poppins* in the theater. *Mary Poppins* had been released in 1964, but was re-released in 1980 for a limited run before it came out on video. This is probably the first movie I actually remember seeing in the theater. From that point on, I was hooked. So what lesson can we apply today? Does the Bible even talk about movies? Well, not specifically, but it definitely talks controlling what we see. Read on.

Movies can be great. A great story, exciting adventure, hilarious comedy or nerve-wracking thriller...they can all be fun and entertaining. However, movies, and even television, can also be dangerous in that we often become numb while watching. We get so wrapped up in the story or plot that we forget what we are allowing ourselves to view. Unfortunately, movies these days are often filled with profanity, violence, drug use, sex and other things that are the opposite of what we should allow into our minds and into our lives. The Bible has many passages teaching against these things. We justify it because we're just watching it, not doing it. But is it really ok to allow that stuff into your mind? As you know, movies have ratings attached to them for a reason. So where do we draw the line? What movie rating is acceptable? That's a good question and one you will have to answer for yourself. Let me just assist be sharing a few Scriptures with you.

"Finally, brothers, whatever is true, whatever is honorable, whatever is just, whatever is pure, whatever is lovely, whatever is commendable, if there is any excellence, if there is anything worthy of praise, think about these things." (Philippians 4:8)

"Put to death therefore what is earthly in you: sexual immorality, impurity, passion, evil desire, and covetousness, which is idolatry." (Colossians 3:5)

"I will not set before my eyes anything that is worthless." (Psalms 101:3)

"The eye is the lamp of the body. So, if your eye is healthy, your whole body will be full of light, but if your eye is bad, your whole body will be full of darkness." (Matthew 6:22-23)

There are many more. I don't share these to make you feel guilty or try and shame you in any way. I'm talking to myself here too. I'll admit that I've watched my fair share of movies that I later felt guilty about. In fact, I had to set a rule for myself a few years ago where I no longer allow myself to see R-rated movies. I had seen way too many, and I realized that I was allowing myself to view things that went against the Bible's teachings. I couldn't justify claiming to be a Christian while allowing myself to watch that stuff. Even with PG-13 movies, I will look online before viewing it to see what kinds of things give it its rating before making the decision to watch it. I don't say this to brag or to be "holier than thou." I still sin and have many things in my life I need to work on, but this is just one area that I'm trying hard to control.

Movies can be great. Most Disney movies are clean and worth watching. But there are many others that honestly shouldn't be viewed if we are really trying to follow the Word of God. I once heard someone say, "Are we really going to sit there and be entertained by the very things that put Jesus on the cross?" That's definitely something to think about. If we are using sin as our entertainment, maybe it's time we reexamined our lives and made some adjustments.

"Pop Century"

We'll have to drive a short distance to get to the next resort, but now we move on to what is my favorite of the values. After staying at all the values, this has been the one I've enjoyed most, simply because of its theme and what all you can see while staying on property. This also happens to be the largest resort on Disney World property as far as number of rooms. There are 2880 guest rooms here which make it not only the largest at Disney, but one of the largest hotels in the state of Florida. So today let's book a stay at the Pop Century Resort.

The Pop Century Resort opened in December of 2003. It features 10 buildings dedicated to pop culture of the 1950's through 1990's. Each of these buildings is four stories instead of the standard three at most of the value resorts, which is the reason there are so many rooms here. As you enter the lobby of this resort to check in, you will notice hundreds of classic toys and other objects from these years that were all part of the pop culture of their time. I could spend hours just in the lobby. You will also find huge pop culture items spread around the resort at each building. This was why I enjoyed my stay so much because a lot of the items were from my childhood of the 70's and 80's. I took an hour one day and just walked around the resort snapping pictures left and right. One of the courtyards features a giant Big Wheel from the 1970's. I used to have one of those! According to the sign on this oversized toy, it could hold a child up to 877 pounds! That's one huge riding toy! In 2017, this resort underwent a massive refurbishment which brought queen sized beds to the rooms and converted one of the two beds to Murphy style so it folds out of the wall.

You may have noticed that the resort only covers from the 1950's on. For that reason, sometimes this resort gets the nickname, the "Pop Half-Century Resort." This was originally going to be two resorts in one covering the entire 1900's. Across the lake behind the resort, was going to be a resort of similar size to cover the 1900's through the 1940's. That resort would have been called the "Legendary Years" while the original would have been known as the "Classic Years." Both would've been connected to each other with the "Generation Gap Bridge" over the water. While Disney built the first Pop Century, they actually started on the 2nd across the water. They got some of the buildings finished as well as the bridge, but then 9/11 happened. After the terrorist attacks of September 2001, tourism went way down. Many people put off family vacations including Disney World for several years. Because of this, Disney put a halt on the second Pop Century resort. The buildings that were finished actually sat abandoned for nearly 10 years while Disney figured out what to do. Eventually, it was decided to turn those buildings into a whole different resort altogether, which we'll talk about next time.

If you've lived long enough, you know that sometimes life is just like that. Sometimes we have great plans, and we think we know exactly how things are going to turn out. We prepare, organize, and schedule things just how we want them to go, and then life throws a big ole' wrench right into the middle of our plans. That's what happened here with this resort. Disney thought they had the perfect plan, and it was a good one. I give them creative points for coming up with the idea to spread the 1900's over two resorts with a bridge in the middle. That was a great idea! However, life threw a curveball at them too. 9/11 changed everything, and they had to go back to the drawing board, which I'm sure was challenging. Sometimes we have to do that too, and it can be very frustrating. It can make you angry enough where you want to give up or quit. But we have to remember that God is on our side, and He has a plan for all of us. Proverbs 16:3 says, "Commit your work to the Lord, and your plans will be established." As long as we involve God in all we do, He will be there to guide our plans, goals and work. He may lead it in a different way than what we thought, but He will be involved, which should be enough. We have to trust in Him to know what's best for our plans. Don't forget Proverbs 3:5-6 which tells us to trust in God, and lean not on our own understanding, and He will direct our paths. Also remember that we are promised suffering in Scripture. It's going to happen. I Peter 5:10 says that after we've suffered a little, God Himself will be there to help us. Romans 5:3-4 adds that suffering will produce good things like character, endurance and hope. Suffering is part of life. If our plans get changed, it may just lead to something better. Yes, it may cause suffering, but in the end, God may have a better idea coming our way.

Next time we'll talk about what Disney did when their plans were changed. Luckily, they didn't give up or quit. They turned their old idea into something even better. We have to be prepared to do the same. We will all face suffering and frustration when our plans get messed up. But as long as we include God every step of the way, it will all turn out ok in the end. Never forget that God is on your side! He's got you and your plans right in the palm of His hand.

"Art of Animation"

Ever heard of Paul Harvey? Some of you young whipper-snappers probably haven't. However, if you're approaching the elder category like myself, you might just know who he is. My dad used to listen to him on the radio every day driving us to school. Harvey would always give his news report and then do a feature called "the rest of the story." During that section, he would tell a true story with some sort of surprising ending, which became the "rest of the story." I say all that to say, today's resort is the "rest of the story." So let's go figure out what in the world Disney did with that abandoned hotel they started. This is the last WDW resort in the value category. Today we cross that bridge to the Art of Animation!

The Art of Animation was the 5th and final value resort built at WDW. It opened in 2012 and was actually the first resort of any kind that had opened in seven years since 9/11. It features 1984 rooms, 1120 of which are family suites. This means that most of the rooms here are more expensive than value, yet this is still considered a value resort because of the section built before 9/11. That section has exterior doors to the rooms, and so they are value priced. The rest of the buildings, built after 9/11, are suites, have interior entrances, and were built with larger families in mind. The 10 buildings at this resort are dedicated to four classic Disney animated films. The value portion, with the outdoor entrances, is all dedicated to *The Little Mermaid*. The other buildings, the suites, are dedicated to *Cars, Finding Nemo* and *The Lion King*. The lobby of this building celebrates the art and history of animation displaying multiple drawings and sketches of famous Disney characters. There are 3 pools at this resort including the largest of all pools at any Disney World resort (not counting water parks). The Big Blue Pool here has over 300,000 gallons of water, and if you swim under the water, you might just hear sounds from *Finding Nemo*. Give that a try! This resort also has more large outdoor sculptures than any other resort making for some great picture spots.

So this resort is the "rest of the story." Instead of becoming the second half of Pop Century, it became a family resort dedicated to celebrating the history of Disney animation. We stayed here once in the Little Mermaid section due to it being value, and the fact that we only needed a one night stay. I would love to go back and try one of the suites, but I can safely report after the one stay that this is a beautiful resort. The larger than life scenes from the timeless films are fantastic. This resort also caters to the needs of the bigger families that visit WDW. While it may have been nice to see the other half of Pop Century, I think Disney did a fine job repurposing this area into a useful resort. Did you know that God also does some repurposing? He certainly has on me.

When I became a teacher 20 years ago, I thought I would be a teacher for life. I had no idea that after 16 years, God would lead me in another direction. But He decided that 16 years was enough, and it was time to repurpose my life. I truly believe God wanted to use me in a different setting. As a paramedic, I now get to influence a whole new set of co-workers. I also get the chance to meet and talk with all different types of people as patients on my ambulance. God needed me in another way. He knew that there would be a lot of different people I could affect in this new capacity, so He redirected my life. It wasn't easy, and there were times I questioned making such a big career change. But my family and I felt I was being called. God was leading me. He was guiding me to a new purpose. I think He also did the same thing with this very book you are reading. For years, I prayed for a way to reach and encourage others...to share my thoughts and words. God had just the way and guided me to follow the steps to communicate through these books. He repurposed me into an author, something I never dreamed of becoming.

Listen to Jeremiah 18:4... "And the vessel he was making of clay was spoiled in the potter's hand, and he reworked it into another vessel, as it seemed good for the potter to do." God is our potter and does just that. He reworks us into another needed vessel when He sees fit to do so. 2 Timothy 2:21 is a very similar passage when it says, "...he will be a vessel for honorable use, set apart as holy, useful to the master of the house, ready for every good work." Also keep in mind Romans 8:28 which says that all things work together for good for those who love God and have been called according to His purpose. Not our purpose, but His. His purpose will lead us to great things and we will see it as good if we are just patient and give God time to work.

Disney repurposed an abandoned hotel into something great with the Art of Animation Resort. Be prepared because God may do the same with you at some point. He may already have. He will change you, redirect you, lead you or guide you to fulfill His purpose for you. It may not be the direction you are expecting. But trust Him and His plans, because it may just end up being something great...something even better than you could have ever imagined. It certainly has for me!

"Caribbean Beach"

Having finished all the value properties, we now move on to the next category...the moderate resorts! There are four of them. My family has been blessed to stay at three of the four. We keep trying to book the last one but our plans get changed, or we find it all booked up. We'll get it soon though. I can tell you that we've absolutely loved all three of the other moderates we've stayed at. They are wonderful, and I can't even decide which one I like the best because they all have something special about them. We are going first to the Caribbean Beach Resort. This place is fabulous, and I could absolutely live there if they'd let me (which they won't). There are so many amazing things about this resort, and I'm thrilled we are stopping here today.

The Caribbean Beach Resort opened in October of 1988. It is designed Caribbean style with very colorful two-story buildings surrounding a 42 acre lake called Barefoot Bay. This resort is fairly centrally located among the four WDW parks. In fact, if you stand in just the right place at the Caribbean Beach, you can see the Epcot nighttime show. The buildings are grouped into five different villages, each named for an island in the Caribbean: Martinique, Barbados, Jamaica, Aruba and Trinidad. Each village has its own pool, and there are a total of 1536 rooms. There used to be over 2000 rooms on property, but some were removed to make way for a new Disney Vacation Club resort on property that we'll get to later. This resort is so big that it has its own internal bus system that will transport you from village to village. In 2009, Disney began refurbishment on this resort and redesigned some of the rooms to a *Finding Nemo* theme. There are also several rooms in the Trinidad section that have a pirate theme complete with boat-shaped beds. This is an all-inclusive resort with many activities, restaurants and rentals available. Just a few of the things you could find here are bike rentals, playgrounds, beaches, hammocks, outdoor movies, activity cruises, fishing, volleyball and a jogging trail. The main pool features water slides and a hot tub and is themed after a Spanish fortress called Port Royale. That is the same fort that happens to also be the setting for both the film and Magic Kingdom attraction "Pirates of the Caribbean."

We have stayed at the Caribbean Beach a couple of times and are planning a week-long stay on our upcoming trip. I absolutely cannot wait. The first time we stayed here, I woke up early one morning before my family. I walked out of our room and took a very short walk to the beach on the shore of the Barefoot Bay. As I laid in one of the many hammocks available, I took a deep breath and tried to just take it all in. The gentle breeze around me, the smooth sand below me, the sound of the water, the birds flying overhead, the sun shining down....it was all just perfect. I wanted to lay there forever. Without a doubt, this is one of the most peaceful and beautiful resorts I've ever stayed at. I really did feel like I was alone, sitting on a beach somewhere remote, even though I was really in the middle of Florida. Have you ever experienced peace like that? If you're like me, those times are rare. I tend to get so caught up in the pandemonium that is work, bills, family, kids, activities, homework, stress, etc., that I often forget to just stop, take a breath and relax. If I got to choose what Heaven would be like, I might just choose that hammock on the shore of Barefoot Bay at the Caribbean Beach Resort. However I'm sure God will prepare it to be much better than even that.

Our lives can get very busy. That's probably inevitable. But if we have our faith rooted in God and are working hard to follow His ways, we can also experience a deep peace. In John 16:33, Jesus says that His words are meant to bring us peace. He then says that we will have trouble at times, but that He has overcome the world. In other words, the trouble, chaos and stress of life won't last forever. Focusing on the words of Jesus can bring us peace. In 2 Thessalonians 3:16, Paul says that our God is a God of peace and can give us peace at all times. Finally, don't forget Philippians 4:7 which reads, "And the peace of God, which surpasses all understanding, will guard your hearts and your minds in Christ Jesus."

I can't remember another time in my life when I felt the peace that I felt that day lying in that hammock. I'm hoping to experience that again in a few weeks. It's hard to imagine being able to have that same feeling in our normal everyday lives, but keep the verses above in mind. All that matters in the long run is that we are part of God's family. If that is true, then everything else will fall into place. God will guide us, protect us and save us in the end. That fact alone should bring us peace every single day. If you ever find yourself overloaded, overworked, or overstressed, just stop, take a deep breath, and focus on God and the words of Christ. Ask God for peace. He'll give it to you and also help you to remember that your relationship with Him is all that really matters.

"Coronado Springs"

Do I have to leave? I guarantee I will ask that, probably out loud, as we approach the end of our next trip. Once I get to the Caribbean Beach, I don't want to leave. But I guess I will...as a thank you for reading this book. But I don't have to be happy about it. So let's hop a bus to the next moderate resort. This is the one I've never stayed at, much to my disappointment. And we've tried, but it just hasn't worked out yet. I've heard great things about this place, and I want to experience it for myself. I enjoyed doing a little research about it for you, and I learned a lot. Come with me as we try out the Coronado Springs Resort!

The Coronado Springs Resort opened in August 1997 with a colonial Spanish and southwestern American theme. This resort is well-known as the convention center resort. It has thousands upon thousands of square feet of meeting space including the largest ballroom in the southeastern U.S. called the "Coronado Ballroom." It has several other large meeting rooms as well as 45 smaller breakout rooms available. It is renowned as one of the largest single level hotel convention centers in the Southeast. Needless to say, you will most likely find a lot of business people during your stay, as a lot of conventions are hosted here. But don't get me wrong, there is fun to be had here too! This resort features suites, restaurants, a gift shop, an arcade, four pools, a salon, fitness center, dance club and the largest outdoor hot tub in all of WDW. The Coronado Springs recently announced a huge expansion with the centerpiece being a new 15 story tower that will house an additional 545 guest rooms including 50 more suites. This brings the grand total of rooms to nearly 2000! The rooms are divided into three sections: Casitas, Ranchos and Cabanas.

This resort was named after the famed 16th century Spanish explorer Francisco Vasquez de Coronado. In 1540, he set sail for the New World in search of the Seven Cities of Cibola, also known as the seven cities of gold. These cities were a popular myth of the time promising riches of gold to those who found the treasure. The seven cities were supposedly in the southwestern portion of the U.S. around where New Mexico is today. He and his group never found the mythical gold of course, but they did find quite a treasure. They were the first known group to find the Grand Canyon, which is of course today one of the most visited and recognized U.S. tourist attractions. I don't know how they felt about that discovery. Maybe they wish it would've been gold. Maybe they didn't realize they had found something even better. This reminds me of a similarity in our own lives that I'd like to discuss today. Imagine that!

How much time do you spend studying the Bible? Think about it. Do you read the Bible more than just while at church? Do you read it daily? Do you actually take the time to study it or just quickly read a few verses to get in your daily quota? I'm asking myself these same questions. I recently made a goal for 2019 to read a chapter a day of the New Testament and Psalms. As of this writing, I have finished the New Testament and am beginning Psalms. I've kept up and enjoyed it, but I'll be honest and say that not much studying has been involved. I've just been reading and trying to re-familiarize myself with those books. Next year, I would like to actually do a more in-depth study using a guide, so I can really get more in depth. I find that the more I study the Bible, and the deeper I dig into a passage, the more I tend to learn and grow.

Read the very first Psalm today. This first chapter of this large book begins by talking about a blessed man. Another translation for the word "blessed" in this passage is "happy." So the first couple of verses basically say that we will be happy if we study the Word of God and think about it daily. In I Timothy 4:13, Paul tells those reading this letter that they should devote themselves to reading Scripture. Read these other passages carefully and pay special attention to the italicized words:

"You will *seek me and find me*, when you *seek me with all your heart*." (Jeremiah 29:13)

"...for whoever would draw near to God must believe that he exists and that he *rewards those who seek him*." (Hebrews 11:6)

"But from there you will seek the LORD your God and you will find him, if you *search after him with all your heart and with all your soul*." (Deuteronomy 4:29)

"I love those who love me, and those who *seek me diligently* find me" (Proverbs 8:17)

Do you see what happens when we diligently study God's Word with our heart and mind? We find God and He rewards us!

I'm not sure if Francisco Vasquez de Coronado knew what kind of a treasure he found in the Grand Canyon. If he knew then how popular it would be today, he might have realized that his searching for mythical gold led to something more valuable. We can also find valuable treasure every time we carefully study the Bible. Make the time every day to do so. Use a study guide or online tool to help you really focus on God's Word. I promise that the more you study, the more you'll find, and the closer you'll grow to God. So go seek Him! Go find your Grand Canyon!

"Port Orleans—Riverside"

We have two moderate resorts to go and the two remaining are like sisters in a way. For a while, the two were actually considered one resort, the largest on property. However, they have now been split into two resorts even though they are right next to each other. And even though their names are similar, we're going to talk about them separately because there are a lot of differences, and each has a unique personality. We'll start with the Port Orleans Resort—Riverside.

This resort, themed around the antebellum South, opened in February of 1992. It features large plantation style buildings with exquisite landscaping and large patches of green space. When it first opened, it was called Disney's Dixie Landings Resort. Today, it is the 2nd largest Disney resort by number of rooms with 2048 total. A few years ago, 500 of those rooms were transformed into what are called "Royal Guestrooms." These rooms have special royalty theming with ornate beds, gold accents and magical fireworks in the headboards that operate with the push of a button. There is a 3.5 acre island here called "Ol' Man Island," which contains the featured swimming pool, water slide and hot tub. There are five other quiet pools on property as well as fishing, bike rentals and horse-drawn carriage rides available. On that island, you'll find the largest living oak tree to ever be transplanted. It was originally on the site where Animal Kingdom is now located approximately 13 miles away. It took hundreds of people over 48 hours to replant the 85 ton tree. Once it was replanted, the island was constructed around it. This resort, along with its sister we'll get to next, also connect to Disney Springs via the Sassagoula River. This 2 ½ mile waterway was completely man-made and created in preparation for these resorts.

When my wife and I went to Disney on our 15th anniversary, we stayed at this resort for the first time and were very surprised to see a cast member waiting at the entrance with our name on a sign. Upon arrival, we were told that we were the "royal family of the day" and were being upgraded to one of the royal guestrooms. We took a carriage ride that night, as well as the boat back and forth to Disney Springs. It was truly a magical stay, and we fell in love with this resort on that trip. We have since been back to stay there with our boys, and it was just as wonderful as before. Needless to say, this resort is one of our favorites.

As you can easily see, it took a lot of work to build this resort. A five story enormous tree was replanted. An island was built around it. A 2 ½ mile waterway was hollowed out and filled. There are bridges constructed as well as bike paths, walking trails, multiple buildings and pools. Need I go on? Needless to say, it took great time and effort to construct this beautiful piece of property. In the same way, it takes a lot of invested time and hard work to be a Christian, at least to do it right. Our Christian lives of course take faith, and that is very important. But we can't just depend on faith alone. Our works are also important. Read James 2:20-24 today. This passage talks specifically about Abraham, when he was asked to sacrifice his son, Isaac. He was willing to do that to show his faith in God. He gathered the materials, climbed the mountain, built the altar, tied up his son and even raised his hand to strike before he was stopped. Abraham did the work. Verse 24 says, "You see that a person is justified by works and not by faith alone." Abraham had strong faith, extremely strong to be willing to do that! However, he also did a lot of hard work, and not just on that day. Paul also worked hard for God all his life. He traveled all over the world of his day and preached constantly, despite many threats and attempts on his life. After all that, look at what he said in Acts 20:24..." But I do not account my life of any value nor as precious to myself, if only I may finish my course and the ministry that I received from the Lord Jesus, to testify to the gospel of the grace of God." The only thing Paul cared about was working hard for God and continuing to preach, even if it cost his life. If you have time, also read Hebrews 11 today. This is the famous faith chapter with a "hall of fame" type list of Bible characters with great faith. If you read carefully, you'll notice that almost every account of a person in that chapter describes the work they did for God.

If you've never stayed at Port Orleans—Riverside, I highly recommend it. It is an absolute magnificent resort with so many wonderful touches. I will definitely stay here again one day. The attention to detail and tremendous hard work that went into it obviously didn't happen overnight. It took a lot of planning, organization, time and effort by a great number of people. Our spiritual life also takes great determination and energy. We have to work hard to remain faithful, to resist temptation, to help others and serve our Father. You can't just sit back, do nothing and expect to be a strong Christian. Decide right now that you are going to put the hard work in and continue to each and every day. I promise it will all be worth it in the end.

"Port Orleans—French Quarter"

Today we go visit the sister. As I mentioned last time, these two moderate resorts are next door, easily within walking distance of each other. Or even better, you can take a boat between the two. The same boat that goes to Disney Springs also stops at each of these resorts. This resort definitely has its own unique qualities and style, so let's reserve a room here today. This is Port Orleans—French Quarter.

This resort actually opened in May of 1991, nearly a year before Riverside. The resort here was originally just called Port Orleans, but added the "French Quarter" moniker when they changed the name of Riverside next door. This resort, as expected, is heavily themed after the famous French Quarter district in the city of New Orleans. There are 1008 rooms here in seven different buildings. These buildings and the surrounding areas resemble what you would see in downtown New Orleans with balconies, wrought-iron railings, cobblestone streets and courtyards. There are also several special additions at this resort that make it feel even more authentic. For example, you can order mouth-watering, genuine-tasting beignets. In addition, the cast members put on an annual Mardi Gras parade for the guests in keeping with the renowned New Orleans celebration. When checking in, take a look at the musical notes spread across the registration desk. They play out the first verse of "When the Saints Go Marching In." There is only one pool at this resort, but it's quite large with a slide and waterfall. There is also a separate hot tub. We have only stayed here once, but we loved it. Shocking! We actually got a room on the backside right on the water, and the location was wonderful. We could watch the boats go by right outside our room which was very tranquil and relaxing.

As mentioned, this resort is set up to mimic the actual French Quarter in New Orleans. In that city, it is a six by thirteen block district steeped in both Spanish and French colonial history. It is the oldest neighborhood in New Orleans, founded in 1718. The city actually developed around this area, also known as the "Old Square." Most of the buildings here were constructed during the late 1700's or early 1800's. The entire district has been designated as a National Historic Landmark and is a prime tourist destination. You may remember that

New Orleans was devastated by Hurricane Katrina in 2005. Most of the city suffered destructive and deadly floods and over 1500 people lost their life in Louisiana alone. The main reason for the flooding was the failure and compromise of the city's levee system. However, the French Quarter of New Orleans was different from most of the city. Due to its distance from areas where the levee was breached as well as the strength and height of its nearest levees, it suffered relatively light damage compared to the rest of the city. This area opened back up a lot quicker after the storm than the rest of New Orleans.

Natural disasters like Hurricane Katrina can be very scary. Sometimes we have to face terrifying catastrophes like hurricanes, tornadoes, floods, fires, earthquakes, etc. In life, we also have to face personal storms in the shape of sickness, death, accidents, disease, tragedies or other types of unexpected suffering. Read Luke 8:22-25 today. This is probably a familiar story to you. Jesus and his disciples are sailing on a lake when a terrible storm strikes them as well. The disciples basically freak out while Jesus sleeps peacefully. He must have been pretty tired. When they start to panic and wake him up, he calms the storm and asks them, "Where is your faith?" While we aren't able to literally make storms calm down, our goal should be to have faith strong enough to face the storms of life. Life is going to deal us some challenging hands sometimes. It's not always going to be calm and peaceful, sitting by the water, watching the boats go by at a Disney resort. But when those tragedies occur, keep in mind Ephesians 6:10 which says, "Finally, be strong in the Lord and in the strength of his might." We have the ability to be strong because we have God on our side.

I want another stay at Port Orleans—French Quarter. Actually I want another stay at a lot of places as you can tell. I also wouldn't mind visiting the actual city of New Orleans again. I've enjoyed the couple of times I've been able to go there. This Disney resort has an authentic feel about it, and you can actually picture yourself in the French Quarter of New Orleans as you walk those cobblestone paths. Keep in mind that famous district and how it withstood one of the deadliest storms in U.S. history. Use that fact as motivation to withstand the terrible storms that will come your way. It's not easy, but it's always possible if you call on God and lean on Him. He will strengthen your levee so you won't be washed away by the flood waters. He will keep you on your feet if you just ask, believe and trust.

"Animal Kingdom Lodge and Villas"

Today's a big day. A deluxe day! It's time for us to make our way through all the deluxe resorts at Disney World. And there are a lot of them for you to choose from, with more on the way, so we're going to be livin' it up in luxury for the next several devotionals. You may wonder why there are so many more deluxe resorts as opposed to value or moderates. One reason is that most of these deluxe resorts have bigger rooms and so there are not as many available as at the values and moderates. Another reason is simply that Disney is a business and there are a lot of people willing to pay more for these rooms. Even though they can be pricey, families are willing to spend due to the special theming, larger space, or amenities offered. So where in the world do we begin? A good question. We're going to travel around and visit these resorts grouped by areas or proximity to parks. We'll start near the Animal Kingdom, then go to the Epcot/Hollywood Studios area, then to Disney Springs and finish out near the Magic Kingdom. Sound good? I'll assume you said yes. Let's start at the Animal Kingdom Lodge and Villas!

This is the only resort in close proximity to the Animal Kingdom although Coronado Springs and the All-Stars aren't very far away. The Animal Kingdom Lodge opened in April 2001, approximately three years after the park. A few years later, the Villas were added as a bonus Disney Vacation Club (DVC) resort. Several of these deluxe resorts have villas attached. Most serve DVC members, and some could be considered separate resorts. However, for the sake of time and space, we will include them with their respective resorts. The main building and original lodge here is now called Jambo House. The Villas are called Kidani Village. These names were added to help distinguish the two and hopefully eliminate confusion. This resort is African themed and includes a 16 foot Ijele mask on display in the lobby. This visually stunning mask is the first ever to leave the country of Nigeria after being created there. This resort includes two large pool areas complete with slides and water play areas for children. There are also some award winning restaurants here including Jiko, Boma and Sanaa. The greatest perk this resort offers is views of nearly 250 different animals right outside the resort or some of the rooms. There are 46 acres of land and four different savannahs surrounding the resort, so there is plenty of room for these animals to roam. Some of the animals you might see include ostriches, zebras, giraffes, kudu, gazelles, hogs, wildebeests, flamingos, pelicans, and many more. There are also several programs available here including animal feedings and night watch explorations.

We have visited several times to eat at Boma because it's one of our favorites. While visiting, we have wandered out back and watched the animals. They are literally right there. I could almost touch the giraffe on one visit! But that would have been a no-no. Touching or feeding an animal can get you in trouble. But just seeing them that close and viewing the beautiful savannahs is reason enough to love being at this resort. I hope to get to stay one day. I think it would be simply amazing to step out on my balcony each morning and see a zebra or giraffe greeting me with the sunrise. Disney seems to have done a really good job in the last 20 years of building this huge area with a whole park and resort dedicated to the animals. They have hundreds of cast members whose job is to properly provide and care for the animals. Moving to our lesson for today, let's talk about God's relationship with animals.

If you read enough Scripture, it's pretty obvious that God cares about animals. God of course cares for everything He created, and if you look back in Genesis 1, you can see where he created all the animals on day six. He then created man to look after and care for the animals. God also uses animals to show His power in the Bible. Look at the story of Jonah in the book of Jonah chapters 1-4. Look at the story of the Lions' Den in Daniel chapter 6. God also uses animals to teach us lessons. Read Matthew 6:25-34, a passage I have to read often. Jesus teaches us all a lesson about being anxious and worrying by looking at birds. He reminds us that if God takes care of even the birds, surely He will take care of us too. Animals are also used to show us compassion. Read 2 Samuel 12:1-14 as well. In this passage, the prophet Nathan uses the story of a lamb to make King David feel compassion. He then twists the same story to teach David a lesson and rebuke him for his sin.

Animals are a wonderful gift from God. If you get a chance to stay at or just visit the Animal Kingdom Lodge, don't miss out. I have no doubt you will enjoy the experience of simply getting to observe these animals in their habitat. They are amazing creatures that God created as a blessing and for our benefit. There are many Biblical examples where God uses animals as object lessons or to show His authority. It's pretty obvious that all creatures are special to God because He created them and has a great purpose for them all. We should also see them as a blessing and do our part to care for them as well.

"Beach Club Resort and Villas"

We're going to move now to the group of resorts that are between Epcot and Hollywood Studios. This section, commonly referred to as the Boardwalk, is one of my favorite areas to visit. These properties are more often described as Epcot resorts, although they are fairly equidistant between the two parks, and you can walk to each. If you've never visited this Boardwalk area, you've missed an important part of Disney World that a lot of people don't know about. I used to be one of them. I went to Disney for over 10 years before I really discovered this area. When I ran the Disney marathon in 2011, part of the course goes around the Boardwalk and past all these resorts. I could hardly believe what I was seeing, viewing it for the first time. I guarantee I wasn't watching the race course at all, with my head swinging side to side trying to take it all in. There are five deluxe resorts in this area, and I've only gotten to stay at one of them! Therefore I've just decided I really need a sponsor so I can visit all these resorts I'm discussing here. Any takers? Anyone? (crickets) Didn't think so. Oh well, let's just keep on with our virtual visits. Today we're staying at the Beach Club Resort and Villas.

The Beach Club is a AAA four diamond award winning resort as are many of Disney's deluxe resorts. In case you're curious, the only five diamond award winner in this area is the Four Seasons Resort, which isn't technically a Disney resort even though it's on Disney property. The Beach Club resort was built in November of 1990 along with the resort next door. Yes, this resort also has a sister resort like the Port Orleans Resorts. These two look very similar and share many amenities and staff. We'll talk about the other resort next time. The Beach Club is themed after the seaside cottages of Newport Beach and has 583 rooms, including several expanded villas. As mentioned, one perk of these resorts is the proximity to Epcot and Hollywood Studios. This resort is the closest to Epcot, about a 5 minute walk, and guests have special access to the park through the International Gateway in the World Showcase area of the park. A walk to Hollywood Studios will take around 15 minutes. You can also access both parks via boat, which is a lot of fun. There are several great restaurants at the Beach Club including one of our favorites, Cape May Café, a wonderful buffet style meal. It also hosts a character breakfast in the mornings. The most famous benefit of this resort is the huge swimming area shared by the two resorts. It's called Stormalong Bay and includes waterfalls, a circular lazy river, poolside restaurants, a kiddie pool, a tanning deck and the largest sand-bottom pool in the world. It also has the "Shipwreck," which is a 230 foot water slide, and one of the highest resort slides available at Disney World. Needless to say, Stormalong Bay is typically hopping with crowds of people, so there are also quiet pools with jacuzzis available at both resorts.

We've never stayed at this resort, but we've certainly visited several times to eat there. I've always admired that huge pool and water area, as well as the slide. It looks like a lot of fun. Unfortunately, I've never been able to get in because there is a large white fence that completely surrounds Stormalong Bay. This was placed by Disney several years ago because they found a lot of guests were coming over to use the pool even though they weren't staying there. Consequently, guests now have to scan their magic bands to enter this fun water area, meaning regular joes like me have to stay out. We are left to just stand outside the fence with our bottom lip sticking out, looking pitiful. Believe it or not, Jesus describes a similar situation in the Bible.

Take a look at John chapter 10 today. In verses 1-18, Jesus describes the reality of who belongs to God and who doesn't. He basically describes a fenced in area like a sheep pen. Jesus says that the only way to get into the pen is through the door which is Jesus himself. He then goes on to say that He knows the sheep and they know Him. Trust me when I say that we want to be in that sheep pen. We want to be inside that fence. The only way to get in is through Jesus. We have to believe in Him, know Him, follow Him and love Him. If we do that, He will let us into the fence. Also compare that passage with Matthew 25:31-46. This is a very important passage which is also Jesus teaching. He is describing Judgment day and basically says we will all be divided into sheep and goats. The sheep will be welcomed into Heaven while the goats will be told "Depart from me, you cursed, into the eternal fire prepared for the devil and his angels." (verse 41) Yes, that's harsh and scary, but it's also reality and part of God's plan. Everyone can't get into the fence. It's reserved for those who follow the laws of God and the plan He's put forth. He's giving you every opportunity to come to Him and know Him. The fact that you're reading this right now is another chance to make your life right.

I've never gotten to go inside the fence at the Beach Club's Stormalong Bay, but I feel confident that I've entered the fold of God with Jesus as the door and the Shepherd. What about you? Are you inside the fence? If not, come in quickly and don't wait. Get to know Jesus now and He'll let you in. You don't want to miss what's inside!

"Yacht Club Resort"

Sitting right next door to the Beach Club is another resort that looks nearly the same. In fact, the only obvious difference at first glance is the color, the Beach Club being a light blue while the other is gray. Both resorts share a lot of the activities available such as nearby jogging trails, volleyball, tennis, an arcade, and a playground. There is a convention center on site available to both resorts, and the marina just adjacent to both has several boat charters available, including a night time Epcot fireworks cruise. However, even though these resorts look similar and share many activities, they are certainly unique in theming and décor. So today, let's visit the other resort, known as the Yacht Club.

The Yacht Club also opened in November of 1990 here in the Boardwalk area between Epcot and Hollywood Studios. There are around 630 rooms in this five story building. The theme here is a New England nautical motif with models of boats and subtle compass designs throughout. The Yacht Club is one of four resorts at Disney World that have recently been made pet friendly, along with Port Orleans—Riverside, Art of Animation and Fort Wilderness, which we'll talk about soon. There are some unique restaurants here at Yacht Club including a high quality and popular establishment called the Yachtsman Steakhouse. Between the resorts, you will also find the highly admired Beaches and Cream restaurant. This is an authentic retro style diner with renowned desserts, including the "Kitchen Sink," which is a dessert literally served in a metal sink with several scoops of ice cream, multiple toppings, and an entire can of whipped cream. It is definitely a dessert to be shared. I've seen it, but never had the stomach, or quite frankly the wallet, to order it. I've only braved the Mini Kitchen Sink available at the Magic Kingdom, which I did eat by myself I'm proud to say.

As you probably could've guessed even if I hadn't said it above, this resort theme is all things nautical. There are many references inside and out to ships, navigation and other items related to sailing and the sea. I've had the absolute pleasure of taking four cruises in my life, two of which were Disney cruises. That, my friends, is definitely my favorite way to travel! It would be my dream to retire and live on a cruise ship. Maybe I'd even bring my wife too. ☺ I just love being on the sea. There's something incredibly peaceful about being on the vast expanse of water with no land in sight. This got me also thinking about boats and sailing in the Bible.

There are many boat references in Scripture. I think about the obvious accounts of Noah, Jonah, Paul and even Jesus. In fact, Jesus was on a boat several times. We recently talked about His calming of the storm when the disciples panicked. Another time, Jesus stepped into a boat just off shore to teach the people because of the severity of the crowds. Today, however, I want to focus on a story from Matthew 14. Read verses 22-33 and refresh yourself on the story of Jesus walking on the water. During yet another storm, the disciples, this time without Jesus, are worried for their lives. To their fear and amazement, they see Jesus walking toward them on the water. Seeing this, Peter requests to join Jesus and walk on the water too. Jesus calls for Peter, and he steps out of the boat and indeed walks on the water for a brief moment. Most people focus on what happens next. Peter takes his eyes off Jesus, remembers the storm and begins to sink. While that makes a good lesson about keeping your eyes on Jesus, I'd rather focus today on what Peter did first. He took that step!

Imagine yourself on a small boat during a storm with the water raging and the wind blasting. Could you take that first step onto the water? Let's change the situation...what about taking the first step to start a Bible study with someone or leading a program to serve those in need? What about taking just a simple step towards a conversation with someone about their faith? Sometimes, we have to be bold like Peter and have the courage to step out of our comfort zone and try something new, especially if it will benefit or serve others. Thankfully, there are some scriptures to help us in this often uncomfortable area. Psalms 27:14 reminds us to wait for the Lord, be strong and let our heart take courage. I Corinthians 16:13 tells us stand firm in our faith, act like men and be strong. In addition, look at what King David said to his son, Solomon, in I Chronicles 28:20. He said, "Be strong and courageous and do it. Do not be afraid and do not be dismayed, for the LORD God, even my God, is with you. He will not leave you or forsake you, until all the work for the service of the house of the LORD is finished."

Sailing is great! However, it can certainly be scary if the sea is rough or there's a fierce storm with strong winds. I realize Peter ended up sinking that night, but for now, let's celebrate the fact that at least he took that first step showing incredible courage. We must do the same. If there's anything at all we can do to serve others or help their faith, we must act! If you are having trouble, ask God for help. He will guide you to be strong and help you build up your courage to pick up your foot and take that first step. Even onto raging waters!

"Boardwalk Inn and Villas"

Checking out of the Yacht Club, we now walk around the boardwalk just a short distance to the area across the water. I highly encourage you again to check out this area, even if you aren't staying in one of these resorts. There is so much to see and do here, and it's so much fun to walk around, sample the various foods and just people watch. The whole area keeps going strong well into the night, so even a late night stroll is worthwhile. With five resorts here, it stands to reason that there should be one named after the boardwalk itself, so that's where we're headed today. Let's go take a look at the Boardwalk Inn and Villas.

This resort, opened in July 1996, is in the same area as the others, but nearer to Hollywood Studios. It is modeled after an early 1900's Atlantic City resort, with several features reminiscent of Coney Island in New York. In the lobby you'll find many interesting old photos and decorations including a miniature carousel model. This model was hand-crafted in the 1920's at Coney Island by a master designer and manufacturer of merry-go-rounds. The main pool here is also themed after an early 1900's carnival. It is called the Luna Park Pool named after the famous amusement park that used to sit on Coney Island. The pool features a 200-foot water slide that looks like an old wooden roller coaster, complete with a huge clown's face at the end of the slide. Those riding the slide actually exit out the clown's mouth into the pool. There are playful elephants nearby to shower you before entering as well as a play area for kids called the "Luna Park Crazy House." If carnival theming or giant clown faces aren't your thing, there are a couple of other quieter pools nearby. On the boardwalk side, this resort is directly above several well-known and loved restaurants and businesses. Guests can enjoy a dueling pianos show at Jellyrolls, a lively nightspot and piano bar. There is dancing available at the Atlantic Dance Hall or even a place to see magic at the AbracadaBar.

I've never stayed here at the Boardwalk, but my family has walked by many times. It is definitely an energetic area, especially at night, with bright lights, spirited music, animated crowds and a lot to see. I've never been to Coney Island in New York either, but apparently the resort here coupled with the boardwalk is very similar to that entertainment destination that has been around since the late 1800's. We already talked several entries ago about how the giant Ferris wheel at DCA Park is a model of the Wonder Wheel on Coney Island as well. Did you know that Coney Island is not even an island? It is a four mile long peninsula on the west side of Long Island, NY. It used to be an island, hence the name, but in the 1920s and 30s, a large section of water was filled in to make a land bridge. This gives the "island" much easier access to the mainland bringing more tourists and a higher economy for the vibrant neighborhood.

Have you ever heard the phrase "no man is an island?" It's a line from a 1624 prose work by English poet, John Donne. The meaning behind it is quite simple. In order for a person to live effectively, they need others around them. Humans tend to struggle when trying to do everything by themselves, and instead need to be a part of a community in order to thrive. Coney Island would not have blossomed and prospered as much if it had remained an island. It was therefore made into a peninsula to connect to the main land and be more a part of a community. We need the same in our spiritual lives in order to succeed and grow.

Take a look at Exodus 17:8-16. This is a wonderful story of the Old Testament that is often forgotten. In these verses, we read where Moses and the Israelites fought against the Amalekites. As long as Moses held his hands in the air, God allowed the Israelites to be successful in battle. However, when he would drop his hands, they would begin to lose. Moses of course got very tired throughout the day and eventually sat down on a rock. Moses's brother, Aaron and another man named Hur, then stood on either side of Moses holding his arms up in the air. The Bible says they did this until the setting of the sun. That's all day long! Because of their assistance, the Israelites won the battle that day. Moses could never have held his arms up alone. He needed the strength of others to succeed. We are exactly the same. We may think that we can always be self-sufficient and do things on our own. That may work for a while, but you'll find it's a lot easier to accomplish goals and get things done when aided by others. Galatians 6:2 reminds us to "Bear one another's burdens, and so fulfill the law of Christ." God intended us to help and serve each other. That's one reason He sent Jesus here...to be an example of a servant to others.

The Boardwalk Inn at Disney World and the area surrounding it are a lot of fun. You'll never be bored visiting there. It is a party atmosphere nearly around the clock each day. I hear Coney Island in New York is the same. Remember today that "no man is an island." We may try to be, but it won't work out for long. Keep in mind that God intended for us to be peninsulas with a bridge. He wants us to make connections with other people, so we can help those in need and allow others, in turn, to help us. Don't be an island. Find your bridge and connect to others!

"Swan Resort"

There are two more resorts in the Epcot/Hollywood Studios/Boardwalk area, and they are sister resorts, built around the same time with many similarities and shared elements. But once again, we are going to discuss them separately due to the fact that they have different names and some distinguishing characteristics. There's also something very unique about both of them compared to all other Disney resorts, the fact that these aren't technically even Disney resorts. Say what? We'll get to that in a second. First, let's check in to the Swan Resort.

The Swan opened in January of 1990 and has 758 rooms available. It is a 12 story rectangular main structure with two 7 story wings. The building is crowned with two 47 foot tall swan statues each weighing in at 56,000 pounds. You might also be able to find a great deal on pricing at this resort and its sister next door. There are times when this resort can be booked for close to $200 per night making it a deluxe resort at the price of a moderate. You typically only get these deals during off season times, but it's still worth checking on. This resort shares a huge grotto pool with the resort next door. This pool is considered by many to be one of the most beautiful on Disney property with gorgeous rock work, in-pool seating, waterfalls and a waterslide. Also available to guests is a spa, arcade, day care program along with multiple gift shops and restaurants.

So you may be wondering why I mentioned above that this technically isn't a Disney resort. Here's the story...In the late 1980's, Disney wanted desperately to increase the amount of hotel rooms available at WDW. The Tishman group was a company that Disney had contracted with to build Epcot, and Disney wanted to keep a good relationship with them. Therefore, a deal was made. The deal says that Disney owns the land, has some say in any refurbishments and receives part of the revenue, but these two hotels technically don't belong to Disney. They still carry the Disney name, and the guests there receive most of the Disney benefits. But the Tishman group owns the buildings and has a 99 year lease on the land. Those who stay at these two resorts get most Disney perks given at the other resorts with 3 exceptions: no magic bands, no magical express from the airport and no charging items to your room outside of the resorts themselves. In addition, you can't use the Disney dining plan at any of the restaurants found at these two resorts.

I stayed at the Swan a long time ago on a family trip when I was 15 years old. My dad had business in Orlando, so mom took us to Hollywood Studios and Typhoon Lagoon which were both fairly new. I don't remember a lot about that trip, but I remember staying at the Swan which was also new. I don't remember our room, but I do remember the pool and thinking how amazing it was. I didn't realize until many years later that these resorts were different, not being owned by Disney. That fact leads to today's lesson.

Do you realize that you own something that technically doesn't belong to you? I'm talking about your body. God has given you a body to borrow while here on Earth. It's yours to do with as you please. But technically, it doesn't belong to you. It belongs to God. Let me show you what I mean...I Corinthians 6:19-20 reads "Or do you not know that your body is a temple of the Holy Spirit within you, whom you have from God? You are not your own, for you were bought with a price. So glorify God in your body." Our bodies are meant to be a temple that hosts the Holy Spirit. God has given us His Spirit to live inside us and guide us. That is the main purpose of our bodies. They are temporary homes for the Spirit to work within us, helping us to live right, be a good example and bring others to God. I Corinthians 3:16-17 echoes this when it says, "Do you not know that you are God's temple and that God's Spirit dwells in you? If anyone destroys God's temple, God will destroy him. For God's temple is holy, and you are that temple." And don't forget Romans 12:1 which instructs us to offer our bodies as living sacrifices as part of our worship. We are basically leasing our bodies from God while we live. We can choose to mess them up if we want, but that displeases God. He intended for our bodies to serve His purpose and to be living sacrifices to Him.

The Swan Hotel, and its sister that we'll talk about next, are unique resorts. They are beautiful and offer a great place to stay on your vacation, but you can't deny that they are a little different in the fact that they aren't owned by Disney. Disney owns the land and gets to put their name on the building, but they are allowing someone else to run the show. God is the same way. He allows us to run our bodies how we want, but our bodies are only borrowed. One day we'll lose them. They'll return to dust in the ground and only the Spirit inside will survive. Treat your body as the sacrifice to God it's supposed to be. Remember that your body is a gift from God so respect it and use it properly. Also use the Spirit God has given you inside to guide you to that Heavenly home that's waiting for us all.

"Dolphin Resort"

So if you're going to name one resort the Swan, what do you name the sister resort next door? I probably would've picked another type of elegant bird, like the flamingo or stork. "Hey kids, we're going to Disney and staying at the Cockatoo!" Naaah, I guess not. Maybe Disney chose wisely in naming the other resort here the Dolphin. Just like the Port Orleans resorts and Yacht and Beach Club resorts, these two are adjacent to each other and share many features. But the Dolphin is special in its own way, so we're going to reside here for today.

The Dolphin Resort opened just a few months after the Swan in June of 1990. It includes a 257 foot tall triangular tower with a bisecting 12 story rectangular building. There are also four 9 story wings to complete the unique architectural shape. On either side of the roof of this resort are two 56 foot tall dolphin statues. This resort has nearly twice as many rooms as the Swan at 1509. The Dolphin was also originally built as a convention-hosting resort, and so it includes thousands of square feet of meeting space. It is now used for several special Disney events as well. While it shares the large Grotto pool with the Swan, there are actually 5 pools between the two resorts as well as 17 places to eat. Within walking distance of both is a mini-golf course called "Fantasia Gardens," and both are known to have super comfy beds, a recent upgrade. Finally, from both resorts you can watch the Epcot fireworks and maybe even Fantasmic at Hollywood Studios. Certain rooms and locations have better views of course, especially the higher you are.

So I wonder why Disney decided to name this resort after a dolphin. Could it possibly be because dolphins are often considered the most intelligent animals? Did you know that dolphins have been known to teach, learn, cooperate, scheme and even grieve? For years, scientists and biologists have studied dolphins and their intelligence. Dolphins have even showed some sense of self-awareness. This has been verified with a mirror test where animals are marked with a dye and then shown a mirror. If the animal then goes back to view the mark in the mirror, it is said to have some aspect of self-awareness. As I'm sure you're aware, dolphins can be taught many commands and instructions. They have incredible intelligence to be able to process and remember direction and training. I could summarize and simply say that dolphins are incredibly intelligent, but their brainpower is nothing compared with what God has blessed you and me with.

Humans are of course the most intelligent creatures in the animal kingdom. Proverbs 2:6 says "For the LORD gives wisdom; from his mouth come knowledge and understanding." At the beginning of Daniel, in chapter 1, verse 17, it says that God blessed Daniel, Shadrach, Meshach and Abednego with "learning and skill in all literature and wisdom." God's design for humans, starting with Adam and Eve in Genesis 1, was to bless them with intelligence, the ability to reason, make decisions and acquire many skills. He has blessed us with that ability as well, and we are strongly encouraged to add knowledge throughout our lives. In 2 Peter 1:5, we are advised to supplement knowledge to our faith. Learning more about God, His Word and simply life in general will help strengthen and solidify our faith. Read the first Proverb today. Solomon makes it clear that the purpose of that book is to elevate our wisdom and instruction. As you may remember, when Solomon was given the chance to request anything from God, he chose wisdom. He became the wisest man to ever live, so maybe it would be wise for us to take his words seriously and study them.

I think the Dolphin is actually a good name for this resort. Have you ever seen a marine show with dolphins? They are fun to watch and their intelligence is pretty incredible. If you ever stay at the Dolphin or get to see one in action, keep in mind the intelligence that God has also blessed us with. He has given us the ability to do so many good things as well as continue to grow in our knowledge. Let's take Him up on that. Seek ways to increase your knowledge, especially the understanding and familiarity with God's Word. That will only help increase your faith and give you a firm foundation in God's kingdom.

"Saratoga Springs Resort"

It's now time to leave the boardwalk and move on to another group of deluxe resorts. Before we go, I have to say just one more time how great this Epcot resort area is. I would absolutely love in the future to stay anywhere on the boardwalk. There is just so much to do and see. Ok, I'm done. We can move on. Let's now go to a smaller group of resorts that you'll find near Disney Springs. In case you forgot, Disney Springs is the mecca of shopping, restaurants and entertainment that attracts thousands of Disney guests daily. There are a couple of deluxe resorts very nearby this huge complex, so let's begin at a beautiful place called Saratoga Springs.

This resort opened in May of 2004 as a Disney Vacation Club (DVC) resort. It provides very easy access to Disney Springs as you can literally walk a short path or take a quick boat ride across the lake. Saratoga Springs includes 18 villa buildings with a total of 1260 rooms. There are five pools available including the High Rock Spring Pool which is the feature pool of the resort. It is designed as a natural spring with trees, rocks, geysers and other decorative touches. It features zero-depth entry, a waterslide, two hot tubs and poolside dining. There is also the Paddock Pool which was added in 2011 due to increased guest capacity. It is basically the same size with most of the same features. There is also a spa and golf course available on site. This resort was built on the former site of the Disney Institute which was a new direction in vacationing that Disney attempted. Guests who booked a stay at the Disney Institute (DI) would sign up for classes on many different topics and learn during their stay at WDW. Unfortunately, the idea did not catch on and the DI didn't last too long.

This resort is named after Saratoga Springs, New York, a city known for several features. First of all, Saratoga Springs has been the site of filming for several famous and award winning movies. It is also the home of a prominent horse racing track which attracts many tourists from around the country. Before racing ever began in this city, however, people were attracted here for another reason...the area's natural mineral springs that are found spread throughout the city. For many years, these springs were believed to have healing powers, and so visitors would come from all around to sample the various waters. Some of the springs are clear freshwater, others are salty and still others have a strong mineral taste. Even today, guests are welcome to bottle the water themselves for personal consumption.

So what do you think? Do these natural springs found all over Sarasota Springs have actual healing powers? Do you remember the story in John 5 of the paralyzed man who was waiting by a pool that was believed to have healing powers? The man was distraught because he had no way to get to the pool for healing. As expected, Jesus had compassion on the man and healed him. I don't know if that pool or the springs in New York had healing powers. However, I do know that our Father in Heaven definitely has the power to heal. We've all heard stories or seen movies where people miraculously recover from a grave disease or injury. There is something very real and true about that. Why do you think we pray for those who are sick or hurt? It's very simple...God heals. Jeremiah 17:14 says, "Heal me O Lord, and I shall be healed." Look at James 5:14-15. It reads, "Is anyone among you sick? Let him call for the elders of the church, and let them pray over him, anointing him with oil in the name of the Lord. And the prayer of faith will save the one who is sick, and the Lord will raise him up." I've heard of churches literally anointing the sick while praying as these verses suggest, only to watch them get better. God listens to our prayers. He considers when we ask for healing and sometimes grants our request. He can literally change the course of someone who is in serious or grave condition if He so chooses. What an awesome God we serve!

It would be great to stay at Saratoga Springs, and I think it would be fun to visit the city in New York it's named after. I would even be so bold as to taste some of the natural spring water. It probably tastes pretty refreshing. At the same time, I wouldn't expect much from it in the way of healing. However, you better believe that I often pray to God for healing in my life or the lives of those I've heard about, know and love. Also keep in mind that God heals us all spiritually. I Peter 2:24 says "by His wounds you have been healed." The death of Jesus on the cross has healed any spiritual sickness and sin we may have. That is an even greater gift than physical healing because it means we have the hope of Heaven. Praise God today for healing us both physically and spiritually!

"Treehouse Villas"

"Dad, can you build me something?" My dad was an architect. I guess technically he still is even though he's been retired for several years now. He used to design and build a lot of things for us to use around the house. Needless to say, my school projects were top notch. But I remember being a kid of about 10 years asking him to build something for me. And what does every boy of that age want? A treehouse! I wanted my own treehouse. And to my extreme surprise and excitement, dad agreed. He was going to build it. Why am I telling you this, you may be asking? Because we're going to make an exception here. We're going to dedicate one devotional to a certain section of villas that are attached to Saratoga Springs. I realize that with every other resort, I've just included the villas with the resort. But I'm doing things different here. Hey, it's my book, and I can do what I want, right? These villas are just too special and unique to group in with their resort. So allow me today to discuss the very creative Treehouse Villas.

Yes, the Treehouse Villas are technically a part of our last entry, Saratoga Springs. But they're so different! They are in a different location, albeit not too far away. They have their own pool. And they have their own boat launch on the Sasagoula River en route to Disney Springs. Plus the fact that they just look different...way different than anything else Disney has to offer. They are treehouses for crying out loud! Each of the 60 treehouses stands 10 feet off the ground and is approximately 1074 square feet in size. Up to nine people can stay in each treehouse which have 3 bedrooms and 2 bathrooms. These treehouses actually first opened in 1975 but were then used as rent lodging, Disney Institute housing and residences for international students. Over time the treehouses began to deteriorate due to hurricane damage and age. Disney decided instead of tearing them down to totally renovate them and offer them up as a perk for DVC members. They reopened in 2009 to what they are today. Guests of these treehouses are welcome to use all facilities and amenities at Saratoga Springs and are offered all the normal Disney perks.

I honestly do remember wanting my own treehouse so badly. I've always thought treehouses were neat, especially creative ones with lifts, pulley systems and slides. So when my dad agreed to build me one, I was excited about what my treehouse would have to offer. One of my best friends growing up was my next door neighbor (shout out to Holli). She and I would play together often, making up clubs that we were a part of. I think we had a spy club at some point, although I don't remember what we spied on. I do recall telling her that I was getting a treehouse, and so we made big plans together. We decided that my treehouse was going to be an enclosed three stories. I think we made plans for a game room as one of the stories. And if I remember right, we were going to convert the treehouse into a school where we would teach neighborhood kids. Needless to say, we weren't able to register any prospective students that I recall. And as you might expect, my dad wasn't exactly in agreement with our plans. Three stories were a little much. I ended up with an open air, two story treehouse. It did have a rope ladder, slide and bench seating. I was pleased and spent a lot of time in it, but it certainly wasn't what I had originally planned. My friend and I thought we had a perfect plan. We spent hours discussing it and thought we knew exactly what the treehouse would look like. But it wasn't a perfect plan. We had overstepped our boundaries just a tad. This leads me to our thought for today.

None of us are perfect. Striving to be perfect is a worthy goal, but we will never succeed. We will all make mistakes and overstep our boundaries at times. Luckily, our God is perfect. Matthew 5:48 tells us this. Psalms 18:30 does as well. We also know that God designed and created this Earth and everything in it, including us. His design is also perfect. Genesis 2:7 says that He formed us from the dust of the ground and breathed life into us. Psalms 139:13-14 even says the He knitted us together and formed our inward parts. It goes on to say we are wonderfully made. So if God is perfect, and He created you and me, that means that we are designed just the way God intended. We still make mistakes and mess up God's perfect plan sometimes, but we should never forget that God made us just the way He wanted us. So be content and happy with who you are. Remember that God doesn't make mistakes so if you trust in His plan, everything will eventually work out for good like it says in Romans 8:28.

I would love to try a stay at the Treehouse Villas. If not, I can just take a trip over to my parents and hang out in my old treehouse. It's over 30 years old, but still standing! Seeing it always reminds me of the plans my friend and I had, and how different things turned out. We can make plans and set goals but they may be flawed. They may not be what God intends. When your plans don't work out, keep in mind that God is perfect. He designed you the way He wants you, so trust in His plan for your life. Be who you are and be happy with God's perfect design.

"Old Key West Resort"

When I was in high school, my family took a trip down to Miami, Florida. We then rented a car and drove a couple of hours down U.S. Highway 1, heading deeper and deeper south. I remember that as a long but fascinating drive. We ended up on the island of Key West, Florida which is the southernmost city in the contiguous 48 states. It was a beautiful place, full of history and interesting sights. I remember visiting the home of famed author, Ernest Hemingway. It's worth a trip if you can get down there, but a great substitute is the next resort whose theme is that famous island. This whole resort has an old, southern feel to it. Today we're renting a room at the Old Key West Resort.

This resort originally opened in December of 1991 and was called the Disney Vacation Club Resort. It was the very first DVC resort. In January 1996, the name and theme changed to resemble Key West. This resort has the largest rooms of all 15 DVC resorts and villas. Most of the rooms here even include a full kitchen and laundry room. This is a large, spread out resort with five inner bus stops. There are four pools on site as well as volleyball, basketball, tennis, golf, shuffleboard, a gym, a fire pit, multiple playgrounds, arcades, cornhole, billiards, ping-pong, foosball, bike rentals and a walking path. Wow! There's a lot to do here! This resort is also found on the Sassagoula River meaning easy access by boat to Disney Springs. The main pool has a large sandcastle slide that spits you out of a hidden Mickey. There is also a sauna on site hidden inside a lighthouse!

As I mentioned, this was the first ever DVC resort. How much do you know about the Disney Vacation Club? I don't claim to fully understand it. I've tried to over the years, asking several friends and family who have bought into it. I know that once you are in, you get first dibs being able to book early at many of these great resorts. There are many other perks as well that I don't have room to discuss. It does take a pretty hefty sum initially to become a member, which is the main reason we've never bought in. By the way, you don't have to be DVC members to stay at a DVC resort. However, a certain allotment of rooms are reserved for members making it often difficult to get in for us regular Disney nerds. Here at Old Key West, there is a hallway full of pictures of families who have bought into the DVC. This and several other features give the resort a real homey feel.

The Disney Vacation Club was intended to be a special organization to reward those who come to Disney a lot. The special incentives make it easier to book reservations along with several special perks given. The whole goal is for Disney to get you to come back again and again. I can tell you right now that Disney has succeeded in that goal with our family, even though we aren't DVC members. I can safely say that we are "regulars" at Disney. So here's the question for today...are you a regular? And I don't mean at Disney although it's great if you are. I'm asking today if you're a regular at church.

I hope you have a church home. I have been so very blessed to have the same church home my entire life. It is a true blessing from God to have a special church family in my life. If you don't have that, I strongly encourage you to get it. Sometimes, even with a church family, we may not attend regularly like we should. Unfortunately, we let life get in the way and find something more important than attending. Look at what the Bible says about going to church. Hebrews 10:24-25 says, "And let us consider how to stir up one another to love and good works, not neglecting to meet together, as is the habit of some, but encouraging one another, and all the more as you see the Day drawing near." Notice is says we are not to neglect meeting together. If your church is meeting and you are physically able to attend, you should. Jesus set up the church for many important reasons. Obviously it is a time meant to worship our Father in Heaven. However, it is also meant for fellowship with others. Acts 2:42 says that the disciples devoted themselves to fellowship with one another as well as prayer and teaching. In Acts 11:25-26, we learn that Paul and Barnabus went to church in Antioch for a year, and that is where they were first called Christians. If you are a true Christian follower of Jesus, you need that bond with other believers. Their encouragement, along with regular attendance, will help keep your faith strong.

The Old Key West Resort is the original, but one of many DVC resorts today. Members of the DVC are meant to feel a strong connection to WDW. Its intention is to make them feel special which entices them to come back often. The church you attend should do the same and make you want to come back often so you can grow in your faith, grow in your relationship with God, and grow in your bond with fellow Christians. Matthew 18:20 says that where two or three are gathered in Jesus' name, He is there with them. Find a church that makes you want to attend regularly with Jesus right there in the middle. Just like the DVC, it will make you feel special to be a part of that spiritual bond. Go to church. Be a part of the church. Be the church!

"Shades of Green"

It's now time to move to our last set of WDW resorts, and we saved the best area for last. The next several resorts are all near the Magic Kingdom, where it all began in 1971. Let's start with what is probably the least familiar of these resorts. Once again, like the Swan and Dolphin, this one isn't technically a Disney resort. But we have to discuss it because it has a very special purpose. You will not be able to even stay here, unless you meet certain qualifications or know someone that does. But we'll make an exception today for everyone reading and check ourselves in to the Shades of Green Resort.

Disney opened this resort way back in 1973 and named it the Golf Resort. It was built just southwest of the MK with a golf course around it, but the occupancy rates didn't match that of the bigger name resorts closer to the park. Guests felt like it wasn't as much a Disney resort with the golf theme, and so in 1986, it was renamed the Disney Inn. The resort was subsequently refurbished with more Disney touches including some Snow White theming in certain rooms. It still never quite had the popularity of the resorts on the monorail line, even though this resort is a mere 10 minute walk from the monorail. In 1994, a big change took place when the U.S. Department of Defense began leasing the property from Disney to use as a retreat for active military and veteran families. After just two years, in 1996, the D.O.D. bought the resort outright, and still own it today. Thought not Disney-owned, the resort must still meet certain Disney standards as guests there have many of the Disney perks shared by the other resorts. However, in similarity to the Swan and Dolphin, there is no Magical Express service to this resort, no Disney dining plan available for its guests, and no charging items to your room off the resort's property. Shades of Green doesn't have a definite theme but simply the look and feel of a modern country club. There are 586 rooms, all of which are large compared to most Disney rooms, as well as 11 suites. The resort also has tennis courts, two pools, a children's pool, hot tub, fitness center and laundry facilities. The resort is still reserved for military families and proof of service must be shown. Those who stay here do so at a reduced rate, although your rate is based on your military rank.

One perk of staying here is that since it is owned by the government, there is no tax on the room or on any merchandise sold on property.

The motto of this resort is "serving those who serve." This resort is simply one way that the government tries to give back and reward the many soldiers who have served our country. Today's lesson should be quite obvious. There are millions of men and women over time who have served in the U.S. military. I'm proud to say that my dad served in Vietnam and my grandfather in World War II. Both of them were able to come home to their families, but there are of course many soldiers who aren't given the same outcome. So many soldiers have died in battle and given their life for our freedom. While it's certainly sad and we need to try and honor and remember them any way we can, it's safe to say that they all knew that death was a possibility. Anyone who serves in the military knows that the possibility is that they might not come home. That's what they sign up for. That's the reality of the situation. They are putting themselves in danger of death to serve others. In the same way, Jesus put Himself in the pathway of death to save not only our country, but every person around the world. The difference is that Jesus knew death was definitely coming.

In Mark 9:31-32, Jesus outright told the disciples that He would die, but they didn't understand. There are several other passages where Jesus foretold of His death. He knew it was God's plan. He knew He had to die as a sacrifice for our sins. He knew it was coming. It's safe to say that He wasn't excited about it. In Matthew 26:39, He says, "My Father, if it be possible, let this cup pass from me," but then adds, "nevertheless, not as I will, but as you will." He wasn't looking forward to the pain and agony He was facing, but He was willing to go through with it if it was truly God's plan. And why was He so willing? Because of His great love for you and me. In John 15:12-13, Jesus says, "This is my commandment, that you love one another as I have loved you. Greater love has no one than this, that someone lay down his life for his friends." Jesus showed us the greatest love possible when He laid down His life for us all. Would you be willing to do the same for someone else?

Even if it doesn't belong to Disney, I'm so glad there is a resort on property to serve those who have served. I'm glad that in just a small way, our military men and women can receive a reward for being willing to give up their life. Never forget our soldiers who put their lives on the line for our freedom. And definitely never forget Jesus who did indeed give up His life for our eternal freedom in Heaven. That sacrifice showed what it truly means to be a friend and was the greatest example of love in history.

"Fort Wilderness Resort and Campground"

If we exit Shades of Green and head east across the man-made Seven Seas Lagoon, the body of water in front of the Magic Kingdom, we come to Bay Lake. On the banks of this natural body of water, we find our next resort. It is a very special place that has been around for many years, almost since Disney World began. It is a fun and unique place to stay with many choices of accommodations. So grab your campin' gear, because today we're making our home at the Fort Wilderness Resort and Campground.

Quick quiz alert! On what date did Disney World begin? Do you know? If you truly love Disney, you probably should. Just in case you don't, I'll tell you. The Magic Kingdom and two resorts opened on October 1, 1971. Fort Wilderness was the third resort to open just a little over a month later on November 19, 1971. The beauty of this resort is that it includes your choice of lodgings. You can stay at the campground and go basic with tent camping or in a camper if you have one. Or you can rent a very nice cabin and have a few more conveniences. There are 799 campsites and 409 cabins available. Fort Wilderness is 750 acres of pine and cypress forest. Did you know that there was a train here within the campground starting in 1974? It was a 3.5 mile loop around the area servicing various sites as well as the River Country Water Park that used to be nearby. However, due to maintenance costs, safety and noise concerns, the railroad's life was short and rarely ran after 1977. Today there is an internal bus system to help guests get around the massive campground. At Fort Wilderness, you can find several playgrounds, two pools, fishing, horseback riding, canoeing, biking, tennis and archery. Golf carts and boats are also available for rent. There is a large passenger boat available to take guests to the Magic Kingdom as well as the resorts around it. Since 1974, this resort has hosted the Hoop-Dee-Doo Musical Revue dinner and stage show. This is one of the longest running stage shows in U.S. history. While I've never stayed at Fort Wilderness, I saw Hoop-Dee-Doo several years ago. I was thoroughly entertained and enjoyed the great food as well. I would gladly go back to see it again. The campground also features the Campfire Sing-Along with Chip 'n Dale. During that performance, a Disney cast member leads songs in an outdoor amphitheater while Chip and Dale entertain the crowd.

In thinking about this massive campground and the vast expanse of land available, we are led to our Biblical thought for today. This resort is called Fort Wilderness for a reason. At one time, it was in fact a wilderness, before it was developed by Disney. This got me thinking about stories in the Bible that happened in a wilderness. If you have time, read Exodus 3 and Matthew 4 today. In Exodus 3, the Bible says that Moses was guiding sheep in a wilderness when he sees a burning bush. The bush is on fire, but it's not burning up. We very soon find out that it is God beginning Moses' path toward freeing the Israelites from slavery and leading them to their promised land. Moses has to be convinced to take on that great task and so God shows His amazing power through a burning bush in the wilderness. I also think about Matthew 4 which says that Jesus was led into a wilderness to be tempted by Satan. Through three separate temptations, Jesus resists the devil's offers and shows His power as well. Two different testaments. Two different stories. Two different men. But both examples show the power of God and Jesus within a wilderness.

God is powerful! I Corinthians 6:14 says He will raise us up by His power. Jesus is powerful! Hebrews 1:3 says that Christ upholds the universe by His power. Even the Holy Spirit is powerful! Romans 15:13 says that by the power of the Holy Spirit, we have hope. God, His Son and His Holy Spirit are all powerful. That is obvious. But did you know that we are powerful too? Acts 1:8 says, "But you will receive power when the Holy Spirit has come upon you." God offers us power by giving us the Holy Spirit when we follow His ways. We then have the power to lead others and guide them to God as well. We also have power to resist Satan and his attempt as temptation in our lives. Finally, we have power to be bold and courageous in our faith regardless of what happens in the world around us.

You might not think much happens out in the wilderness, but Disney turned it into a fantastic resort in Fort Wilderness. And God used the wilderness twice to show us His power and how He gives power to people like Jesus, as well as you and me. Take time today to thank God for His power and the fact that He gives you power through His Spirit. If you aren't feeling that power today, ask God for to lead you to it so you can be ready to face the world and whatever it has to offer.

"Wilderness Lodge and Villas"

If you aren't into camping and rustic cabins at Fort Wilderness, perhaps you'd like to take a very short walking path to our next resort. There ain't no camping here! At this place, you'll have all the accommodations, frills, and extras you'll need to be quite satisfied. Also nestled on the shore of Bay Lake, but a little closer to the Magic Kingdom, stands the large and picturesque resort called the Wilderness Lodge and Villas. There are five of these deluxe resorts that I've had the privilege to stay at. I already mentioned staying at the Swan, and this is number two. My entire extended family stayed here almost 15 years ago and had a wonderful time. So I'm very excited to travel back there today as we discuss the Wilderness Lodge.

This resort opened in May of 1994 near Fort Wilderness. The main building was modeled after the Old Faithful Inn at Yellowstone National Park. The Grand Californian also shares the same look and theme. Over time, two sets of villas have been added to the Wilderness Lodge including the Boulder Ridge Villas and Copper Creek Villas and Cabins. The cabins include 26 luxurious cottages right on the shoreline of Bay Lake with gorgeous views. Just like the Old Faithful Inn at Yellowstone, this resort has a geyser right outside. As part of its theming, there is an artificial hot spring that begins right in the lobby and runs behind the resort leading to an artificial geyser. The Fire Rock Geyser is an incredible sight shooting water 120 feet into the air on the hour throughout the day. If you've never been in the lobby of this resort, I would bet on the fact that your mouth will fall open the first time you see it. It is absolutely breath-taking to see this eight story indoor wonder complete with an 82 foot tall colorful fireplace, as well as 55 foot authentic totem poles. The lobby was actually built with 85 truckloads of pine logs that were brought in from Oregon and Montana. One final fun fact is that every day, one family is chosen for the incredible honor of being the "flag family." This means a cast member takes you to the roof of the main building where you get to raise the flags atop this massive lodge that represent America, Florida, Disney World and the Wilderness Lodge itself.

As mentioned, the Wilderness Lodge was modeled after the Old Faithful Inn. That famous hotel was built way back in 1904 in

Yellowstone with views of the famous geyser. Over one million eruptions have been recorded of Old Faithful since it was named way back in 1870. It was so named because its eruptions are very regular and predictable, each occurring between 60 and 110 minutes apart. The Wilderness Lodge also has a very predictable geyser. I realize it's man-made, but you can know when it's coming and anticipate the explosion of water. Maybe you can see the lesson coming today with talk of Old Faithful and the assurance of the eruptions. Let's talk about faith today.

Read Hebrews 11 today. This is commonly known as the faith chapter. It begins with a definition saying that faith is the assurance of things hoped for and the evidence of things not seen. In other words, faith means you are sure that what you hope for will happen. It also means you believe something is true even when you can't see it. I cannot stress the following statement enough: Having faith in God in our lives is so very important! Faith is the basis for our relationship with God. Faith is what we have to use to fight against Satan as well as those who don't believe in God or persecute us for our beliefs. It's pretty simple...we can't see God, and we won't see Him until we are blessed to in Heaven. There are many people out there who find it too difficult to believe in something they can't see. And I realize it's not always easy. It can be very hard to maintain a belief in something unseen. It can be easy to doubt or give in to pressure from others not to believe, especially during difficult times or tragedy. But we must believe. We must have faith. Hebrews 11:6 says, "without faith it is impossible to please him, for whoever would draw near to God must believe that he exists and that he rewards those who seek him." Having a strong faith and belief in God is vital to our spiritual survival. So how do we get or strengthen our faith? Romans 10:17 says that faith comes from hearing the Word of God. The more we read and study the Bible, the stronger our faith becomes.

In Luke 17:5, the disciples beg Jesus and say, "Increase our faith!" They knew that having a strong faith and foundation in God was so important. We need to do the same. When you say your daily prayers to God, beg Him from the bottom of your heart to increase your faith too. Ask Him to help you to always know that He is real, He is present and He is what we hope and strive for. Ask Him to help you keep your faith strong, especially when times get tough and doubts begin to creep in. Ask Him to help your faith not to waiver when others oppress or shame you for it. If you ever get a chance to see the Wilderness Lodge and its geyser, or even the original Old Faithful in action, remember how faithful we need to be. Just like those geysers can be depended on, we need to depend on and trust in God. We must believe that He is real and always have strong faith in everything He's done and will do for us.

"Contemporary Resort"

Take a deep breath! Today's a big day! It's finally time to move to the best of the best. The cream of the crop. The tour de force. Ok, so I had to look that last one up, but it means something really good. The point is...we're moving to the best resorts Disney has to offer. The resorts that everyone wants to stay at. Yes, we're heading to the monorail resorts! These resorts are very special because the Disney monorail comes right up to them, or even through them! As you might expect, they have many other amazing qualities and some interesting facts as well. Let's start with a resort that is very special to me. I'm very excited to invite you to today to Disney's Contemporary Resort.

The first time I ever remember going to WDW, I was around 6. I remember seeing the Contemporary for the first time and being simply amazed. To see the monorail go in one side of the building and come out the other looked like something from the future. The design of the building was adapted from plans that Walt Disney had for Epcot as an all-inclusive city. In fact, his plan for a shopping center there had a monorail going through it. This resort was one of only two that opened with the park on October 1, 1971. A unique design idea was used to construct this building during the two years prior. Each of the rooms was created off-site and then lifted by crane to fit into the steel frame of the building. You can actually see pictures of this happening online and it's pretty incredible. Behind the main building, there used to be two wings of rooms extending backwards. These rooms don't offer as great of a view, but are much quieter as the main tower can be loud at times with the monorail and crowds inside. The north wing was eventually torn down to build another resort which we'll talk about next time. When staying at the Contemporary, it almost feels like you are on an island being nearly surrounded by water. The Seven Seas Lagoon is out the front side while Bay Lake is out the back. Guests here have the option to walk to the Magic Kingdom, a short 10 minute stroll. The top floor of the resort houses the California Grill, a numerous award-winning restaurant with great views of the Magic Kingdom. This resort was also the site of a famous press conference when former President Richard Nixon declared to the public, "I am not a crook." He had been attending a convention at the hotel and felt he needed to talk to the press amid rumors of criminal activity. He would go on to resign the presidency less than a year later. This resort was originally going to be called the Tempo Bay Hotel, but that name was axed by Roy Disney, Walt's brother. Everyone had gotten used to calling it the Contemporary during construction as that was its working title. Roy thought the other name sounded "phony" and the simpler name was better.

This is where my wife and I stayed on our honeymoon. We couldn't get a room in the main building and so we were placed in the north wing. We had the very end room which had a balcony and great view of Bay Lake. We loved our room and were sad to see it torn down and replaced a few years ago. I had always wanted to stay there since I had seen it as a young boy. To get to finally fulfill that dream, and with my wife on our honeymoon, makes this resort one of my very favorites. I love simply visiting there during each of our trips. There are several great places to eat inside, and it is always hopping with crowds of people. The Contemporary is still just as popular today as it was on opening day, which leads me to our Biblical lesson.

The name "Contemporary" is a very fitting title for this resort. I'm glad they stuck with that instead of Tempo Bay. Contemporary means "belonging to or occurring in the present." When this hotel first opened, people were intrigued and amazed, just like I was. And even today its admiration and reputation are of the highest among resorts. It was relevant and significant nearly 50 years ago, and it's the same today. I can think of something else which has stood the test of time like that, but for much longer. The Bible has been around for nearly 2000 years and is still as popular as ever. It is estimated that over 5 billion Bibles have been sold in just the last two centuries. It is by far the most popular book of all time currently selling approximately 100 million copies annually. Even being as old as it is, much older than anything at Disney World, people still find the Bible relatable, significant, helpful and important. In Matthew 24:35, Jesus said that this world and the universe will eventually pass away, but His words would never. Similarly, Isaiah 40:8 says the Word of God will stand forever. Finally Hebrews 4:12 tells us that God's Word is living and active. There is so much to be gained from reading and studying God's Word. It has stood the test of time and always will which is what God intended.

It's safe to say that the Contemporary Resort is a Disney icon. It's unique design with the monorail going through make it something that people recognize as distinctly Disney. The Bible is the ultimate icon. People know it. They recognize it. They buy it and use it. I encourage you today to use it also, and use it often. It will never fail you. It will stand the test of time. And it will lead you to God.

"Bay Lake Tower"

As I mentioned last time, there used to be two garden wings at the Contemporary. These rooms were originally built as a quieter alternative to staying in the main A-frame. While the main building offers great views of the Magic Kingdom on the front side, or Bay Lake on the back, some guests prefer the wings because they are cheaper and more private. My wife and I found that to be true on our honeymoon and would have gladly stayed in the same room again. Unfortunately, we can't do that because it's gone. In 2006, plans were announced for a DVC resort to be built on this property. In 2009, the Bay Lake Tower opened as the first DVC resort on the monorail loop. Technically, this hotel is an extension of and belongs to the Contemporary. But once again, it's just too big and iconic to combine so let's visit the Bay Lake Tower today.

As mentioned, the Contemporary was the first monorail resort to have a DVC property. Today, all three have DVC property of some form. During construction, this resort was called Kingdom Tower. It connects to the Contemporary with a covered sky bridge giving guests there access to everything, including the monorail. Guests at Bay Lake Tower can use anything at the Contemporary including the pool. However, the opposite is not true. Contemporary guests aren't allowed to use the pool at Bay Lake which features a giant slide and zero-entry. Several of the rooms at this large tower offer stunning views of the Magic Kingdom and the nightly fireworks. Some guests can even watch the display from the comfort of their bathtub! At the very top of this resort is the Top of the World Lounge, an exclusive facility for DVC guests only which offers superb views with large windows and a balcony.

This is deluxe resort 4 of 5 that I've gotten to stay at. My wife's family took us to Disney about ten years ago and booked rooms at Bay Lake Tower. It was the ultimate treat as we had a room facing the Magic Kingdom. It was by far the nicest room and the best view I have ever experienced at Disney World. For that reason, I have mixed feelings about this resort. I definitely loved staying there, but part of me still hates that they tore down part of the iconic Contemporary to build it. Many others have felt the same way, especially when Bay Lake Tower was first built. Some called it an "eyesore" or "sadly conventional."

Some said it diminished or ruined the traditional and established view of the Contemporary. I think a lot of those criticisms have died down, and today it is more accepted. But at the time of its completion, it was considered by many to be a disappointment. It was designed by famed architect Charles Gwathmey. He was well-known in the field of architecture for many unique and creative projects. Coincidently, he died the day before Bay Lake Tower was to open to the public. It's a little sad that this resort, being one of his last designs, was so criticized. Luckily, he is still remembered for being an elite architect. Let's talk briefly today about another architect, the pinnacle designer and the ultimate creator.

Our Father in Heaven has a lot of titles, but have you ever thought of Him as an architect? The Bible makes several references to this. Read Psalms 139 today. Pay particular attention to verses 13-14 which we've discussed before. In those verses David commends God for forming us and knitting us together. David praises God saying he was "fearfully and wonderfully made." God designed our complex bodies to work and function correctly. How anyone could ever believe we were made without a creator is beyond me. God also was the architect of the Bible. 2 Timothy 3:16 says that all Scripture is breathed out by God. Men may have written the Bible, but it was composed completely of the words of God. He guided all of those men to write what He wanted to say. He designed the Bible. Finally, God is the architect of something we haven't even seen yet. Hebrews 11:10 says, "For he was looking forward to the city that has foundations, whose designer and builder is God." This verse is talking about Abraham, a man of great faith, but who often had to move and live in tents on foreign land. Consequently, he looked forward to the day he could live in Heaven, which this verse says God designed and built. God is the architect of Heaven.

I hold no ill feelings toward Bay Lake Tower. We thoroughly enjoyed our stay there. I don't mind that Disney placed it there as it provides some great rooms with remarkable views. If the architect were still alive today, hopefully he would be pleased with his design. Thankfully, the architect of our bodies, the Bible and Heaven is still very alive and well today. God designed all those things and so much more. He designed a plan for our lives as well. It's perfect too and right in front of us through His Word. Thank God today for creating and forming us. Thank Him for his plan and giving it to us through Scripture. Most of all thank Him for the perfect design of Heaven which we will all hopefully get to see one day.

"Polynesian Village Resort and Villas"

Since we're staying at the monorail resorts, we might as well hop on the monorail to get to the next one. So follow me as we walk out of Bay Lake Tower and across the sky bridge. We'll head into the Contemporary and take the escalator up to the monorail. After boarding and hearing our favorite phrase, "Please stand clear of the doors. Por favor manténgase alejado de las puertas," our first stop will be the Ticket and Transportation Center. We'll stay onboard to get to the next stop which is our next deluxe resort. This also happens to be the last of the five I've stayed at, as well as the most recent. Let's exit the monorail and walk toward those sliding glass doors. Right when they open, it happens! Do you know what I'm talking about? Ahhhh! That smell! It's one of the best in the world. We've made it! We're at the Poly!

The Polynesian Village Resort was the other resort available on opening day, October 1, 1971. The original plan of Disney was to pattern these monorail resorts after the lands of the Magic Kingdom. The Contemporary was supposed to represent Tomorrowland and this was to symbolize Adventureland. Unfortunately, that's as far as they got. The Polynesian, as you might expect, has a Southern Pacific theme. Original plans called for a 12-story high-rise hotel to be built here, but they instead opted for several buildings surrounding a central hub called the Great Ceremonial House. Inside that building, itself designed after a Tahitian royal assembly lodge, you'll find several restaurants, shops, registration, as well as abundant greenery and décor. You will also find a Kukui Nut tree on site which is the only one of its kind in the state of Florida. The tree was transplanted all the way from its native state of Hawaii. This resort used the same design and method as the Contemporary with rooms built offsite. However, the rooms here were stacked and then the frame and concrete were built around them. In 2015, twenty bungalows were built on the shoreline here as DVC properties. They offer fantastic views of the Magic Kingdom sitting literally in the water of the Seven Seas Lagoon. There are a couple of interesting historical facts about the Polynesian. A couple of weeks after opening, there was a grand opening ceremony complete with a luau on the beach. Among the many celebrities attending were Lucille Ball and Bob Hope. On December 29, 1974, John Lennon signed the documents while staying here that effectively ended the Beatles, arguably the greatest rock 'n' roll band of all time.

On our most recent Disney trip, my wife and I met her sister and our nephew at the Poly for a mini-vacation. We had visited the resort on several occasions to eat, but had never stayed there. Imagine our complete surprise when we were given a room upgrade and didn't even know it. We were expecting a garden view but walked in our room to find a park view. It was magnificent and we had a great time. During that trip, we noted several times between us what I mentioned above regarding the smell. One reason I love going to this resort is the distinct and wonderful scent you get when walking into the main building. I don't even know how to describe it, but I want it for my house. My house smells like teenage boys. It's not quite the same. I have heard many Disney diehards talk about the smell of the Poly. There's apparently a candle out there that claims to replicate it. It's just a very pleasing fragrance that makes me want to camp out in the lobby at all times. So let's use that as our spiritual message today.

Did you know life began for man through his nose? Genesis 2:7 says that God breathed life into Adam through his nostrils. The Bible even talks about God's nose. In Genesis 8, we read of Noah and his family exiting the ark after the flood. Noah built an altar to make a sacrifice offering to God, and in verse 21 it says that God smelled the pleasing aroma. It was at that point that God made a covenant never to flood the Earth again. Did you also know that we can be a pleasing smell to God as well? Jesus came to this Earth to show us how to do that. In Ephesians 5:2 it says, "And walk in love, as Christ loved us and gave himself up for us, a fragrant offering and sacrifice to God." We are to imitate Christ and give ourselves to God. In doing so, we become a living sacrifice to Him and are like the offering that smelled pleasing to God. Look at 2 Corinthians 2:15 which reads, "For we are the aroma of Christ to God among those who are being saved and among those who are perishing." Since Jesus is no longer on Earth, we have taken His place as God's children here in this world. When we give of ourselves to God, live like He wants and spread his Word, we become a pleasing aroma as Christ was.

I wish I could bottle up that Polynesian Resort smell and take it home with me. If you haven't smelled it, take a trip to the Poly just to breathe. When you get to enjoy that pleasant aroma or anything that smells good, remember our life's mission. We are to be a pleasing smell to God by becoming a living sacrifice to Him. Give God your life and let Him take control. Become a fragrant offering to God.

"Grand Floridian Resort and Spa"

On around the monorail we go to our final deluxe resort. Did we save the best for last? Maybe. I've never stayed here, so I can't give a definitive answer. I know we saved the most expensive for last, and what is considered to be Disney's flagship and most opulent resort. And I know we saved a beautiful, elegant and grand resort. I can't deny that. So maybe it is fitting that we end with Disney's Grand Floridian Resort and Spa.

Yes, that's the full name. Disney dorks like me call it the Grand Flo. That's probably not an acceptable nickname by Disney standards. The Grand Floridian opened in June 1988 as the Grand Floridian Beach Resort. The "beach" was later dropped as the theme here is a Victorian luxury hotel. There are 867 rooms on property along with 147 villas. Just stepping into this place, you get the feel of high-class, sophistication and style. Every detail at this resort is made to perfection. During daytime hours, a grand pianist performs in the main lobby while a house orchestra plays on the balcony at night. This is probably the closest resort to the Magic Kingdom, but currently you cannot walk to the park due to a waterway. However, as of this writing Disney has recently announced plans to build a bridge to fix that very problem. On site here you'll find the Fairy Tale Wedding Pavilion where many dream weddings are held. You'll also find eleven original maps of Florida dated from as early as 1775 near the entrance to Victoria and Albert's Restaurant. The Beach Boys filmed the music video for their well-known song "Kokomo" here at this resort. Standing behind the resort, you can watch the classic and timeless Electric Water Pageant that has been traveling through the Seven Seas Lagoon since just a couple of weeks after the Magic Kingdom began. You can actually see this famous boat parade from any of the resorts on the monorail or Bay Lake. Finally, you will also find a small lighthouse tribute here that was placed not too long ago to remember Lane Graves. He was the child who was tragically killed by an alligator while playing in the water behind this very resort. Disney has since put up fencing all around the Lagoon along with this touching remembrance.

We have never stayed at the Grand Floridian. As usual, we have visited many times to eat, shop, watch the fireworks and enjoy the scenery. As mentioned, this resort is considered to be the most lavish and luxurious that Disney has to offer. Some might say you'd have to be rich to stay here. I'd say not necessarily, but it certainly helps. I'm definitely not rich, but I could stay here, Of course I'd have to save up for a while because let's be honest, it takes a lot of money. Let's talk about money and how the Bible defines being rich.

There's nothing wrong with staying at the Grand Floridian. Hats off to those who do. I'm jealous...in a loving, Christian way of course. There's also nothing wrong with being rich. Some people work hard for their money, and if that means they have a lot of it, then good for them. But let's look at some important Scriptures today. Read the story found in Luke 18:18-27. In these verses, a rich man came to Jesus and asked what he must do to go to Heaven. Jesus first told him to keep the commandments which the man agreed he had done. Jesus then told him he needed to sell everything he owned. The man left distraught because he loved his wealth too much. Does this story mean it's wrong to be rich and we should sell all we have? I don't think so. I think it means we should be willing to give up material things if needed and shouldn't love our money more than God. Matthew 6:24 is pretty plain when it says we can't serve God and money. We must choose. I Timothy 6:10 says the love of money is the root of all evil. It doesn't say money is evil, but the love of it. That verse goes on to say that people that crave money tend to wander away from their faith. Matthew 6:19-20 tells us not to store up treasures on Earth but in Heaven instead. Again, it's all about our focus and priorities. As long as we are putting God and our service to Him first, we will all be rich one day. 2 Corinthians 8:9 says that even though Jesus was rich, he became poor so that we may become rich. And look at James 2:5 which says, "Listen, my beloved brothers, has not God chosen those who are poor in the world to be rich in faith and heirs of the kingdom, which he has promised to those who love him?" Jesus could have lived a life of luxury here on Earth but instead chose a life of poverty so that we could all be rich in Heaven one day. His sacrifice and death on the cross means we all have the hope of a lavish life in Heaven.

The Grand Floridian is a beautiful resort, and there's nothing wrong with paying a little extra to stay there if you can. The important thing is to make sure we don't get too caught up in money and riches. If you end up with a lot of money, great! Use it for good. Give some back to God, and serve others with it. If you don't have money, that's fine. Keep your focus on God and one day I promise you'll be richer than anyone you know. I also know that your eternal home will be much more luxurious than the Grand Floridian or any other place on Earth.

"Riviera Resort"

I told you after finishing Disneyland that I can't stop this book on an odd or weird number. We can't just have 82 devotionals. It's got to be 100. So what now? We did all the attractions at Disneyland. And now we've finished all the resorts on both coasts. So where do we go from here? I thought we might spend the next few devotionals talking about the future and what's coming. Disney is always planning, building and announcing new resorts, attractions and refurbishments. There are actually three resorts being planned at Disney World as of this writing, and there's enough information out there to use them as a devotional topic. One is nearly finished, and the other two are in varying stages of construction. Today we're going to focus on the one that's almost open for business. It's time to make a reservation at Disney's Riviera Resort.

The Riviera Resort is scheduled to open on December 16, 2019 which is the future for me, but it should already be open when you are reading this. This will be the 15th DVC property at WDW and the first entirely new DVC resort since 2011. While the Riviera will be in the same vicinity as the moderate resort, Caribbean Beach, it will not be attached to another deluxe property like many of the DVC rooms and villas. However, it does have a prime location being basically equidistant between Epcot and Hollywood Studios. There will be 300 available rooms in all different categories. Some of the rooms will be called Tower Studios and will feature flexible living space with a private balcony. They will be priced lower than the deluxe studios and will allow guests a deluxe stay at a more affordable price. There will be several restaurants on site, but the pinnacle (literally) will be Topolino's Terrace on the top floor of the building. From this elegant eatery, you will be able to see the fireworks of Epcot and Hollywood Studios. By the way, Topolino is the Italian name for Mickey Mouse! The main pool at this resort will feature stucco facades completely surrounding you, so you will feel as if you are basking in an exotic location. There will be an interactive splash area for children as well as a large wraparound slide for all ages. Staying at the Caribbean Beach fairly recently, we have watched this resort rise out of construction. It looks to be a beautiful resort with wonderful amenities and a great location.

The theme of the Riviera Resort will celebrate the grandeur of Europe. As you may or may not know, Walt Disney fell in love with Europe and used inspiration from several European locations in his films. This resort is meant to capture the spirit of Europe that Walt knew and loved since so many of his great stories, fairy tales and castles were inspired by the magic of Europe. Have you ever been to Europe? I was blessed to go to Italy with a group my junior year of high school. I then went to England, France and Belgium with my family right before I went to college. Finally, one of my favorite trips of all time was a Mediterranean cruise with my parents and great aunt about 10 years ago. During that and all my European trips, I have gotten to see some amazing sights and just a small part of the beauty that inspired Walt Disney and this resort. Did you know that Europe is a major setting of many Biblical stories? Let's talk about some of those today.

While the Bible doesn't specifically mention the word "Europe," it certainly talks about several countries included there. Most of this occurs in the New Testament. Jesus himself talks about the Roman Emperor Caesar when the people ask Him about paying taxes. Many of the stories in Europe involve Paul and his missionary journeys. He travels throughout Rome and Greece preaching to the people and remembering them with his letters in the New Testament. Paul's life story is a true inspiration. He went from being a persecutor of Christians to a baptized believer of God to a world traveler converting many souls to Christ. This is what we are all called to do. In Mark 16:15, we are commanded to go into all the world and proclaim the Gospel to everyone. In John 20:21, Jesus told the apostles, "As the Father has sent Me, so I am sending you." He's not just talking to the 12 apostles. He's talking to you and me. Now that He's gone, we are to carry on His work and message. Right before Jesus ascended into Heaven, in Acts 1:8 He said, "But you will receive power when the Holy Spirit has come upon you, and you will be my witnesses in Jerusalem and in all Judea and Samaria, and to the end of the earth."

Disney may see Europe as a place of beauty and inspiration for fairy tales and new resorts, and it certainly is. But I also see Europe as a place where mission work began with Paul and other disciples of Jesus. We are all called to go into the world and teach people about God. That doesn't mean we have to go to Europe, but I strongly admire those who do choose to be missionaries and truly go into all the world. For us, it can mean just teaching people around us. It can mean seeking out friends and family who don't know God, or even co-workers, school friends or anyone we come in contact with. Make it a goal to choose just one person you can talk to about God. Just one. You might just be the one to make an eternal difference for them.

"Disney Skyliner"

I bet you thought we were done with rides, didn't you? We covered all the rides in Disney World in book one and all the Disneyland rides in this book. But surprise! There's one more. Disney World has recently added a ride of sorts that we simply can't ignore, and it's appropriate to insert it here as it can be found at the resort we just finished. It has just opened as of this writing and actually experienced some problematic issues the very night I'm writing this. Let's hope Disney gets all the kinks worked out because I can't wait to ride it soon. So come with me on one final ride as we hop aboard the Disney's Skyliner.

Disneyland, Disney World and even Toyko Disney used to have a skybucket ride in their parks. Do you remember those? If you're a Nashvillian like myself, you may also remember our former native park, Opryland having this ride. Oh how I miss Opryland. I could so go off on a tangent right now about how our beloved Opryland was replaced by another dumb mall, but I won't torture you. Like they tortured us! Stupid mall! Anyways, back to Disney. As a sort of tribute to the sky-buckets of the past, Disney has recently added the Skyliner servicing four resorts and two parks. Opening in September 2019, there are five different stations where you can board this "highway in the sky" and have another way to be transported around WDW. You can find stations at Epcot near the boardwalk resorts and another station at Hollywood Studios. The other three stations can be found at the Riviera, Caribbean Beach and on the bridge between Pop Century and Art of Animation. The station at Caribbean Beach serves as the central hub where you can choose your path. From there, you will find six miles of cable taking you in all different directions. There are 300 possible gondolas each holding a maximum of ten guests. Each gondola features a different Disney character that serve as a decoration, but also as a sun shield. The gondolas are not air-conditioned, a fact that worried some potential riders, so the characters placed also block the hot Florida sun. There is also ventilation in each gondola so that air can move through as it travels. The complex loading system allows for a secondary zone so that the gondola can be halted for disabled guests. Once they are properly loaded, the gondola can then be placed back in motion in the proper rotation.

There used to be skyway rides at three different parks. The Disneyland, Tokyo Disney and Disney World versions all closed in 1994, 1998, and 1999 respectively. All three served as a shortcut between Tomorrowland and Fantasyland and provided birds-eye views of the parks. We discussed how the Disneyland version traveled through the mountain on the Matterhorn ride. I wish they were still in operation. However, maintenance and worn out parts made it difficult to keep them open. Some have been skeptical on the necessity of this new version, but I am excited to try it and see Disney from a new viewpoint. We are staying at the Caribbean Beach on our next trip, and so I hope we can use them to get to and from the parks. Once again, they serve as a shortcut to avoid bus lines and crowds at other transportation sites. This leads me to our thought for today as we talk about taking shortcuts in our spiritual life.

We've talked at length about the importance of our relationship with God. We've discussed our purpose in life...to get to Heaven and bring as many with us on our journey. We've seen how the only way to get there is through Jesus. He is the gate and door to Heaven. Following Him and living as He did is the only way we'll get there. (John 14:6) And this fact can't be stated enough...there are no shortcuts! Read the story in Acts 19:1-20. Starting in verse 11 we read that God was doing many miracles through the hands of Paul. At one place, there were seven men who claimed to be exorcists, casting out demons from various individuals. When they saw Paul and the fact that he was doing miracles in God's name, they tried the same. They began casting our demons using God's name, but it backfired on them and got them into trouble. They were trying a shortcut, using God without really knowing Him. They weren't successful because they didn't take the proper steps to God. The same will happen to us if we try to get to Heaven the wrong way. Proverbs 19:2 says, "Desire without knowledge is not good, and whoever makes haste with his feet misses his way." A couple of chapters later in Proverbs 21:5, we read, "The plans of the diligent lead surely to abundance, but everyone who is hasty comes only to poverty." If we are too hasty and try a shortcut, thinking we can make our spiritual walk without the knowledge of God, it won't work. A proper relationship with God takes time, planning, dedication and most importantly, a strong relationship with Jesus.

As mentioned, while writing this there was an incident on the new Skyliner where some of the gondolas got stuck and passengers were briefly trapped. It looks like nobody was injured, and I'm sure Disney will get the issues resolved. It is said to be quick-loading, so I'm looking forward to this alternative and shortcut around Disney. But keep in mind there are no shortcuts on our journey to Heaven. We must take the proper steps laid out in Scripture, staying on the narrow path, with Jesus as our focus.

"Star Wars: Galactic Starcruiser"

That little Skyliner ride detour was certainly fun and relaxing, but now it's time to get back to the resorts. We still have a couple of them that have been announced and are nowhere near completion as of this writing. I'm not sure which of these two will end up opening first as they have both basically just cleared the land are in the very first stages of construction. So we'll just begin in a galaxy far, far away. Know what I mean? The details on this resort are a bit sketchy, and Disney has purposely not revealed too much, but from what I've heard so far, this experience (and I stress that word) is going to be unbelievable. So let's do something I hope and pray I can do for real one day... let's prepare to take flight at Star Wars: Galactic Starcruiser.

Yes, that is the name of the resort that is coming to an area just outside of Hollywood Studios. As you are well aware I'm sure, Disney recently opened Star Wars: Galaxy's Edge which is the new section of Hollywood Studios that allows you to become immersed in the Star Wars experience. This resort will do the same, but on a much greater level. Again, the details have been few and will most likely change or be tweaked along the way, but the following is what has been reported. According to renderings, the new hotel will be shaped like a Star Wars starship. Disney will offer a two-night itinerary where guests will arrive and depart together, similar to a Disney cruise. Upon "boarding" the resort, you will enter a lobby decorated in the style of a spaceship interior and be shown your "cabin" which holds up to four people. Once everyone is on board, you will then experience your ship "taking off" with simulated views out the windows, sounds and effects. The ship you are on will be called the "Halcyon" and every window, including those in your cabin, will have a view of the galaxy outside. The views will change throughout your stay as the Halcyon travels from place to place. Other planned features include Star Wars creatures and droids acting as hotel staff, lightsaber training and duels, the chance to explore and pilot the spacecraft, secret missions personalized toward each guest and the ability to interact with other hotel features. It will pretty much seem like a large-scale, interactive theme park attraction within your resort. Guests will also have direct access to Galaxy's Edge in Hollywood Studios, although it's uncertain if it will be a direct entrance to the park or some sort of galactic travel system.

Bob Chapek, the Disney chairman of parks, experiences and products was quoted as saying that Star Wars: Galactic Starcruiser will be a "100% immersive experience that will culminate in a unique journey for every person who visits." Every description, rendering and projection that has been announced make this resort look completely interactive. This will not be just booking a stay at a resort. This will be reserving your place in a completely enveloping, mesmerizing and captivating experience. You will actually feel as though you are on a spacecraft cruising through the galaxy in some futuristic, sci-fi event. In short, it will seem totally and entirely real..."100% immersive" as Bob Chapek said. So here's my question to consider today...what if it was real?

I don't know if you will ever get to experience space travel. Some of you kiddos reading this might live to see the reality of human space flight. I don't expect to experience it myself. But I know one thing...I do plan to travel to another world one day. I am planning to experience a 100% immersive flight" to another place, but mine will be completely real. Read the end of I Corinthians 15. Starting in verse 50, we read what will happen when this Earth ends. It says that those of us in Christ will be changed. It says we will be immortal, and the dead shall rise. Philippians 3:20-21 says that our citizenship is in Heaven and God will transform our bodies to be like His. Also take time to read Revelation 21 today which describes what Heaven will look like. In short, it will be glorious, magnificent and breath-taking. I promise you Heaven is real, and it will be like nothing we've ever experienced or even can imagine. Don't you want to see that? Don't you want to experience that?

I Corinthians 2:9 says, "What no eye has seen, nor ear heard, nor the heart of man imagined, what God has prepared for those who love him." We can't even imagine what God has in store for those who follow and love Him. But I can tell you that it won't be done with special effects and window projections. It will be real. I can tell you that we won't just have costumes and props. Our bodies will be transformed and changed. I can tell you that it won't just be a two day experience. It will be forever. I want a 100% immersive forever Heaven experience. Nothing else in my life really matters. I'm working as hard as I can to get there. I have to get there. I will get there. Please get there with me. Let's have a total, interactive, Heaven experience together!

"Reflections—A Disney Lakeside Lodge"

Today we move on to the final property currently being built at Walt Disney World. That's not to say that something else won't pop up before this book even gets published. You know the saying...if Disney builds it, they will come. Ok, so maybe that was the *Field of Dreams* movie, but it certainly applies to Disney too. The demand continues to be there, so Disney continues to build. This final DVC property has barely begun. As of this writing, the land has been cleared and permits have been filed, but there's not a whole lot of information out there. But we'll at least discuss what we do know because once again, it looks to be a beautiful resort. Do we really expect anything different from Disney? This one is going to be called Reflections—A Disney Lakeside Lodge.

Set to open in 2022, Reflections, to shorten the name a bit, will be the 16th DVC resort on Disney World property. It is being constructed on Bay Lake between Wilderness Lodge and the Fort Wilderness Campground. It has been announced that the resort will feature 900 rooms and be a celebration of Walt Disney's lifelong love and respect for nature. Many of the renderings released appear to highlight nature as well with outdoor elements shown inside, as well as a possible large Pocahontas statue in the lobby. Just recently it was announced that the resort will include a table service restaurant dedicated to Disney's *Princess and the Frog*. Just what exactly it will entail is still being kept secret, but that news brought joy to many, as that film hasn't had a whole lot of representation in the parks. Reflections is being built on the former site of Disney's first water park. River Country was a water park on the shores of Bay Lake that operated from 1976 until 2001. For nearly two decades after that, it became a sort of ghost town as Disney chose not to tear it down but simply leave it abandoned. They put a fence around it, but apparently it wasn't too difficult to sneak in. You can probably still find YouTube videos of people exploring this deserted water park. Even ten or so years after closure there was still music playing and the water fountains still worked. Creepy! But you won't find that anymore. The water park was finally torn down when this new lodge began construction not too long ago.

I find the name of this new resort to be interesting. "Reflections" was a song from the Disney film *Mulan* during which Mulan looked at herself in the water to try and see who she really was. Reflection was also a big part of *The Lion King* when Rafiki wanted Simba to look at himself in the water and be honest with who he was. My guess is that the name here is simply meant to call to mind a beautiful reflection on the waters of Bay Lake. This may sound strange, but I have an activity for you today. That's right...we're getting interactive on these devotionals now. If you have the time or opportunity, I want you to pause this reading and go look at yourself in a mirror. Don't use your phone...that's cheating. Use an actual mirror. Go on! I'll wait. Now, what did you see? Did you like what you saw? My guess is that you focused on your outer appearance, mainly how your face looks, right? What I really want to know is what kind of person did you see staring back at you? Did you like the kind of person you saw? Did what you saw reflect inner beauty? Did what you saw reflect God?

As you probably know, Genesis 1:27 says that God made all of us in His own image. You were created to reflect God. So, do you? Do others see God in you? Do they see the hands and feet of Jesus in your hands and feet? Do they see evidence of a servant heart like He had? If the answer is no, the good news is that you can start right now to change that. Galatians 6:3-4 reads, "For if anyone thinks he is something, when he is nothing, he deceives himself. But let each one test his own work, and then his reason to boast will be in himself alone and not in his neighbor." One of our jobs as Christians is to self-reflect daily. We must constantly test and evaluate ourselves to make sure we are reflecting the image of God to others. 2 Corinthians 13:5 also tells us to test and examine ourselves to see if we are in the faith. I Corinthians 11:28 tells us to examine ourselves before we take communion with God. While we are to strive for perfection like Jesus, we can never get there. There's always something we can change or make better.

Reflections—A Disney Lakeside Lodge will be beautiful I'm sure. I have no doubt that the reflection it brings into Bay Lake will be a picturesque scene that will draw in crowds for years to come. Let me encourage you to take time daily to reflect on yourself. Look in a mirror every day. Don't worry so much about the outward appearance. Focus on what reflects to others from inside you. Do people really see God in you? Examine yourself. Test yourself. Change yourself if needed. Reflect God to others so they will desire to do the same.

"Vero Beach Resort"

Well, we're back to that ever popular question...where do we go now? We've exhausted all Disney resorts, both current and future. So are there any others at Disneyland or Disney World? No, I don't think so. Not for now anyways. We could go international, but that opens up a huge can of worms with several new parks, resorts and attractions. I'm not ready for that book (or books) yet! However, did you know there are three more Disney resorts within the United States that aren't at a Disney park? Can you name them? I know one is in the title just above, you cheater, but do you know the other two without looking ahead? I thought we'd talk these three and relate a lesson from each. We'll go in order of when they were built, so today we're starting with a stay at Disney's Vero Beach Resort.

Vero Beach is a city in Florida on the Atlantic Ocean about midway down the state, almost in line with Orlando. It was settled in the late 1800's and incorporated around 1920. Disney decided this was the location to open their first ever stand-alone DVC resort outside of Orlando or Anaheim. It opened in October of 1995 and includes rooms with ocean and garden views. There are studios available as well as one and two bedroom villas. There are also some three bedroom free-standing ocean view cottages. The resort includes a Mickey-shaped pool, one of only two on Disney property. The other is at the Shades of Green resort. The pool here also has a large slide called Pirates Plunge and is surrounded by a nine-hole Peter Pan themed miniature golf course. You will also find a community hall complete with board games, Ping-Pong and crafts as well as a fitness center, massage studio and rental shop. One of the highlights of this resort are the turtle nesting grounds nearby. Hatching season typically runs August through October and guests here are invited to participate. There are opportunities to learn and participate in the conservation and tracking of these turtles, and Disney contributes to the efforts as well.

This resort ranks very high on trip planning websites. Many of the positive comments reflect the fact that one can get the Disney benefits and attention to detail without the crowds, lines and busyness of the parks. I've never been to this resort, but it is said to be very peaceful and relaxing with excellent service, amenities and activities available. For those reasons, this resort draws in a large part of the tourists that visit the city of Vero Beach. It's safe to say that without Disney, Vero Beach as a city would not have the volume of tourism and economy that they enjoy. In short, Disney brings people in. Thinking along those lines, I want to encourage you to be like Disney. We are going to focus today on being more welcoming to those seeking to know God.

I hope you have a church family. If not, I strongly encourage you to attend regularly so you can have one. I can't stress enough the benefits and blessing of a church family around you, especially in difficult times. If you do have a church, think about today how welcoming you are to others while there, especially to visitors. Do you actively seek out visitors? Do you make an effort to speak to those you don't know, whether they are visiting or not? What about when you're not at church? Do you invite others to attend your church? There are many verses we find in Scripture talking about being welcoming to others or showing hospitality. Consider these:

"Contribute to the needs of the saints and seek to show hospitality." (Romans 12:13)

"Therefore welcome one another as Christ has welcomed you, for the glory of God." (Romans 15:7)

"Show hospitality to one another without grumbling." (I Peter 4:9)

"Do not neglect to show hospitality to strangers, for thereby some have entertained angels unawares."

That one is from Hebrews 13:2 and makes you wonder. Maybe God disguises angels as visitors to test us in showing hospitality and friendliness to others. Even Jesus himself discussed this when in Matthew 25, He is talking to the people about Judgment Day. In verses 35-36, he talks about some of the things we may be asked about, including feeding the hungry, clothing the poor, visiting the sick and welcoming strangers. It may be a little out of our comfort zone, but welcoming those who are new, unfamiliar, lost or in need is one of God's expectations of us as Christians.

You can't deny that Disney does an excellent job of bringing people in. Whether it's the parks, the restaurants, the shops or even a random, stand-alone resort in Vero Beach, people come because they love Disney. We can take an example from that and be the Disney to those seeking God. Unless you were brought up in the church, you were a visitor once too. Maybe you are currently a visitor seeking a church home. Isn't it nice and so much easier when others are kind and welcoming to you? Set as a goal and make the effort to be extra hospitable and welcoming to others, especially at church or anywhere you can find a soul seeking God.

"Hilton Head Island Resort"

I've been looking forward to this particular devotional since I began planning this book. This location is special to me, and it has nothing to do with the Disney resort because I've never stayed there. Oh, I've visited, swam in the resort pool and used their beach house, but I've never reserved a room myself. The reason this entry is so special is because this Disney resort is found in one of my favorite places in the world. My family grew up vacationing there. We have many friends that travel there. My wife, sons and I have been there several times as well. This is our place...second to Disney of course. Therefore, I'm very excited to check in to our room today at Disney's Hilton Head Island Resort.

Hilton Head is a very special island in southern South Carolina. It is 20 miles northeast of Savannah, Georgia, itself a beautiful town. Hilton Head is also the location of Disney's 2nd stand-alone DVC resort, opening in March of 1996. The resort can be found on a smaller 15 acre island in the Shelter Cove harbor area of Hilton Head. The resort itself is not on the Atlantic Ocean side of the island and therefore not on a beach. However, Disney does own a beach house on the ocean complete with its own pool, snack bar and shaded parking, that is approximately a mile or so away, with transportation offered. The resort itself has beautiful views of the harbor and is very family friendly with multiple hammocks and grills on site. You will also find many activities for children there including nature programs, campfires, magic shows, crabbing, pool games, biking, kayaking, tennis and much more.

My family has been using Hilton Head as our vacation spot for years. I'm actually very anxious to go back as it's now been a while since I've made it there, due to our Disney addiction. ☺ On one family trip a few years ago, my wife's sister and family were staying at Disney's Hilton Head Resort while we were staying across the street. So we visited them one day, toured their room and also took advantage of the pool for a few hours. It was, as expected a beautiful resort, and I'd love to stay there. If you've never been to Hilton Head, it is a wonderful vacation destination. The island is so well managed, exceedingly clean and environmentally friendly. Certain standards and laws make it a very attractive and appealing place. For example, all business signs have height limits and must be wooden in appearance. There are no neon lights or cheap tourist attractions allowed. The island features 12 miles of beachfront on the Atlantic Ocean with many different resorts and private beach houses available. The island thrives on tourists receiving millions into the local economy annually.

As mentioned, my family grew up going to Hilton Head every year, and there are several home videos at my parents' house to prove it. There is one in particular I want to mention. This video involves my older sister, Allison and my younger sister, Abigail. I'll pause here to give them both a shout out, which Allison in particular will be thrilled about. She's been begging me for a shout out or dedication page for months. So, hey Allison! Here you go! Enjoy your moment! Ok, it's done. Anyways, in this particular video, Allison was around 12 trying to teach 2 year old Abigail to jump into the pool. After failing to coax her to jump, Allison lifted her down into the water only to lose her balance and fall right on top of her. Typical Allison. Abigail came up crying for a moment, but ended up being fine. Allison looked scared to death.

That video made us laugh for years and still does today as I remember. But it also reminds me of some Bible verses. I'm sure Allison didn't mean to fall on her, but maybe she wasn't as qualified to teach Abigail to jump in as she thought. Maybe Abigail needed a better trained instructor. In a similar way, we need to be very careful who we choose to teach and instruct us when it comes to God's Word. In Matthew 7:15, Jesus warns of false teachers who may appear in sheep's clothing only to be ravenous wolves. In 2 Corinthians 11:13-15, Paul says even Satan disguises himself as an angel to deceive us. Finally, In 2 Timothy 4:3-4, Paul warns again saying, "For the time is coming when people will not endure sound teaching, but having itching ears they will accumulate for themselves teachers to suit their own passions, and will turn away from listening to the truth and wander off into myths." Folks, I think that time is now. There is so much false teaching in the world today which is made to look right and appealing, but obviously goes against the Bible and God's desires. We must be very careful.

Hilton Head Island is one of my favorite places in the world. It is fantastic, as is the Disney resort there. Disney did well to choose this popular tourist spot. I have many great memories growing up there with family, as well as recent trips with my wife and sons. Today I remember my sisters and their little mishap at the Hilton Head pool. Watch out for false teachers who may appear knowledgeable, but know nothing about what God truly wants for His people to know and learn. Make sure you are evaluating and testing anyone who is teaching you Godly lessons to make sure they are following the Bible in everything they say. Otherwise, you will eventually be deceived and led in the wrong direction.

"Aulani"

Ok, we're going to have to travel a little ways for the next resort, because it's over 4700 miles away! Before we depart, make sure to pack your grass skirts, flowered shirt and a ukulele, because today we're headin' to Hawaii. Yes, ladies and gentlemen, our final resort in this book is found on the island of Oahu in the great state of Hawaii. When Disney goes big, they go huge, and I think we saved the ultimate resort for last. Are you ready? I am! I'm always ready for this one. Let's go check into Aulani!

Disney's Aulani is a 16 story beachside resort sitting on 21 acres of land that opened in August of 2011. It contains 359 hotel rooms, 460 time share villas and was designed by famed Disney Imagineer Joe Rohde, who also designed Animal Kingdom. When building and creating this resort, Disney wanted it to be as authentically Hawaiian as possible. Therefore, they created an advisory council of Hawaiian elders to ensure that this happens. Apparently the motto is "Big H, Little D," which means big emphasis on Hawaiian traditions with just a little Disney fairy dust sprinkled throughout. Aulani features one of the largest private collections of contemporary Hawaiian art in the world. Those who stay here can enjoy the Rainbow Reef which is the only private snorkeling lagoon on the island of Oahu with more than 1300 brightly colored fish. There is also a water playground, several pools, water slides, a lazy river and a fun play area known as the Menehune bridge. Speaking of the Menehunes, which are the traditional "little people" tribe of Hawaii, there are over 300 Menehune statues hidden around the resort. Many of them are hidden low to the ground so that kids will have an easier time finding them. Sitting by the pool at Aulani, you might just enjoy a visit from one of many Disney characters such as Mickey, Minnie, Donald, Pluto, Moana and of course Lilo and Stitch. There are character meals available, as well as traditional luaus for guests to enjoy.

The word "Aulani" is a Hawaiian word that is loosely translated as "the place that speaks for the great ones" or "with deep messages." Basically it means "a message from the chief," and if you're delivering a message from the chief, you know how important that message is. That reminds me of a Bible story. Take the time to read I Samuel 3 today. This is the story of Samuel as a young boy. One night he is lying down alone when he hears a voice call out his name. Samuel replies, "Here I am" and runs to his mentor, Eli, thinking he's the one calling out. This happens three times before Eli finally figures out that God is the one calling Samuel. Finally, when God calls the fourth time, Samuel says, "Speak, for your servant hears." God then proceeds to tell Samuel what he has in store for him. Samuel becomes a great prophet of God, and the Lord is with him throughout his life.

In a sense, Samuel was called by God and became Aulani, a messenger for the chief. His willingness, even as a young boy, to do whatever God called him to do, is to be admired and an example to us all. We need to all be willing to answer when God calls on us. Like Samuel, we should be ready to reply, "Speak, for your servant hears." We are called to be the messengers for our chief, which is our Holy Father in Heaven. 2 Corinthians 5:20 says, "Therefore, we are ambassadors for Christ, God making his appeal through us." It is up to us to deliver whatever message God needs us to communicate to others. If we take the time and effort to study God's Word and talk to others about Him, He can speak through us and get His message through to those who need it.

It is definitely on my bucket list to one day stay at Aulani. My family is trying very hard to make that happen. It would be very special and an absolute dream come true. I went to Hawaii once with my family at age 10, but I really want to go back with my wife and sons and do it Disney-style at Aulani. Don't forget that Aulani means a messenger for the chief. We are called to be God's messengers throughout our lives. Seek to know what God wants to say to others and communicate that. In Isaiah 6:8, it says, "And I heard the voice of the Lord saying, 'Whom shall I send, and who will go for us?' Then I said, 'Here I am! Send me.'" Next time you talk to God, tell Him that too. Be willing to go where God wants you to go. Be willing to say what God wants you to say. Be willing to do what God wants you to do. Wherever, whenever and whatever God needs of us, we should be willing to boldly and proudly proclaim, "Here I am! Send me!"

"Disney Magic"

Here we go again with that same ol' question...where do we go now? We've done all the attractions. We've done all the resorts, old, new, on property and off. What now? I thought we'd try a different area of Disney altogether. A few devotionals back, I mentioned that my favorite way to travel is cruising. I have taken four of them, two of which have been Disney cruises. All four have been wonderful, but there is something special about a Disney cruise. If you've taken one, you know what I mean. Yes, they are a little more expensive than regular cruises (ok, maybe a lot more), but it's worth it in my opinion, especially if you are a Disney fanatic like this guy. So for the next few devotionals, I thought we'd look at Disney's fleet of cruise ships. There are four of them with three more apparently on the way. We'll begin today with the very first Disney ship that took its maiden voyage in July of 1998. When you board a Disney cruise ship, your family is actually announced over the P.A. system as you enter the grand atrium lobby, just one of the many special touches. So Ahoy, mateys! It's my honor to welcome (insert your family's name here) aboard the Disney Magic!

When you enter the Magic, you'll see a statue of Mickey waiting for you. Each ship has a different character statue in the main lobby, as well as a different godmother and character on the rear of the ship. The Magic has Patricia Disney as its godmother, the wife of Walt's nephew, Roy E. Disney. On the back of this ship, you'll find Goofy painting the logo. The Magic has 11 decks and 875 staterooms. It can accommodate around 2700 passengers and has around 950 crew members. In the early years, the Magic took voyages around the Caribbean and all around the east coast. In 2005, however, the ship was sent to the west coast to celebrate Disneyland's 50th birthday and had some itineraries out there. In 2007, the Magic took her first international voyage across the Atlantic to the Mediterranean region and began offering summer trips there. Each of Disney's four current ships were built in Italy. The Magic was actually built in two halves one hundred miles apart and then perfectly joined and welded together. The ship measures 964 feet in length which is longer than Main Street at the Magic Kingdom. The Magic also features the only "Aquadunk" water slide, which is 3 stories tall and has you stand and wait for a trap door to fall out beneath you. You then travel 212 feet swirling out over the ocean before landing in a pool on the top deck.

Each of the four Disney ships are similar in appearance, sharing the same basic color scheme and look. However, upon examination and exploration, you'll find that each has its own unique traits and characteristics. They have different itineraries, shows offered, entertainment options and just personalities in general. Each also has a different name of course, and it's fitting that Magic was chosen for the first Disney ship. Magic is probably the adjective most often used to describe a Disney vacation. There's just something very unique and special about the way Disney does things, that it often appears to be magical. Disney is able to make things move that you don't expect to move. They are able to make wishes and dreams come true that nobody ever thought possible. They are able to surprise you many times during your stay whether at a park, a resort or even on a cruise ship. In a word, Disney is magical. Now, I think we all know deep down that there isn't any real magic going on. If you didn't know, sorry to be a spoiler. Disney isn't magic. They are just very creative and clever in the way they do things, making it appear as magic. There is an individual that also does that in our lives, but he doesn't mean it for good and happiness. He is purely evil in his intent to appear magical.

When we first meet the devil in Genesis 3:1, it says that he was more crafty than any other beast. Ephesians 6:11 warns us to put on the full armor of God so we can stand up against the schemes of the devil. In I Peter 5:8, we are told to be sober and watchful because the devil prowls around like a lion, seeking someone to devour. In just those three verses alone, we see that Satan is crafty. We see that he schemes against us. And we see that he stalks us quietly, lurking in the shadows, waiting for a time to pounce when we are most vulnerable. Let's be honest here... Satan is smart. Satan is clever. Satan is sneaky. And in a sense, Satan is magical. He is able to make evil things look good. He is able to tempt us into doing things we never meant to do. He makes sin look fun. That's what magic is...creating the unexpected. It is making something look different than what it appears to be. It's tricks. It's deceptions. It's scams. And it's a trap when it comes to Satan! Don't fall for it!

If you get to travel the Disney Magic or any of their ships, you will be shown things that you can probably only chalk up to magic. The shows are incredible. The entertainment is brilliant. The personal touches are magnificent. It will all appear magical, and that kind of magic is great. But keep in mind that Satan also uses magic against us making bad things appear good. Don't fall into his traps, because it's often hard to escape. Be ready for his deceptive magic!

"Disney Wonder"

I Wonder which ship we'll go to next. That was a hint...you see because I said "wonder," and because it was capitalized. Trying to make it punny here, people! Guess I'll keep trying. For today, we're going to go on to Disney 2nd ship, which is nearly identical at first glance to the Magic. But as I mentioned last time, there are always many subtle and some obvious differences. So get your passport ready, because today we are setting sail on the Disney Wonder!

This ship had its maiden voyage in August of 1999. It can hold up to 2400 passengers but is nearly the same size as the Magic. The statue inside the grand lobby is *The Little Mermaid's* Ariel, the godmother is Tinkerbell, and on the back of the ship you'll find Donald Duck suspended while painting. His nephew, Huey, is there too about to cut Donald's rope. The Wonder's maiden voyage was to the Bahamas but over time, it has sailed a variety of itineraries including Alaska, Hawaii, the Mexican Riviera and the Panama Canal. The Wonder and all the Disney ships are marked by their yellow lifeboats instead of the traditional regulation orange. Disney had to get special permission from the U.S. Coast Guard to use that color in keeping with the theme of the ship. All four ships also claim four different captains: Captain Mickey, Captain Hook, Captain Jack Sparrow and the actual human captain of course. This ship can make 500,000 gallons of fresh water from seawater every day. This is also the only one of the four ships that doesn't include a major ride or slide, although there is a small one for kids. It does, however, currently feature the *Frozen* show that we talked about a while back. Finally, this was the first Disney ship to have an onboard incident when a 24-year-old cast member disappeared in March of 2011. It is assumed that she fell or jumped overboard.

Once again Disney has picked an intriguing name for their ship. Wonder can mean many things. You are certainly filled with wonder onboard a Disney ship which is probably the intention of the name. However, wonder can also be used to describe our curiosity, imagination and interest. Therefore, I suppose the name of this ship could also be directed at wondering what adventures you'll have while on board. Or wondering how much fun you'll have and what all you will get to do. Or wondering if you can afford another Disney cruise even though you just got back. I'm sure Disney is hoping your wonder and curiosity will lead you to book an adventure with them, especially if it's your first. Our lives are often filled with wonder as we are naturally curious creatures. We like to know the answers to questions, how things work and why they sometimes don't. Speaking from a spiritual sense, we often wonder about life, what's our purpose and why God does certain things. I don't know about you, but I have a lot of questions for God that I'm hoping to ask one day. You may as well. But praise God today because there is one thing we don't have to wonder about, and that's our eternal future.

I remember sitting in a Bible class in college when our professor asked, "How many of you know you are going to Heaven?" He then had us raise our hands for three possible answers: yes, no or unsure. At that point, my hand went up for unsure. A part of me wanted to raise my hand for yes, but I didn't want to seem boastful or arrogant. Shame on my college self! If we have followed God and the steps for salvation laid out in his Word, the answer is of course yes! The Bible makes it clear that we can then know we are saved. We don't have to wonder. 2 Corinthians 1:22 says that God has put His seal on us and given us His Spirit in our hearts as a guarantee. A guarantee! A few chapters later in 2 Corinthians 5:1-5, it talks about Heaven and then says God has given us the Spirit as a guarantee of our home there. A guarantee! Ephesians 1:13-14 says that we were sealed with the promised Holy Spirit who is the guarantee of our eternal inheritance. The guarantee! And in I John 5:13, John says, "I write these things to you who believe in the name of the Son of God, that you may know that you have eternal life." That we may know! Do you need any more evidence?

The Disney ship Wonder may fill you with just that. You may be in complete awe, astonishment and wonder just stepping foot into the lobby. Or you may see friends' vacation photos on a Disney cruise and wonder if you can do the same. Disney is hoping you wonder yourself right into their next cruise destination. You also may wonder many things about God, the Bible and your spiritual life. But thank God today that you don't have to wonder about your eternity and salvation. If you are living for God, have followed His Word and have His Spirit living inside, then you have the guarantee. You can know where you are going when this short life ends. Praise God that we don't have to wonder! Praise God that we can know! Praise God for the guarantee!

"Disney Dream"

Let's skip ahead ten years. Actually, it was a little more than ten years before Disney cruise ships 3 and 4 were born. For the first decade of this century, Disney only operated the two. Eventually the word got out, however, and Disney cruising was quickly becoming a popular way to travel. So Disney decided to double the fleet and add two more ships. Today we board the third ship which took its maiden voyage in January of 2011. This one is very special to me because both of my Disney cruises have taken place aboard the ship we're discussing today. So listen carefully! Hear that familiar toot of the horn? That's the first 7 notes of "When You Wish Upon a Star." That means it's time to board the Disney Dream.

Actually all four ships use that tune as their main whistle, but the horn is capable of several other Disney classics like "It's a Small World," "Be Our Guest," "A Pirates' Life for Me," and "A Dream is a Wish Your Heart Makes," among a few others. The Disney Dream has almost always been a Caribbean/Bahaman cruise line offering 3, 4, and 5 night cruises in that area. Ships 3 and 4 were built 40% larger than the first two which means the Disney Dream has 14 decks, 1250 staterooms and can hold a maximum of 4000 passengers. It also of course has a bigger crew with over 1450 on board. The Dream's lobby statue is my favorite character, Donald Duck (another reason I love the Dream) dressed in his admiral costume, and you'll find Sorcerer Mickey on the rear of the ship. This ship's godmother is Grammy and Oscar winner, Jennifer Hudson who actually worked on the Disney Wonder before her career skyrocketed. The Dream was the first ship to have a water coaster ride which was copied on ship 4 as well. It is called the AquaDuck and allows guests to board an inflatable raft for an enclosed tube ride around the top deck. The ride is raised off the ground which allows the top deck to be multi-purposed. Finally, the Dream has been involved in a couple of "traffic" incidents. In January of 2012, it was involved in a near-miss with a Royal Caribbean ship at Port Canaveral. In September of 2017, the stern of the Dream was slightly damaged after a collision with the dock in Nassau, Bahamas. Who's steering this thing, for crying out loud?

Our first trip on the Dream took place in 2012. We enjoyed it so much that we did the exact same cruise again in 2018. On the second trip, we splurged and got a stateroom with an expanded veranda. When I make it to Heaven, I would not be all surprised if after passing through the Pearly Gates, Saint Peter himself points me to that very stateroom for an eternal stay. Oh yeah, it was that good! I was actually sad when I first saw it because I knew it was going to end in a few days. Is that weird? Yeah, it is. There's something wrong with me. But anyways, the Dream is...well...a dream! I'm sure all four ships are, and we probably should've branched out a little and tried a different one. But we had such a good first experience on the Dream so why mess with success? So let's talk about dreams today. Can you think of stories in the Bible that include dreams? I bet you can.

There are several dream stories in the Bible, but I want to focus on two Josephs, one from each Testament. Read Genesis 40 and Matthew 2:13-23 as a reminder of these stories. In the first one, Joseph has been thrown into prison after being sold by his brothers and falsely accused by Potiphar. He is at about the lowest point one could be. But then God sends him a gift, the ability to interpret dreams. He interprets a butler and baker's dream there in prison which eventually leads to his freedom and rise to power. In the second story, Joseph, the earthly father of Jesus, has a dream warning him to take Jesus and flee to Egypt. At that time, King Herod was about to go on a killing rampage, and God wanted Jesus to be kept safe. In both of these stories, God used dreams to provide for his children. He used dreams in Genesis to provide Joseph with a unique ability, eventually leading to his power. He used a dream in Matthew to provide Joseph a warning and save Jesus which would lead to the salvation of us all. The point is 3 P's... God always provides. God always protects. And nothing can stop God's plan. Philippians 4:19 says that God will supply all our needs. Psalms 34:10 says that those who seek God lack nothing. 2 Thessalonians 3:3 says that God will guard us against the evil one. He protects. He provides. His plan is perfect.

It was a dream to be on the Dream, and I dream of another dream cruise on the Dream. How about that sentence? I'll take any Disney ship though, and one day I'll be back. Today, however, I'm thinking about Biblical dreams and how those two Bible stories demonstrate how God provides and protects. God has a plan for our lives, and it will be done. It will be on His timetable, so be patient with Him and accept His plan for your life. In the meantime, never forget that He's there to provide for your needs and if you need protection. One final P...Prayer. Talk to God often and ask Him to provide. Ask Him to protect. And tell Him you accept His plan for your life.

"Disney Fantasy"

Today we embark on our final Disney cruise as we board the fourth and final ship that Disney owns and operates. However, remember there are three more ships coming, so there will plenty of opportunities in the future to go sailing Disney-style. Today we'll be having our nautical adventure on the Dream's sister ship. They are nearly identical and were released around the same time. This one had its first voyage in March of 2012. So follow me as we walk through those giant Mickey ears (yes, you get to do that), across the gang-plank and onto the Disney Fantasy.

Upon entering the Fantasy, you'll see a statue of Minnie Mouse in her fancy dress. You'll see a giant Dumbo and his pal Timothy Mouse on the back of this ship. There are a few celebrities associated with the Fantasy. Mariah Carey serves as godmother, and when it had its grand opening ceremony, Neil Patrick Harris hosted and Jerry Seinfeld performed. Like the Dream, the Fantasy has 14 decks with a 4000 passenger maximum. It cost 900 million dollars and took 747 days to build. In addition to the AquaDuck ride, you'll also find the AquaLab which is unique to the Fantasy. It is a water play area that offers all kinds of interactive sprayers and water cannons. This ship also features "magical portholes" for those with interior staterooms. These "portholes" are monitors that broadcast real-time views of the outside world via cameras placed on the exterior of the ship. The magical part is getting to see Dumbo, Mr. Potato Head, Peter Pan or another Disney character fly by.

Have you ever noticed that Disney uses the word "fantasy" a lot? Besides this ship, they have Fantasyland, a Festival of Fantasy Parade, and we've already talked about the Fantasy Faire experience at Disneyland. Just like magic, wonder and dream, here is yet another ship name which also happens to be what Disney provides when you arrive on property. Have you ever heard someone start a speech with the cliché, "Webster defines...?" That's a pet peeve of mine just because it's so old-fashioned. Do kids these days even know who Webster is? Sorry...brief tangent. But I'm going to break my own rule here, because Webster defines "fantasy" as creating unrealistic or improbable mental images in response to psychological need. Say what? Basically, that means a fantasy is something make-believe, something made up, or something fake that is created for enjoyment. Disney does fantasy well, but unfortunately when it comes to spiritual things, there are a lot of people that also think God and the Bible are nothing but fantasies.

Think about the Bible for a second and all the incredible people and fascinating stories it contains. At face value, I can kind of understand why to some it may all seem like fantasy. God creating the world in 6 days? Forming man from dust? A flood that covers the Earth? God talking from a burning bush? Moses parting the Red Sea in half? Elijah riding a fiery chariot into Heaven? Three men thrown into a furnace survive? A man spends the night with hungry lions and lives? A man is swallowed by a giant fish and doesn't die? Oh, and best of all...God's own son is born to a virgin girl? He walks on water? He multiplies food? He heals people? He calms storms? And the icing on the cake...after he dies and is buried for three days, he rises again? And then ascends into Heaven? Really? You think all that is true? Because it all sounds like a bunch of stuff that Disney could make up. It all sounds like fantasy. That's what a lot of people say. And you know what? They are right.

They are right that it sounds like fantasy. It all sounds made up, not real, not true and even impossible. But let me tell you something, and read this very carefully. I promise you that all of that is 100% real. Every single word in the Bible is true. It all happened. You ask me how I know? It's because of a little something called faith. Faith is absolutely vital to followers of God. Read Hebrews 11 again. Hebrews 11:1 is the definition of faith. It is being sure and convicted of what we cannot see. Now read verse 6. It says, "And without faith it is impossible to please Him, for whoever would draw near to God must believe that He exists and that He rewards those who seek Him." That's all you need to know right there! Without faith, it's impossible to please God. Without faith, it's impossible to have a relationship with God. 2 Corinthians 5:7 simply says we walk by faith and not by sight. Faith is how we live our lives with God through Jesus. Who cares what others think? Who cares if everyone around us thinks God and the Bible are just fantasy? What matters is our faith! If you want a relationship with God, and if you want to live with Him eternally one day, you must have faith that He exists. You must believe that His Word, the Bible is all true.

When it comes to fantasy, Disney is king. They have mastered the art of creating unbelievable things and making the impossible come to life. Even though we know it's not real, they can make it appear to be true. But God and the Bible are not from Disney. They are not fantasy. They are as real as real can be. I urge and implore you to have strong faith in God that never wavers. No matter what anyone says or does to you, keep your faith strong. It is critical and essential to your salvation. God is real! The Bible is real! Heaven is real! And there's nothing fantasy about them!

"Castaway Cay"

Yes, it's sad that we're done with the four Disney cruise ships, but I've saved an incredible part of the cruising journey for last. If you take a Caribbean Disney cruise, chances are that one of your stops, or "ports of call" as we veteran cruisers say, will be Disney's private island. Of course they have one. What doesn't Disney have? I'm sure they'll soon be announcing their own planet. I've enjoyed visiting the island three times. I would love to change up the redundancy here and tell you the island is hideous and disgusting, but I can't lie. As you would expect from Disney and every place I've talked about so far, the island is beautiful. It's magic. A dream. A wonder. All those ship words. Ok, it's not fantasy, because it's totally real, and it's totally magnificent. In my mind right now, I am traveling there to talk about it with you, so thank you for allowing me to go back to Castaway Cay!

If you're a Disney rookie, you just pronounced it Castaway "kay" in your head, but it's actually pronounced like "key." Don't ask me why. This island, originally called Gorda Cay, was originally settled in 1783 and was once used as a stop in the 1930's for bootleggers and drug runners. Yikes! Thankfully, it's not used for that anymore. Good job, Disney. In 1997, Disney purchased a 99 year lease on the island from the Bahaman government meaning Disney doesn't technically own the island. Castaway Cay, as Disney renamed it, is 3.1 miles long and 2.2 miles wide. It's 1000 acres of land, but only 55 of them have been developed and are in use. The island is 258.9 miles, to be exact, from Port Canaveral, where many of the Caribbean cruises depart. Disney spent 25 million dollars and 18 months on redevelopment and construction which included trudging 50,000 truckloads of sand from the Atlantic Ocean. During that time, they also added a massive dock so that ships can pull right up to the island and guests do not have to take tender boats to get there. This is the first private island in the cruise ship industry that allows for that. Castaway Cay has anywhere from 60-140 permanent residents, depending on the season, that live and maintain the island. Ok, let me just stop right here and announce that this is my dream job. If I could make a decent living working on this island, I would so do it. Unfortunately, I don't think I could adequately support my family at this point living there. Plus the fact that I wouldn't see my family. I guess that's kind of important. Ok, back to the island. These residents are provided with food and supplies brought by each cruise ship, and since there is no fresh water on the island, sea water is desalinated for drinking. Before Disney opened the island in July of 1998, it was used for the movie *Splash* with Tom Hanks and Daryl Hannah. Part of the film *Pirates of the Caribbean: The Curse of the Black* Pearl was also filmed there.

Upon your arrival to Castaway Cay, you will find a huge variety of activities. You will notice that the island has been developed in the theme of a castaway community with buildings made to look improvised after a shipwreck. All food and drink, with the exception of alcohol, is free. There is a working post office where you can mail a post card to friends back home. There is also a free 5K race that you can participate in, and all finishers get a souvenir medal. My younger son and I did this on our last trip and had a blast. Helpful hint—if you do the 5K, you get on the island before any other passengers. Other activities include bike rental, personal watercraft, massage, snorkeling, parasailing, volleyball and basketball. There are three beaches for guests: one for families, one for cabana renters, and one exclusively for adults. Two submarines from the 20,000 Leagues Under the Sea ride that closed at the Magic Kingdom, lie underwater in the snorkeling area.

Speaking of Tom Hanks earlier, have you ever seen the movie *Castaway* where he becomes stranded on an island alone for 4 years? I realize it's just a movie, but picturing the realization of that happening is disturbing. While I would love to live and work with others on Castaway Cay, I would not want to be lost and abandoned on an island alone. That would be scary. One passage for you today...Read Matthew 25. It is divided into three sections. In the first section, we read about five who were not ready when Jesus came. In verse 12, they are told "I do not know you." Frightening! In the second part, we read about one man who didn't use the talent given to him. In verse 30, it says, "cast the worthless servant into the outer darkness. In that place, there will be weeping and gnashing of teeth." Horrifying! The final section talks about what's coming one day for us...Judgment Day, when some will be told from verse 41, "Depart from me, you cursed, into the eternal fire prepared for the devil and his angels." Verse 46 says they will go away to eternal punishment. In other words, they will be cast away. Absolutely terrifying!

While I love being "castaway" on Disney's island, I don't want to be cast away from God, and I know you don't either. Unfortunately, some will. We will be separated into two groups on that day. One will be given eternal life with God, and one will be cast away to punishment for all eternity. Which will happen to you? Only you can decide.

"Disney Wish/Lighthouse Point"

I bet you thought we were done cruising. Well, you were wrong. We're going to give one more devotional to cruising because some very exciting news has just recently been announced. At least for me it has. You may be reading this way in the future and thinking, 'Old news! Boring!' I hope not. I hope you are as excited as I am to hear Disney has announced their fifth ship!! Not only that, but in a surprise twist, they also announced a new Disney-owned port! A new island! A new exotic location! A new way to spend lots and lots of money! Hooray! The details and information accompanying these announcements is minimal, but I thought we would just put the two together for a devotional here. So come aboard the Disney Wish as we sail to Lighthouse Point.

Yes, Disney has announced their fifth ship will be called the Wish, and it's projected to set sail in January 2022. It is currently being built in Germany and will be about the same size as the Dream and Fantasy. As of this writing, we know that the main atrium will feature a grand staircase with an oversized chandelier. The rear of the ship, also known as the stern or aft (Oh yeah, I know the lingo) will feature Rapunzel from the movie *Tangled* as well as her sidekick, Pascal. It has also been announced that this ship will feature more character encounters than ever before.

When Disney announced the name of this ship, they also announced that they had purchased new land in the Bahamas to serve as a new port of call for their cruises. Sixty miles south of Castaway Cay, there is a Bahaman island called Eleuthera. Disney has purchased a 700 acre tract of land on the tip of that island called Lighthouse Point. It is estimated that they will spend between 250 and 400 million to develop the property. They have agreed to donate 190 of those acres to the Bahaman government to serve as a national park. There are currently around 11,000 people that live on this island, and Disney will give them the opportunity to weigh in on any plans before construction. Disney looks to break ground in 2020 with a possible completion in 2022 or 2023. Joe Rohde, the designer of Animal Kingdom and Aulani, is working on this project. He has already begun studying the history and culture of the Bahamas on which the theme of this new destination will be based.

Well thanks Disney! Just one more thing for my Disney bucket list, which is now about as long as this book. Maybe one day when my wife and I are old and gray, (well, she'll be gray. I'll still be bald.) and don't have two rugrats to support that eat like horses, we can take the Wish to Lighthouse Point. I like the new names. Once again, Disney has chosen a ship name that conveys what they are all about. There are many people who make it their wish to be at Disney. How many videos have you seen online where people are surprised with a Disney vacation? Even the SuperBowl MVPs make it their wish to go to Disney. By the way, did you know the players get well into six figures just to say those five words? Must be nice! Anyways, it's even better seeing Disney grant wishes to kids, especially the sick or struggling children through the Make-a-Wish foundation. Those stories always tug at your heartstrings when you see someone's wish granted. That leads to my question today...what is your one wish?

I think I asked that question in the first book, but it bears repeating. What if you were granted one wish? Forget three wishes like Aladdin. That's too generous. I'm just giving you one today. So what is it? Believe it or not, I just recently found my one wish. I already knew what it was, but I found it worded perfectly in Scripture. I just happened to be reading Psalms the other night, read this verse, and it hit me. That's my wish! The verse is Psalms 27:4 and it says, "One thing have I asked of the Lord, that will I seek after: that I may dwell in the house of the Lord all the days of my life, to gaze upon the beauty of the Lord and to inquire in his temple." That's it right there. That's all I want. In writing this, David said it's the one thing he's asked of God. One thing. That's his one wish too! Nothing else matters to me. I just want to be with God. Ok, I want my family there too. And I want you there. I hope that's your one wish.

I am working hard to make my wish come true. I'm also trying to be a lighthouse to those around me, so it can be their wish. Matthew 5:16 tells us to let our light shine so others may see our good works and give glory to God. In other words, we can be the lighthouse point to help others get their wish granted. You see what I did there? You see how I tied in both the ship name and the new island location? Sometimes I even amaze myself. ☺ I hope you agree with me that nothing in this life really matters. This life is temporary. Our eternal life is what counts. That should be our wish. And if we are truly living for God outwardly, our light will shine and influence others to strive for that wish too. Be a lighthouse. Show others the way. Grant as many wishes as you can, especially your own.

"Backstage Magic Tour"

These last five devotionals are a combination of points of interest that hopefully you can learn from. Just a random mix of topics. A hodge-podge if you will. Ok, I think that's the first time I've ever actually used that word. And it's weird. Who says hodge-podge? Anyways, I thought we'd start by talking about some of the tours offered at Disney World. What do you think? I'm going to assume you gave an emphatic "Sounds great, Albert!" After all, we did talk about a tour at Disneyland in devotional #2 of this book, so I feel we need to spread the love and talk about a couple at WDW. We'll start with the granddaddy of them all... the mega-tour! Today we are joining the Backstage Magic Tour.

There are literally dozens of tours you can take at Walt Disney World. I wish I had room to talk about them all, but that would almost be another book! I chose to highlight this tour because it covers a lot more ground than most, showcasing something at all four parks. I also chose it because it's one of the longer and more involved tours available. And when I say longer, I'm talking 7 hours! Yep, this is pretty much an all-day experience, and it ain't cheap either...$275 per person! Luckily there is no additional pack ticket required for this tour as there is on some. This tour includes transportation in an air-conditioned bus which is a definite perk, especially with Florida's typical warm weather. As mentioned, this tour includes a stop at each park. It begins with a backstage tour of the American Adventure at Epcot. Guests get to see just how that show works and the complicated mechanism involved. Also, as this tour begins before the World Showcase opens, guests get to walk through that area with no other park guests around. The next stop is Magic Kingdom with highlights of Main Street and a visit to the underground Utilidors (more about these in the next devotional). At Hollywood Studios, tour guests visit Creative Costuming and learn what goes into preparing and creating the various character costumes. The tour then moves to what are called the Central Shops. These are the buildings where Imagineers build and maintain all props, ride vehicles and audio-animatronics. This includes a look at the first audio-animatronic ever, one of the birds from the Tiki Room show. The final stop on the tour is Animal Kingdom where guests enjoy an included meal at Tiffin's, the fairly new and exquisite restaurant in the Pandora section. The tour then finishes with a look behind the scenes at the inner-workings of the Rivers of Light nighttime show.

I have not done this tour as of this writing, but we are strongly considering it in the near future. According to online descriptions and reviews, there are many details and secrets shared. Being a total Disney geek, I know I would enjoy that. Reading questions and reviews online, it is also obvious that some people are wary of tours like this because they don't want the magic to be ruined. Obviously there is no real magic at Disney, and some feel if they saw how the magic was created, it would forever spoil the experience for them. That's a legitimate concern, but I think for most people, including myself, taking a tour like this would only make me appreciate more what Disney has accomplished. While I haven't taken this tour, I've taken a few others and each one only enhances my future experiences and time in the parks. However, going backstage at Disney, you are definitely shown that there is no real magic. Seeing the mechanics and methods of the various attractions proves that everything at Disney happens for a reason. That is also very true when we think about our lives.

The apostle Paul, as you probably know, went through many difficult times throughout his life. He was mocked, beaten, stoned, cursed, shipwrecked and even snake-bit, among much more. Yet in Philippians 1:12 he says, "I want you to know, brothers, that what has happened to me has really served to advance the gospel." Paul knew that God had a plan for his life which sometimes included suffering and troubles, but he also knew that it all led to the spreading of God's Word. God has a reason for what happens to us too, including the hard times. Sometimes difficulty makes us stronger, teaches us important lessons or even leads to something better. Paul also said in Romans 8:28, "And we know that for those who love God all things work together for good, for those who are called according to his purpose." If we are working hard to stay on the narrow path to God, everything will eventually work out. God will plan and shape our lives which will eventually lead to good, but we may have to travel through some bad along the way.

I strongly recommend taking a tour at Disney. Look through all the options and pick one that fits your interest and wallet. Yes, through the tour you may see that Disney is not quite as magical as you thought, and that everything happens for a reason, but it will also help you to appreciate Disney so much more. Always remember that things happen in our life for a reason too...God's reason. Be patient and give Him control, and He will eventually lead you to Him. There will be bumps along the way, but it will definitely be worth the journey.

"Keys to the Kingdom Tour—Part 1"

I really debated in my head which tours to talk about. There are so many choices out there, and they all look fun and interesting, at least to me. We have done a few of them over the years. The first one we ever did was when my wife and I tried the Behind the Seeds Tour at Epcot's Land Pavilion. We loved that one so much that we repeated it a couple years later with our boys. That one includes getting to learn about and even sample some of the fresh and delicious vegetables grown there at Epcot. But today I want to focus on another tour that my wife and I did a couple of years ago. This is another fairly long and involved tour, but its concentration is just the Magic Kingdom. If I can narrow my review down to one word, which isn't easy, this tour was outstanding! We didn't want it to end and can't wait to take our boys on this one. Therefore I'm very excited to take you with me today on the Keys to the Kingdom Tour.

This tour is slightly more reasonable at 5 hours long and $99 each, however, park admission to Magic Kingdom is also required. For this tour, guests must be at least 16, which is why we haven't gotten to take our sons yet. Since my wife and I took part fairly recently, I can tell you about it in first person today. We started by entering the Magic Kingdom and registering at Tony's Town Square restaurant near the entrance. There we were presented with a keepsake name badge and were given the opportunity to choose our lunch meal. We were then each given a headset that connected to a microphone our two guides were wearing. This allowed for a little space between the group as we walked through the park. Speaking of walking, you need some good walking shoes for this tour because you're going to put in the miles! Our tour began with us slowly walking down Main Street as the guides gave us a ton of information about the beginnings of the park and Walt's vision. We also heard many stories behind the names you see on each window. We then made our way over to Adventureland where the tour typically takes a private ride on the Jungle Cruise. Unfortunately for us, Jungle Cruise had been completely drained that day for maintenance and was obviously not running. However, as a bonus, our guides led us into the queue line where we got to see what it looked like with no water. Jungle Cruise is actually very shallow! By the way, on any Disney tour, you are allowed to take pictures in public areas, but not backstage. Somebody in our group wasn't sure if a shut-down ride qualified as backstage, so he might have snapped a secret picture. I'll let you figure out who that was. We then slowly made our way backstage over behind Splash Mountain where we toured the warehouse full of the parade floats. This was absolutely fascinating, especially since we got to see those same floats later that day in the Festival of Fantasy Parade. We were then taken to Haunted Mansion where our tour guides gave us a thorough explanation of the ride and all the hidden details before taking us inside through a secret entrance. We then got to go right to the front of the line and hop right on the ride so that we could look for all that had been discussed. We then slowly made our way to the Tomorrowland Terrace restaurant, learning all along the way, where our prepared lunch was waiting. The absolute highlight of the tour was near the end when we were taken in a secret door near the Winnie the Pooh ride and down a flight of stairs into the Utilidors below the park. I can't tell you how incredible it was to be down there. We saw cast members going all different directions. It's huge down there! We even saw Peter Pan fully dressed but obviously not in character. We saw the secret elevator directly below the castle where Tinkerbell makes her way to the top each night for her Happily Ever After flight. We were down there for a good half hour or so before ascending and exiting a door back into Town Square at the front of the park. We had walked completely underneath the park from back to front! Wow! We were given a special pin to commemorate the tour and were given the opportunity to ask questions before the tour ended. There is so much more we got to see and hear, but there simply isn't room to put it here. It was an excellent tour and a wonderful day.

So you may have noticed in the title that this is a "part one." That's because after writing this devotional, I realized it was just way too long. I tried to edit and cut some things, but I found that too difficult. I didn't want to cut any of the tour description because it was just so amazing getting to experience all that. And I definitely didn't want to cut any of the Biblical application because this one is super important. You'll see. So the spiritual message for today comes in the next devotional. Read on if you want. Or save it for tomorrow. It's up to you. I realize that means there's no lesson in this one, so if you need a quick message for today, here you go...Be good and follow God. How's that? That's basically all you need to do. But I promise a great message is coming in the next entry. To be continued...

"Keys to the Kingdom Tour—Part 2"

We talked all about the tour last time, and I apologize if it was too detailed. I probably wrote way too much, but all of those specifics were just too good to leave out. So today, I present you with a little more tour information and the very important spiritual message, a message that can also be controversial and debatable, even among Christians. Therefore, I humbly ask you to just read and consider what I have to say. You can then decide if you agree or not.

One of the things stressed during the tour were the four keys that all cast members at Disney must follow: safety, courtesy, show and efficiency. For example, in the "safety" category we learned that there are buttons on the outside of all parade floats that can be pressed to quickly stop the float if there is any danger. For "show" we learned that there is an actual line painted on the ground at the point where guests can first see the parade floats. Once that line is crossed, cast members on the floats must go into full show mode and keep it up until they cross another line at the end of the parade route. For courtesy, we were told about how cast members must always treat guests with kindness no matter what. Did you know that cast members aren't even allowed to point with one finger when giving directions because that can be considered rude? They must always do a Disney classic two-finger point. We heard examples of efficiency as well, but the point was that those four qualities are the keys to the success of the Magic Kingdom. Today I want to discuss some even more important keys. When I was growing up in Sunday School, these were always on the wall in the actual shape of keys. And the name of this tour was always above them as a title, with one word changed. Let's talk about the "Keys to God's Kingdom."

Do you know how to get to Heaven? Do you know how to tell others to get there? I present the following as what I believe is the way to get there, and it's taken straight from the Bible. Growing up, I always heard there were six steps to salvation. Six keys. Six things we must do to get to Heaven one day. As mentioned, some will debate these or even disagree. But after reading and studying the Bible myself for many years, I believe these are spot on. Therefore I present these to you to study yourself and share with others. The keys to God's Kingdom in order are:

HEAR—Romans 10:17 says that faith comes from hearing. In John 5:24, Jesus said, "whoever hears my Word and believes Him who sent me, has eternal life." The first thing we must do is hear the Word of God. We must read, study, learn and obey the Bible.

BELIEVE—In John 8:24, Jesus again speaking said, "for unless you believe that I am He you will die in your sins." That's pretty clear and blunt, but obviously believing and having faith in God and Jesus is vital.

REPENT—Acts 17:30 reads, "The times of ignorance God overlooked, but now he commands all people everywhere to repent." God commands us to repent which means to make the decision to change our life and live always for Him. It also means to turn away from any sin that has a hold of us.

CONFESS—Romans 10:9 says, "because, if you confess with your mouth that Jesus is Lord and believe in your heart that God raised him from the dead, you will be saved." We must be willing to confess and tell others that we believe in God and belong to Him. We should never be ashamed of our faith or belief but be willing to state it publically.

BAPTISM—Acts 2:38 says, "Repent and be baptized every one of you." Mark 16:16 says, "Whoever believes and is baptized will be saved." This is the one that some would argue isn't necessary, and yes, there are certainly verses that talk about salvation without mentioning baptism. But can you just ignore the ones above and many others that do mention baptism? And if we are truly trying to follow Jesus and live like Him, why would we not be baptized like He was in Matthew 3, Mark 1 and Luke 3?

REMAIN FAITHFUL—Revelation 2:10 says, "Be faithful unto death, and I will give you the crown of life." I've seen steps to salvation that stop at five, but I think this last one is just as important. We must continue to stay faithful to God throughout our lives. This doesn't mean we won't make mistakes, but we must always be striving to serve Him and follow His Word.

So there you go...the keys to God's Kingdom. Disney has its four keys to success at the Magic Kingdom, and I was thrilled to learn all about them and so much more through this fascinating tour. But those four keys pale in importance to the keys we must follow to get into God's Kingdom. There are so many verses in Scripture about these six keys and the importance of following them. It's hard to deny that this is the plan God has laid out for us to get into Heaven and be with Him for eternity. I hope you'll consider them, study them and decide for yourself if you agree. If so, I hope you'll choose to follow them so that we can all one day enter that Heavenly Kingdom together!

"Club 33"

For the last two devotionals, we're catching a flight back to the beginning...in two ways. The beginning of this book and the beginning of it all. I'm talking about Disneyland. We're going back to the original park because I've saved two very special topics that originated there and both speak to the history of Disneyland. Have you ever been in a club? Maybe it was a school or college club. Maybe it was a club you made up with friends or siblings. Maybe it was a club for your professional career. Did you know that Disney has a secret club? Well, the secret's out and has been for a while. At this point I would normally say come join me as we go visit this attraction, resort, ship or tour today. But I don't think we can participate in this one, not even virtually. This club is too exclusive. We'll just have to stand at the door, stare and dream because chances are most of us will never be a part of Club 33.

Club 33 began at Disneyland in May of 1967 as a secret club for corporate sponsors and elite individuals. Today it is a group of private clubs as there are additional locations at the parks in Tokyo, Shanghai and all four WDW parks. There are two explanations for the origin of the name. One theory is that it's simply named after the address where the original door was found, at 33 Royal Street in New Orleans Square at Disneyland. The other theory is that it was named to honor the 33 corporate sponsors at Disneyland during the year when the club was being built. This club was Walt Disney's idea, but he never got to see it realized as he died six months before it officially opened. The idea came while he was working with various corporate sponsors for his attractions at the 1964-1965 New York World's Fair. He noted that there were several VIP Lounges provided for them which gave him the idea for his own selective club. Walt even wanted to incorporate audio-animatronic technology inside the club, but this dream was never realized due to his death. His idea was to listen in on club members' conversations via hidden microphones in light fixtures. A cast member would then respond to them through audio-animatronic characters. To this day, there is an audio-animatronic vulture in the club's upstairs lobby that was to be used.

While it was intended solely for corporate sponsors, Disney began offering individual memberships to Club 33 as well and still do. Any guess to the cost of joining this exclusive organization? At Disney World, the initial fee is $33,000 versus $40,000 at Disneyland since it's the more original and "prestigious" version. But wait, there's more! After that, there are annual dues that amount to $15,000 at Disney World and between $10,000 and $25,000 at Disneyland depending on what member level you are. So just what do you get for these hefty fees? Well, besides access inside the club with special food and drinks, each member gets a premiere passport for themselves and their families. This allows entry into Disneyland or WDW. They also get unlimited PhotoPass downloads, free parking, and exclusive discounts on dining, merchandise, recreation and tours. In addition, they receive 50 one-day park hopper tickets, 5 daylong VIP guided tours, a certain number of fastpass reservations and access to private concierge service. Club 33 has very strict rules, especially when it comes to privacy and social media. There have even been cases of certain individuals being kicked out of the club for violating these policies.

So you ready to join? Got the money? Well, you'll have to be patient because the waiting list is at least four years long at this point. Unless I find Aladdin's lamp, I think this will continue to be just a dream for me. I haven't been invited to Club 33. Luckily I have been invited to join another more important club. And you have too. Read Jesus' parable in Matthew 22:1-14. It is the story of a king giving a wedding feast. When the original invited guests don't show, the king gives orders to invite anyone, good or bad. However, one man shows up improperly dressed and is ordered to be cast out. Jesus' lesson was that everyone has been invited to follow God into eternity in Heaven. However, even though we've been invited, we have to follow the proper steps to be chosen. If we are like the one improperly dressed and don't follow the steps God has laid out, the same steps we talked about in the last devotional, we will also be cast out. But the good news is that you've been invited and there's still time to take advantage. I Peter 2:9 says that you've been chosen and have been called out of darkness into the light. You are being shown the light right now! It's an invitation. What are you going to do with it?

On our most recent Disneyland trip, my goal was to find the door to this "secret" Club 33, and I succeeded. I found it, but I certainly couldn't go through. I never will. But there's another door I'm more interested in. In Revelation 3:20, Jesus said, "Behold, I stand at the door and knock. If anyone hears my voice and opens the door, I will come in to him and eat with him, and he with me." Jesus is at your door waiting for you to let Him in. He wants you to join His club. It's called the Kingdom of God. All you have to do is follow the steps and you'll get your membership card on Judgment Day. So now are you ready to join? All it cost is your life. Just give it to Him and come join the club!

"Walt's Bench"

OK, you have to sing this part: "Now it's time to say goodbye to all our company. M-I-C (see ya real soon!) K-E-Y (why, because we like you!) M-O-U-S-E!" That's how they closed the Mickey Mouse Club, and it's also what they sing on the Magical Express on the way back to the airport. Makes me want to cry every time. Here's another reason to cry...this is the last devotional of Book 2! Bawl your eyes out. Ok, so maybe the emotion is not quite as strong as leaving Disney, but I do hope you've enjoyed this book. I hope you've learned a few things about Disney and a lot about the Bible and God's message. Writing this has been a great way for me to study Scripture as well, so thank you! Once again, I purposely saved something very special for last. We started this book in Disneyland, which was where it all began, but now we're going to go even more specific. We're going to discuss not the park where it all began, but the exact spot. Let's talk about Walt's bench.

If you go to Disneyland Park, walk into Town Square and enter the Main Street Opera House. There you will see what looks like an ordinary wooden bench. But it's definitely not ordinary. In fact, it's very extraordinary. When Walt Disney's two daughters were young, he used to take them on Saturdays to Griffith Park in Los Angeles to ride the Merry-Go-Round. According to a later interview, Walt said that Saturday was "Daddy's Day," and he loved taking his girls to the park. However, adults were not allowed to ride so Walt would sit on a bench nearby and watch his daughters go round and round. While sitting on that bench and seeing the smiles on their faces, he got the idea to create his own amusement park. He dreamed of a place where adults could ride with their kids. He envisioned a place on a much larger scale where whole families could be entertained and celebrate together. So it was there, on that bench where the dream and idea of Disneyland came to realization. Many years later, when Disneyland was completed, that same bench was acquired and placed here on Main Street as a tribute to where it all began. Did you know that originally Walt was going to call it "Mickey Mouse Park," and build it near his studios in Burbank, CA? But as plans developed, the name and location were changed to the Disneyland in Anaheim that we know and love today. The Main Street Opera House, where the bench rests, is the oldest building at Disneyland and formerly served as the park's lumber mill. The building also features a carousel horse from the Griffith Park Merry-Go-Round that Walt's daughters loved. You'll also find a scale model of how Disneyland looked on opening day in 1955.

That special bench is the beginning. Yes, Disney and his movies were already active, but if we're talking anything park related, it all began on a park bench. That's where Walt formed the idea and began the path to creating his magical place. One of Walt Disney's famous quotes is, "I hope we never lose sight of one thing—that it was all started by a mouse." Yes, that's true Mr. Disney, and we'll never forget Mickey Mouse. But you know what? Someone had to create the mouse.

Someone also had to create you and me. God not only created us, he chose us from the beginning. We are His original idea. He thought of us, formed us and developed us to follow Him and further His Kingdom. Read these verses as proof:

"...even as He chose us in Him before the foundation of the world, that we should be holy and blameless before Him. In love, He pre-destined us for adoption to Himself as sons through Jesus Christ, according to the purpose of His will." (Ephesians 1:4-5)

"But when He who had set me apart before I was born, and who called me by his grace." (Galatians 1:15)

"For those whom He foreknew he also predestined to be conformed to the image of His Son, in order that he might be the firstborn among many brothers. And those whom He predestined He also called, and those whom He called he also justified, and those whom He justified He also glorified." (Romans 8:29-30)

Do you see that? Those verses say that God chose us before we were born. He chose us even before he created the world! He predestined us to be His adopted children. And why did He choose us? In John 15:16, Jesus said, "You did not choose me, but I chose you and appointed you that you should go and bear fruit..." We were chosen to bear fruit. That means we were chosen to spread the good news of Jesus. We were chosen to tell others about our faith in God. We were chosen to lead others down the narrow path to Heaven. That's why He created us.

On your next trip to Disneyland, you definitely have to stop in and see Walt's bench and where it all began. That's where his idea was formed, shaped and developed. And look what that one idea has grown into! God also had you in mind from the very beginning, and He's waiting to see what you will grow into. He chose you! He's invited you into His club! He wants you to lead others to Him. Won't you please accept His invitation, follow His path and spread His Word? I hope we never lose sight of one thing—it was all started by God. And God is so good!

About the Author

After 16 years as a school teacher and coach, Albert took a leap of faith and went back to school to pursue his dream of being a paramedic. He is also active at his church where he has served as a deacon, Bible class teacher, and assistant youth minister. In his free time, he can often be found planning his next Disney vacation, buying another Disney souvenir to add to his collection, or listening to a Disney podcast. He has completed the Goofy Challenge Marathon Event at Walt Disney World and continues to visit the parks several times each year. He works full-time as a paramedic in Nashville, Tennessee, where he resides with his wife, two teenage sons, and their dog, Molly.

Albert's first book, the best-selling *Disney Devotionals* (Walt Disney World edition) was published by Theme Park Press in 2019.

About Theme Park Press

Theme Park Press publishes books primarily about the Disney company, its history, culture, films, animation, and theme parks, as well as theme parks in general.

Our authors include noted historians, animators, Imagineers, and experts in the theme park industry.

We also publish many books by first-time authors, with topics ranging from fiction to theme park guides.

And we're always looking for new talent. If you'd like to write for us, or if you're interested in the many other titles in our catalog, please visit:

www.ThemeParkPress.com

....

Theme Park Press Newsletter

Subscribe to our free email newsletter and enjoy:

- ◆ Free book downloads and giveaways
- ◆ Access to excerpts from our many books
- ◆ Announcements of forthcoming releases
- ◆ Exclusive additional content and chapters
- ◆ And more good stuff available nowhere else

To subscribe, visit www.ThemeParkPress.com, or send email to newsletter@themeparkpress.com.

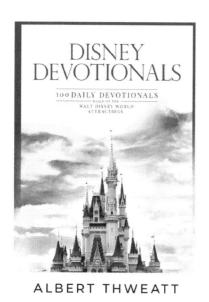

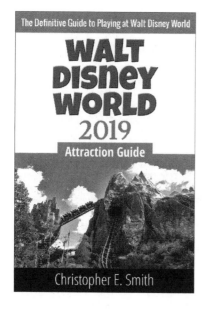

Read more about these books
and our many other titles at:

www.ThemeParkPress.com

Made in the USA
Columbia, SC
24 August 2020